ARMAGEDDON 2015

ARMAGEDDON 2015:

What You Don't Know About Bible Prophecy Will Kill You

ISBN: 978-0-9566254-0-3

Spirit and Truth Publishing

Cover design and book layout: Custom-book-tique

For bulk order prices or any other inquiries, please contact david@spiritandtruthrevival.org

www.armageddon2015.com

What you don't know about
Bible prophecy will kill you

ARMAGEDDON 2015

DAVID J WALTERS

SPIRIT AND TRUTH PUBLISHING

Table of Contents

Preface   5

Acknowledgements   7

Introduction   8

Can We Really Know When Jesus Will Return?   13

The End Time Players   19

Where Is The King Of The West?   34

God's Divine Calendar   51

God's Punctuality   82

Development of the Timeline   96

Armageddon 2015 Countdown Checklist   100

Event Analysis and Justification   107

Spiritual Survival Guide   148

About the Author   165

Appendix A – Solar and Lunar Eclipse Analysis   166

Appendix B - The Re-Birth of Israel and its Amazing Time-Line
Corresponding to the Jubilees and the Golden Proportion   170

Preface to the Second Edition

As I have gone through the process of revising and updating this second edition of Armageddon 2015 I realised that there were a number of interpretations and assumptions that I had made in the original which were invalid and needed correction. But I was even more struck by the number of events which had been completed according to the predicted timeline of the end time countdown. And as I reviewed my research I discovered a fourth independent witness, built into the very growth algorithm of nature itself, which declares the exact day of the announcement of the return of Jesus.

I would also like to thank Bonnie Gaunt for her research into the Jubilee year cycles and the golden proportion. This has been invaluable in helping me identify the end time prophetic anchor point.

We are now two years closer to the time of the end. The curse of Deuteronomy chapter 28 is coming more and more to the forefront of our awareness. As the west pulls further and further away from Israel, natural and technological disasters impact our countries with increasing intensity. Please read this book with an open mind and a seeking heart. If you are drawn to end time prophecy study well, challenge everything and most importantly of all – prove all things from the Holy Scriptures so that you may avoid being deceived by Satan and his false ministers. Time is far shorter than you may think. Do not be like the people at the time of Noah who were still living their lives oblivious to their impending destruction when the rains began to fall!

David J. Walters
Lincoln
May 2010

Original Preface

When I started to write this book last October I was not sure whether my research would hold up against the scrutiny of scripture. At the same time I was concerned that my understanding that America and Britain would cease to exist as sovereign countries and that the third world war would start within 24 months was just too outlandish to be taken seriously. But with the hindsight of six month recent history, I am now totally convinced that what we have witnessed in the collapse of the global economy is the natural pre-cursor for the devastating events which are yet to come.

Please read this book with an open mind. Challenge everything I have written and most importantly of all check the scriptures and prove all things for yourself. When you have done that, if you choose to dismiss this information as the outpouring of another crackpot doomsayer, then may your peace be with you. However, if you are convicted by the words of the Bible and the interpretation and illumination I have provided here, please get close to the Lord and ask Him with heartfelt supplications what you need to do with the information you now have.

And remember, many are called but few are chosen. If you are convicted by this book and all those around you are naysayers and ridicule your understanding hold fast in your faith and again take it to the Lord to strengthen you and encourage you. In doing so you may find yourself numbered among the very few who the Lord calls His saints, those who follow the Lamb wherever He goes!

As a quick side note – all the scriptures I quote in this book are taken from the Authorised or King James Version (KJV). I'm not a member of the King James only school, I actually prefer the New King James Version (NKJV) but for copyright reasons I've used the KJV throughout. All Bibles have some errors in them – either accidental through mistranslation or deliberate through a modern revisionist desire to make the Word of God politically correct (which is why I shy away from the modern translations and paraphrases Bibles). With everything we have learned or been taught in the past – now is the time to challenge what you've been told.

May God open your eyes to see, your ears to hear, your mind to understand and your heart to return to Him so that you are able to worship Him as He commands in Spirit and in Truth.

Acknowledgements

Firstly I would like to thank two people who I have never met but through whose work in this area I came to study end time prophecy with the fervour needed to complete this book.

Tim McHyde has written a book called "Know the Future – a Bible prophecy breakthrough from overlooked keys in the words of Jesus". Although as a result of my studies there are several areas where I disagree with Tim's conclusions, it was his work, and brave stance in identifying possible prophetic dates, that sparked my interest in preparing a detailed chronology of the end time countdown. As I said, my research and Biblical understanding have brought me to different conclusions to Tim, but nonetheless if you truly want to study the apocalyptical chronology Tim's work is worth reading. You can find his information at www.escapeallthesethings.com.

The second person I must thank is Pastor Mark Biltz of www.elshaddaiministries.us. Mark brought the understanding of prophetic significance of the Tetrad moons to public awareness. The statistical improbability of three tetrads occurring in a period of less than 70 years, and each tetrad pointing to a significant event in the land of Israel – the formation of modern Israel in 1948, the Yom Kippur war in 1967 and the return of Messiah in 2015 is astounding. Also the revised analysis of Daniel's 70 week prophecy which provides a second, independent witness to the date in 2015 was published by Mark. If you feel drawn to the Hebrew roots of the Christian faith, and the richness in worship that this awareness provides cannot be underestimated, you should visit mark's ministry website and explore the many teaching materials he has on this subject.

It is with the deepest of affection that I give my thanks to the many brothers and sisters in the faith who have helped, encouraged and assisted me in producing this book. I especially want to thank my dear friends Terry and Sondra for the insight they have given me in preparing this material; Ken and Marie for their diligence in commenting on the manuscript and the many challenges they set out for me to answer; and to my brother in Messiah, Jim, whose endorsement has given me the confidence to finally publish this work so that those whom God may be calling in these end times may have a reference to the support their understanding and challenge their pre-conceived notions. I pray that as the time of the end draws near they may quickly come to an accurate understanding of the righteousness God requires of His saints.

I would like to thank my wife Yve for her unfailing support while I have been writing this book, and her constant nudging and encouragement when my motivation flagged about halfway through the process. I would like to thank all my brothers and sisters, the children of YHWH, in the many assemblies, fellowships and congregations whom I have had the privilege to meet and learn from so that I had the knowledge and Biblical understanding to produce this work.

Finally, I must give thanks to the Lord, for He is good. Without His grace, blessing and calling I would never have come to the knowledge of the truth He openly reveals to us in the pages of His Holy Bible.

Chapter 1

Introduction

According to Bible prophecy the second coming of Christ will be at the culmination of a period of massive destruction and persecution known as the Great Tribulation. This will end with the battle of Armageddon in which all those who fight against Jesus at His return will be killed.

Unfortunately many churches shy away from these hard Biblical prophecies because they feel that the message is too uncomfortable for their parishioners to hear, or that we are not supposed to study these events too deeply as Jesus tells us, *"No man knows the day or the hour."*

But what would you do if you learned that Daniel's prophecy which was *"sealed to the end of time"* is now being accurately interpreted? And that signs in the heavens agree exactly with the timing of the return of Christ prophesied by Daniel over 2,500 years ago. Would you want to know what the Bible teaches us – *and warns us* – about this period?

Has God already started to allow the end time events to unfold? If I told you that God's number for completeness is seven and that prophetic events frequently occur on the Biblical Holy days known as the Feasts of the Lord and that when God wants to get the attention of a specific people He attacks their false gods. What would you make of this information?

In 2008, on the first day of the 7th Biblical month, known as the Feast of Trumpets (which signifies God sounding the alarm to His people) the Dow Jones Industrial Average (a bellwether of US stocks) dropped 777.7 points, which is a 7% loss of $1.2 trillion after the failed $700 billion financial bailout. Do you think God is trying to send us a message that we are coming to the end of the age of corporate greed and human excess?

If you discovered that the Bible indicates that in a little under 7 years from October 2008 (the time of writing the first edition):

- The economies of the West have collapsed (in progress as we speak)
- There has been a nuclear war in the Middle East started by Israel
- America (and NATO) has lost the third world war
- 90% of the English speaking peoples have been killed

- A global saviour (false messiah/Antichrist) has arisen out of the chaos of WW3
- The Jews regained control over all Jerusalem and started sacrificial worship on the temple mount (Spring 2012)
- The Antichrist betrayed the Jews and proclaimed himself as god from the temple in Jerusalem (Spring 2012)
- Proclaiming your faith in the true Jesus of the Bible will be punishable by beheading (from Spring 2012)
- Over 4 billion people have died (Autumn/Fall 2015)
- A small group of true believers has been supernaturally protected by God throughout all this destruction (from Spring 2012)

What would you do with this new knowledge?

Would you put this new found Biblical wisdom to good use to protect yourself, your children, family members and as many of those in your church and community as you can get to listen?

Or will you be like the foolish virgins – not preparing yourself for the return of the Messiah and ending up being left behind in a world of chaos and destruction just as the people did in the times of Noah and the great flood.

The choice is yours. You can study the Bible prophecies and be warned of the coming devastation, or you can pretend that everything is going to be just fine and carry on as it always has done.

Remember – the Bible is split into three more or less equal subject areas – history, doctrine and prophecy (and a large portion of prophecy is end times related). If God took the effort to devote 1/3 of His inspired word to talking about prophecy – don't you think He intended for us to read it and learn from it?

Today, with two recent prophetic discoveries we can identify the probable time for the return of Messiah. By using this information as a prophetic anchor point we can develop the entire plan for the final 7 years of human misrule of the earth.

Now at this point I need to give you a warning – Satan will deceive the whole world – and that includes you and I. The last thing I want you to do is believe what I reveal to you in this book – don't believe anything I write. If you blindly follow the things that I write in this book you'll easily be duped by the next person who comes along with another great sounding tale. Don't fall for it!

Please get your Bible out, get on the internet follow the links I give you and study the scriptures to prove all things.

If you do take time to prove these things to your own satisfaction and believe what is written here – then you have some serious decisions to make.

Alternatively, if you can't be bothered to prove these things – just pull up your chair, surf the TV channels for another game show or reality TV programme, order a pizza and get yourself a beer. Put this book down and don't worry. For as in the days of Noah, it would be cruel of me to disturb you out of your slumber. But if you've read this book, checked out the supporting information I've provided and won't (or can't) believe what has been presented, please get on your knees and ask the Lord for guidance. He may give you further revelation to provide you with the proof you need.

It doesn't matter what version of the Bible you use, please check everything, ask questions, prove all things and do not be deceived. **You life does depend on it!**

How to Use This Book

The core information of this book is found in chapter 9 – Armageddon 2015 Countdown Checklist. This is where the detailed information about the probable date for the return of Messiah is provided. Also there is a checklist of the events you need to be watching for to help you understand what is going on in the world around you from the perspective of Bible prophecy.

And I want to emphasise this point – the countdown checklist is a guide for you to identify the signs we need to be watching for. The Bible tells us to watch and pray that you may be counted worthy to escape all the things [in the end time prophecy] so this information will help you discern the times and seasons.

Don't Get Stupid

There is no point giving up your job, selling your homes and heading to the hills – by all means take prudent and reasonable precautions but please don't panic. Running to the hills will do you no good whatsoever during the pre-emptive nuclear attack on the West and taking up arms against your neighbours will only result in more death – remember the Bible admonition – *"he who lives by the sword will die by the sword"*.

And when the satanically inspired Antichrist comes to impose a one world religion – no amount of guns, ammo, dried food or water purification tablets will save you. The only safety will come from the divine protection that God will provide for those people who love Him, witness to the true testimony of the Biblical Jesus and do what He tells them to do!

If you're going to survive the coming 7 years of destruction and be in a position to protect your family and friends you need to look to God for His protection. In chapter 10 you will find the spiritual survival guide which will help you come to understand the things God is looking for in those people He will choose to miraculously protect during this period.

Many people will read this book for their human craving for knowing the future and the sensationalism of predicting dates and times – that's not the primary purpose of the book. The dates are actually co-incidental to the key message. The Bible teaches us to watch for the signs of the times, not to mark calendars and blindly follow the teaching of a man. Over the past centuries many Churches have predicted the date of the return of Messiah, and so far all have been proven wrong. Statistically there is a high probability that the dates provided in this analysis of end time prophecy could also be proved wrong. But from the information provided in the Bible, the unfolding alignment of world events and the feeling of urgency that many devout Christians are reporting, I believe the dates in this book are extremely credible. We live by the clock and use calendars to provide a convenient way to order our lives. The end time countdown naturally uses today's calendar for convenience in referencing the major prophetic events. However, please do not get fixated on the dates. Jesus may advance or delay His return depending on the attitude He finds on the earth. Do not blindly follow the dates in this book. Simply use the calendar as an indexing system so that you can be aware of the sequence of events once you see the beginning of the signs of His return.

If we study the history of Bible prophecy we see that the Lord is amazingly accurate at fulfilling His prophetic statements – so accurate that in many cases prophecies spanning hundreds of years are fulfilled to the day and the hour! However, even if this book is absolutely 100% accurate in the analysis of every prophetic statement and every assumption made turns out to be correct, the Lord can still choose to change the actual fulfilment depending on the behaviour of the people.

Remember the Bible states *"where there are prophecies they will fail"*. The story of Jonah gives a clear example of this. Jonah was sent to prophesy destruction on Nineveh, all the people, from the king to the lowest peasant, covered themselves in sackcloth and ashes and fasted as an act of repentance (even the cattle were not allowed to eat or drink). And God saw their repentance and relented from His prophetic intention to destroy Nineveh. No matter how accurately we may think we have identified prophetic fulfilment, if our people repent and return to God, He may still relent and delay the prophesied destruction of our nations. Although given the present degenerate state of our society, I hold out little hope that this will actually come to pass.

This book is intended to give you information about the signs to watch out for. If we use the analogy of the tornado alert system – this is not meant to be a "Warning" - giving you immediate cause to take cover. Rather this book is declaring a prophetic "Watch" for the signs of the seasons and times which will herald the return of Messiah.

Before you can make the best use of the information in this book you will need to understand some of the Biblical background to the end time prophecies. In the next few chapters we will discuss the present day identities of the end time players, where the "lost tribes of Israel" have been found; the Biblical way God defines His calendar; how accurately He has fulfilled prophecy so far and the rationale behind the development of the countdown to Armageddon.

Many Pastors warn their congregations against spending too much time studying prophecy as Jesus said, **"But of that day and hour knoweth no man, no, not the angels of heaven, but my Father only." (Mt 24:36).** They say, if Jesus doesn't know, then how can we possibly know – so what's the point of even trying to understand. But if we read our Bibles and understand the purpose of Jesus ministry we read, **"... worship God: for the**

testimony of Jesus is the spirit of prophecy" (Rev 19:10). If Jesus' testimony is the spirit of prophecy – should we be ignoring the spiritual, prophetic intent behind His teachings?

Finally reading this book can be a spiritual blessing or a cursing. I'm not claiming that it has the same divine authority of the Book of Revelation which promises a blessing – **"Blessed is he that readeth, and they that hear the words of this prophecy, and keep those things which are written therein: for the time is at hand."** (Rev 1:3) and a cursing **"For I testify unto every man that heareth the words of the prophecy of this book, If any man shall add unto these things, God shall add unto him the plagues that are written in this book: And if any man shall take away from the words of the book of this prophecy, God shall take away his part out of the book of life, and out of the holy city, and from the things which are written in this book."** (Rev 22:18-19). But reading this book will give you a blessing – if you prove all things and take action on what you discover to put off worldly distractions and get close to Him.

It will be a curse to you if you read this book and choose to ignore its warning or deny the Biblical statements which you find in here. Remember what Jesus said, **"Then some of the Pharisees who were with Him heard these words, and said to Him, "Are we blind also?" Jesus said to them, "If you were blind, you would have no sin; but now you say, 'We see.' Therefore your sin remains."** (Jn 9:40-41).

Please, before you go any further, decide whether you will use this book wisely to receive the blessing Jesus wants you to have or whether you'll continue on your way "as in the days of Noah" and bring greater destruction and condemnation upon yourself. If this is your attitude, please put this book down now, don't read any further because it would be better to die in your ignorance than say "we see" and let your sin remain!

If you are willing to humble yourself and put off your preconceived ideas and unscriptural notions and come before the Lord honestly seeking Him, then read on to Chapter 2 and let's discuss – *"Can we really know when Jesus will return?*

Chapter 2

Can We Really Know When Jesus Will Return?

In the book of Matthew Chapter 24 we read, **"But of that day and hour no one knows, not even the angels of heaven, but My Father only."** (Mt 24:36) This statement is used by many churches and pastors to stop people studying end time prophecy. Their position is that because no one knows (and some Bible versions also include Jesus among those who do not know), there is no point studying as it would be pure speculation and it takes us away from our primary mission (saving souls, preaching the word, baptizing, doing good works – or whatever other priority is declared by a specific denomination).

But a couple of verses earlier, Jesus said this, **"Now learn this parable from the fig tree: When its branch has already become tender and puts forth leaves, you know that summer is near. So you also, when you see all these things, know that it is near—at the doors! Assuredly, I say to you, this generation will by no means pass away till all these things take place. (Mt 24:32-34)** Here Jesus is saying that we can know when His return is imminent (at the doors!) because we can see the signs.

Jesus is referring to the signs of His second coming and at the time He gave the prophetic teaching in Matthew 24, no man or angel knew the time He was talking about. There is also evidence in the New Testament that the Apostles did not know when Messiah would return. The First book of Thessalonians chapter 4 states, **"For this we say to you by the word of the Lord, that we who are alive and remain until the coming of the Lord will by no means precede those who are asleep."** (1 Thes 4:15) This can be clearly understood that Paul was including himself in the group who were alive. Obviously this was written almost 2,000 years ago and the Apostle Paul has long since been dead and Jesus has not yet returned.

Is the Bible wrong? Is Jesus contradicting Himself? Surely His ministry was to reveal all things. Why would He not reveal this information – even to the Apostle Paul who was personally tutored by Jesus for 3 ½ years?

Let's look at these questions in reverse order. If the first century church knew that there would be 2,000 years to wait before Messiah returned, do you think they would have had the same zeal and motivation as if they thought Jesus could return at any time? Obviously not! It is extremely difficult to motivate any group of people to work towards a goal that is more than a couple of years ahead. We live in the present and the vast majority of people want instant gratification. To expect the new converts to work zealously and stay faithful to His word was expecting too much of human nature.

In fact, at the end of this chapter, Jesus gives us a very direct warning – **"But if that evil servant says in his heart, 'My master is delaying his coming and begins to beat his fellow servants and to eat and drink with the drunkards the master of that servant will come on a day when he is not looking for him and at an hour that he is not aware of,"** (Mt 24:48-50). Jesus clearly understands human nature and by allowing them to believe that He could return at any time, He ensured that they would remain focused on the task which He had set for them.

But does this not contradict Jesus ministry to reveal all things? No it doesn't, because Jesus never came to reveal all things. Many people say that Jesus spoke in parables so the uneducated peasants could understand His words. But is this what the Bible teaches? In Luke chapter 8 we read, **"Then His disciples asked Him, saying, "What does this parable mean?" And He said, "To you it has been given to know the mysteries of the kingdom of God, but to the rest it is given in parables, that 'Seeing they may not see and hearing they may not understand.'"** (Lk 8:9-10) Jesus is clearly saying that it is not His intention that everyone understands His teaching and the parables were, in fact, meant to hide His message from those who were not called at that time.

The book of Proverbs adds a second witness **"It is the glory of God to conceal a matter, but the glory of kings is to search out a matter".** (Pr 25:2) As potential kings and priests of the living God, He has set us the challenge of searching out the true meaning of His Word from among all the scriptures. And the prophet Isaiah further explains this, **"But the word of the LORD was to them, "Precept upon precept, precept upon precept, line upon line, line upon line, here a little, there a little," That they might go and fall backward, and be broken and snared and caught."** (Is 28:13) Those who love God and truly desire to do His will put the time and effort in to learn His Word and understand the true meaning of His message. Those who are merely "playing church" won't put in the necessary effort, rather they would follow the teachings of a man or corporate organization, and in doing so they run the risk of being deceived, to be snared and caught in the coming tribulation.

Can men know the specific timing of prophetic end time events? Yes they can! If they're willing to put in the effort to search the scriptures and add precept to precept, line to line.

Let's start by getting a better understanding about the purpose of prophecy and look at one of the most dramatic prophetic events covered in the Bible. As I mentioned before, many Pastors shy away from prophecy stating that it detracts from the works Jesus set for us. But is studying prophecy contrary to Jesus' teaching? This scripture from the book of Revelation, **"Worship God! For the testimony of Jesus is the spirit of prophecy"** (Rev 19:10b) clearly indicates that Jesus' testimony was all about prophecy! How can they say that studying prophecy detracts from Jesus' commission? And what is the purpose of Bible prophecy? The prophet Amos tells us, **"Shall a trumpet be blown in the city, and the people not be afraid? Shall there be evil in a city, and the LORD hath not done it? Surely the Lord GOD will do nothing, but he revealeth his secret unto his servants the prophets. (Amos 3:6-7)** Surely the Lord will do nothing but He reveals His secret to His servants the prophets. If you want to know what is going to happen in the end times, where do you look? To the prophets of course!

But can we really trust Bible prophecy? Is there any way we can identify whether it is really an accurate pre-telling of events or is Bible prophecy made up of just vague and confusing generalisations which we can massage to fit our own expectations and assumptions? Let's start by looking at one of the most prolific and accurate prophets of the Bible – the prophet Daniel.

In the third year of the reign of king Belshazzar a vision appeared unto me, even unto me Daniel, after that which appeared unto me at the first. And I saw in a vision; and it came to pass, when I saw, that I was at Shushan in the palace, which is in the province of Elam; and I saw in a vision, and I was by the river of Ulai. Then I lifted up mine eyes, and saw, and, behold, there stood before the river a ram which had two horns: and the two horns were high; but one was higher than the other, and the higher came up last. I saw the ram pushing westward, and northward, and southward; so that no beasts might stand before him, neither was there any that could deliver out of his hand; but he did according to his will, and became great. And as I was considering, behold, an he goat came from the west on the face of the whole earth, and touched not the ground: and the goat had a notable horn between his eyes. And he came to the ram that had two horns, which I had seen standing before the river, and ran unto him in the fury of his power. And I saw him come close unto the ram, and he was moved with choler against him, and smote the ram, and brake his two horns: and there was no power in the ram to stand before him, but he cast him down to the ground, and stamped upon him: and there was none that could deliver the ram out of his hand. Therefore the he goat waxed very great: and when he was strong, the great horn was broken; and for it came up four notable ones toward the four winds of heaven. And out of one of them came forth a little horn, which waxed exceeding great, toward the south, and toward the east, and toward the pleasant land. And it waxed great, even to the host of heaven; and it cast down some of the host and of the stars to the ground, and stamped upon them. Yea, he magnified himself even to the prince of the host, and by him the daily sacrifice was taken away, and the place of his sanctuary was cast down. (Dan 8:1-11)

A ram with two horns, a goat with one great horn which produced four notable horns; one of these became great and cast down the host and took away sacrifice. But what does this all mean? Thankfully Gabriel tells in the next verses "**And he said, Behold, I will make thee know what shall be in the last end of the indignation: for at the time appointed the end shall be. The ram which thou sawest having two horns are the kings of Media and Persia. And the rough goat is the king of Grecia: and the great horn that is between his eyes is the first king. Now that being broken, whereas four stood up for it, four kingdoms shall stand up out of the nation, but not in his power. And in the latter time of their kingdom, when the transgressors are come to the full, a king of fierce countenance, and understanding dark sentences, shall stand up. (Dan 8:19-23)**

If we remember from Daniel chapter 5, Belshazzar King of the Chaldeans, ruler of Babylon was killed and Darius the Mede took his place. Then the Persian side of the alliance grew strong and Cyrus King of Persia took control (the ram with 2 horns). The Medo-Persian Empire lasted from 559 to 331 BC. In 333 BC Alexander the Great commenced his assault on the Medo-Persian Empire and by 331 BC he has gained complete domination (the goat with a great horn). Alexander died in 323 BC to have his empire split between his four generals Lysimachus, Cassander, Seleucus, and Ptolemy (four kingdoms out of the nation). Seleucus emerged as the dominant force and the Seleucid line produced Antiochus IV, also known as Antiochus Epiphanies. This was the King who murdered many Jews in his attempt to Hellenize Judea. He defiled the temple and committed the abomination of sacrificing a pig before the statue of Zeus which he had set up. This ultimately resulted in the Maccabean revolt of 168 BC with the Seleucid Empire collapsing in a little over 100 years later in 63BC, to be replaced by Roman authority. We can see the literal, line by line fulfilment of Daniel's prophecy spanning 350 BC to 63 BC. But what is so amazing is that the book of Daniel was written around 600 BC, a full 250 years before the beginning of the prophetic fulfilment.

Matthew Chapter 24 states, **"Therefore when you see the 'abomination of desolation' spoken of by Daniel the prophet, standing in the holy place"** (whoever reads, let him understand), **"then let those who are in Judea flee to the mountains. Let him who is on the housetop not go down to take anything out of his house. And let him who is in the field not go back to get his clothes". (Mt 25:15-18)**

And Daniel Chapter 12 states, **"And from the time that the daily sacrifice is taken away, and the abomination of desolation is set up, there shall be one thousand two hundred and ninety days". (Dan 12:11)** Here we can identify an explicit timing point relating to end time prophecy. Exactly 1290 days after the "abomination of desolation" is set up Jesus will return.

Let's look at another example, this time from the book of Revelation. **"And I will give power unto my two witnesses, and they shall prophesy a thousand two hundred and threescore days, clothed in sackcloth. ... And when they shall have finished their testimony, the beast that ascendeth out of the bottomless pit shall make war against them, and shall overcome them, and kill them. And their dead bodies shall lie in the street of the great city, which spiritually is called Sodom and Egypt, where also our Lord was crucified. And they of the people and kindreds and tongues and nations shall see their dead bodies three days and an half, and shall not suffer their dead bodies to be put in graves. And they that dwell upon the earth shall rejoice over them, and make merry, and shall send gifts one to another; because these two prophets tormented them that dwelt on the earth. And after three days and an half the Spirit of life from God entered into them, and they stood upon their feet; and great fear fell upon them which saw them. And they heard a great voice from heaven saying unto them, Come up hither. And they ascended up to heaven in a cloud; and their enemies beheld them." (Rev 11:3, 7-12)**

Here we are told that the two witnesses will prophecy 1,260 days in sackcloth. They will be killed and their bodies will lie in the street for 3½ days after which time they will be resurrected. We know from other scriptures that those raised up in the first resurrection will join Jesus in the clouds as He returns. On the day we see the two witnesses start their ministry we know there will be between 1,260 and 1,263½ days to the first resurrection and the return of Jesus. Now there may be some initial confusion about who they are and when their ministry actually starts, so the actual start point for timing the 1,260 days could be debated, but when they die in Jerusalem we know there are exactly 3½ days before the return of Messiah.

Depending from where on the prophetic timeline we are observing the event determines how clearly we can identify the time being talked of. And the closer we get to the event the more certain and accurate our observations can be. Is the Bible wrong? Or was Jesus lying? Neither! When that prophetic word was given by Jesus during His earthly ministry, almost 2,000 years ago, the additional information (precepts and lines) required to understand the prophecy had not been revealed. Look again at Daniel Chapter 12, **"Although I heard, I did not understand. Then I said, "My lord, what shall be the end of these things?" And he said, "Go your way, Daniel, for the words are closed up and sealed till the time of the end. Many shall be purified, made white, and refined, but the wicked shall do wickedly; and none of the wicked shall understand, but the wise shall understand. (Dan 12:8-10)**

Daniel was one of the most accurate and prolific prophets in the Bible. He was personally instructed by the Archangel Gabriel and yet he did not understand this end time prophecy. When he asked God for understanding he was told that the prophecy was "closed up and sealed till the time of the end". If we are now entering the end times, as many believe, would it not make sense that God would open the seals (of understanding) on these prophetic statements of Daniel? Yes it would! In fact the Bible goes one step further, not only will the prophetic meaning be revealed, the wise *SHALL* understand.

Now some people are taught that we can have a general understanding of end time events, but not the specifics, but does the Bible teach this? Let's look again at Matthew Chapter 24, **"But of that day and hour no one knows, not even the angels of heaven, but My Father only." (Mt 24:36)** Even if this scripture is still applicable to us today, it says we cannot know the day and hour – but it does not prevent us from knowing the year, month and even down to a specific week.

Why is it important that we know the time of Jesus return? In Luke Chapter 21, the parallel recording of the Olivet prophecy we have been studying from the book of Matthew, we read the following, **"But take heed to yourselves, lest your hearts be weighed down with carousing, drunkenness, and cares of this life, and that Day come on you unexpectedly. For it will come as a snare on all those who dwell on the face of the whole earth. Watch therefore, and pray always that you may be counted worthy to escape all these things that will come to pass, and to stand before the Son of Man." (Lk 21:34-36)**

Here we see the same admonition which was given to the wicked servant and a warning about this day coming as a snare on the whole earth. But then we are given additional instructions - to watch and pray that we may be counted worthy to escape.

Jesus is clearly telling us that we can escape from the end time tribulation – if we watch for the signs of the times and pray for guidance.

The book of Proverbs gives us a second witness to this as Chapter 22 states "**A prudent man foresees evil and hides himself, but the simple pass on and are punished.**" (Pr 22:3) Also, as if the Lord is giving this statement real emphasis, the admonition is repeated word for word a few chapters later in Proverbs 27:12.

Not only can we know when Jesus will return (to within a few days), we are instructed to be watching for the signs of His coming, so that we can escape the tribulation which is to come upon the whole earth. Please:

- Do not be deceived!
- Do not be lulled into a false sense of security!
- WATCH for the signs.
- Be ready to do what the Lord instructs you when you see the day approaching.

In Chapter 3 - "*The End Time Players*" we identify to whom we need to be paying particular attention as these end time events unfold.

Chapter 3

The End Time Players

There are a number of individuals and organizations identified in the books of Revelation and Daniel who have key roles to play in the end time sequence of events. If you have not studied Bible prophecy before these can be extremely confusing. In this chapter we will provide a brief description of the individuals and organizations we expect to be fulfilling these prophetic roles. Let's start with possibly the most widely used imagery from the Book of Revelation – the four horsemen of the apocalypse.

3.1   The Four Horsemen

a. The White Horse

"And I saw when the Lamb opened one of the seals, and I heard, as it were the noise of thunder, one of the four beasts saying, come and see. And I saw, and behold a white horse: and he that sat on him had a bow; and a crown was given unto him: and he went forth conquering, and to conquer." (Rev 6:1-2)

The opening of the 1st seal of Revelation reveals a rider on a white horse, carrying a bow and wearing a crown. This rider goes forth to conquer. The white horse is similar to the expected return of the conquering Messiah in Revelation Chapter 19. But in this case the rider is carrying a bow which is symbolic of Ishmael (Genesis 21:20) the ancestral father of the Arab tribes. The white horse symbolizes a false Islamic messiah who will bring war to the earth.

This description has been accepted by many Muslim scholars as identifying the 12th Imam or Mahdi (the Islamic Messiah). On the website Answering-Islam.org we find the following information – *"Ka'b al-Ahbar is supported in his view that this description of the rider on the white horse as found in the Book of Revelation is indeed the Mahdi by two well known Egyptian authors, Muhammad Ibn 'Izzat and Muhammad 'Arif in their book Al Mahdi and the End of Time. 'Izzat and Arif quote Ka'b al Ahbar as saying: I find the Mahdi recorded in the books of the Prophets... For instance, the Book of Revelation says: "And I saw and behold a white horse. He that sat on him... went forth conquering and to conquer."*
(http://www.answering-islam.org/Authors/JR/Future/ch04_the_mahdi.htm).

b. The Red Horse

"And when he had opened the second seal, I heard the second beast say, Come and see. And there went out another horse that was red: and power was given to him that sat thereon to take peace from the earth, and that they should kill one another: and there was given unto him a great sword." (Rev 6:3-4)

The 20th Century could be described as the century of Communism. From the Bolshevik revolution in 1917 to the (supposed) fall of Communism with the destruction of the Berlin wall in 1989. Global politics have been focused around East/West relations, the Cold War and threat posed by the Red army and communist China (as well and North Korea, Vietnam, Cuba, the Warsaw Pact etc). The defining colour of Communism is RED and the defining characteristic is violent repression of the people trapped under its godless regimes. Joseph Stalin killed over 20 million of his own people to enforce his control of the Soviet Union and Mao Zedong is estimated to have killed over 40 million during his reign of terror in China.

c. The Black Horse

"And when he had opened the third seal, I heard the third beast say, come and see. And I beheld, and lo a black horse; and he that sat on him had a pair of balances in his hand. And I heard a voice in the midst of the four beasts say, a measure of wheat for a penny, and three measures of barley for a penny; and see thou hurt not the oil and the wine".(Rev 6:5-6)

The black horse is not representative of a political system as we have seen in the previous two examples. In this case, the black horse represents global famine. The scales indicate selling of food and the cost – a penny was equivalent to a days wage for the working man in the time of Jesus – indicates a global food shortage due to the massively high prices. The oil and the wine are more luxurious goods way beyond the means of an average labourer's basic necessities, and therefore remain unharmed. Pastor Biltz makes an interesting comparison between this scripture and the recent collapse of bee colonies around the world. One third of all food stuff, especially fruit and vegetables, are pollinated by bees. With the collapse of the bee colonies these crops will fail, and interestingly although staples of the Mediterranean diet, they are not mentioned in this scripture. Wheat, barley, olives and grapes are wind pollinated so would not be affected by the extinction of the bees. Listen to the message at http://www.elshaddaiministries.us/audio/torahclub5768/20080811tc44.html.

Famine is a natural result from large scale warfare. After the Second World War rationing did not end in Britain until 4 July 1954 – almost 9 years after hostilities had ended. The impact on the global food supply will be even more devastating after the economic and climatic disruption of all out nuclear war.

d. The Pale Horse

"And when he had opened the fourth seal, I heard the voice of the fourth beast say, come and see. And I looked, and behold a pale horse: and his name that sat on him was Death, and Hell followed with him. And power was given unto them over the fourth part of the earth, to kill with sword, and with hunger, and with death, and with the beasts of the earth". (Rev 6:7-8)

The pale horse again symbolises a social condition rather than a political entity. In this case there will be death on a massive scale (possibly as high as 25% of the global population – over 1.5 billion people) due to violent repression, famine and disease. All of which are natural consequences of a global nuclear war.

Also a brief digression here – the word Hell in this scripture does not mean a place of eternal torment – it actually comes from the Greek word *Hades* which is the translation of the Hebrew *Sheol*, both of which mean the abode of the dead – or the grave.

3.2   The Three Kings

The books of Daniel and Revelation clearly identify 3 kings (or political entities) – the King of the North, the King of the South and the Kings of the East which are active in the end times. A very cursory look at the scriptures allows us to identify the present day manifestations of these three kings.

a. The Kings of the East

"And the sixth angel sounded, and I heard a voice from the four horns of the golden altar which is before God, saying to the sixth angel which had the trumpet, loose the four angels which are bound in the great river Euphrates. And the four angels were loosed, which were prepared for an hour, and a day, and a month, and a year, for to slay the third part of men. And the number of the army of the horsemen were two hundred thousand thousand: and I heard the number of them. And thus I saw the horses in the vision, and them that sat on them, having breastplates of fire, and of jacinth, and brimstone: and the heads of the horses were as the heads of lions; and out of their mouths issued fire and smoke and brimstone. By these three was the third part of men killed, by the fire, and by the smoke, and by the brimstone, which issued out of their mouths". (Rev 9:13-18)

"And the sixth angel poured out his vial upon the great river Euphrates; and the water thereof was dried up, that the way of the kings of the east might be prepared". (Rev 16:12)

From Revelation chapter 16 we learn that the way of the Kings of the East is blocked by the river Euphrates and it takes the angel pouring out the contents of the 6th Bowl of Wrath to open the route for these Kings to complete their journey. The Euphrates runs from northern Turkey through Iraq into the Persian Gulf. It creates a natural obstacle for any army wanting to attack the Arabian Peninsula from the east.

In Revelation Chapter 9 we learn about an army of 200 million men which had been divinely constrained by 4 angels at the river Euphrates and was then released to kill one third of mankind (that's over 2 billion people). If we look due east of Jerusalem (the perspective of nearly all Biblical prophecy is based around Jerusalem) we find China. China has a standing army of over 2.5 million with an additional 800,000 reserves also it is the only country in the world capable of fielding a 200 million man army. This could easily be achieved by rapidly conscripting the male population aged between 15 and 44 (the typical age for military service) to give a potential fighting population of over 331 million men. The People's Republic of China (and possibly other nations allied with China) is represented by the Biblical "Kings of the East".

b. The King of the North

The whole of Chapter 11 of Daniel describes the ongoing war between two rival political entities – the King of the South and the King of the North. The prophecy was literally fulfilled line by line between 530BC and 4 BC. You can read a blow by blow account of this incredibly accurate prophecy at this website – http://users.aristotle.net/~bhuie/Daniel11.htm.

And as we read about the Kings of the South and North constantly struggling against each other we see the two entities emerge as the Seleucid kings in the north and the Ptolemaic kings in the south. The Seleucid's eventually gave way to the Roman Empire and the Ptolemaic kings maintained their power base from Syria and Egypt. Now although the amazing accuracy of this prophecy gives a clear indication that God is in control of all human affairs, it is not history we are here to study but the future!

Let's look at Daniel Chapter 11, starting at verse 40.

"And at the time of the end shall the king of the south push at him: and the king of the north shall come against him like a whirlwind, with chariots, and with horsemen, and with many ships; and he shall enter into the countries, and shall overflow and pass over. He shall enter also into the glorious land, and many countries shall be overthrown: but these shall escape out of his hand, even Edom, and Moab, and the chief of the children of Ammon. He shall stretch forth his hand also upon the countries: and the land of Egypt shall not escape. But he shall have power over the treasures of gold and of silver, and over all the precious things of Egypt: and the Libyans and the Ethiopians shall be at his steps. But tidings out of the east and out of the north shall trouble him: therefore he shall go forth with great fury to destroy and utterly to make away many. And he shall

plant the tabernacles of his palace between the seas in the glorious holy mountain; yet he shall come to his end, and none shall help him". (Dan 11:40-45)

We can see that this scripture is a talking about the end times, so there is a dual fulfilment for this section. But who is going to fill the role of the King of the North in the end times? There are two clues in this scripture. Firstly we know that this prophecy is a continuation from the earlier fulfilment – thus the final King of the North will be a continuation of the earlier Roman Empire. Have a look at some of the proclamations from the European Union and their ambition to recreate the glory of the former Roman Empire!

Also notice the description of how the King of the North makes war – like a whirlwind – that is with great speed and massive destruction. We have experienced this form of warfare already in the 20th century – it was called Blitzkrieg – lightening assaults by Nazi Germany against the unprepared countries on its boarders. The end time King of the North is a German led military machine out of resurgent European Union. A very good source of information on this topic is the DVD "The Rape of Europe" by David Hathaway which you can view an excerpt from here – http://www.propheticvision.org.uk/products.htm.

c. The King of the South

Using the same logic that the political continuation of the earlier King of the South (the power based around Egypt) it is easy to identify that the Sunni Muslim confederation primarily consisting of Egypt, Saudi Arabia, Jordan and the West Bank Palestinians as the end time King of the South.

The Shia Muslims in Lebanon, Syria, Iraq and Iran (the Persian crescent) have a key role in end time prophecy (which we will discuss later) but they are not members of the King of the South confederacy.

3.3   The Two Beasts of Revelation

a. The Beast from the Sea

Revelation Chapter 13 talks about two beasts – one which rises from the sea and the other from the land. What (or who) do these two beasts represent? Let's look at the first beast – the one which rises from the sea.

"And I stood upon the sand of the sea, and saw a beast rise up out of the sea, having seven heads and ten horns, and upon his horns ten crowns, and upon his heads the name of blasphemy. And the beast which I saw was like unto a leopard, and his feet were as the feet of a bear, and his mouth as the mouth of a lion: and the dragon gave him his power, and his seat, and great authority. And I saw one of his heads as it were wounded to death; and his deadly wound was

healed: and all the world wondered after the beast. And they worshipped the dragon which gave power unto the beast: and they worshipped the beast, saying, who is like unto the beast? Who is able to make war with him? (Rev 13:1-4)

Firstly, let us understand that the dragon that gives the beast its power is Satan. Revelation chapter 12 verse 9 clearly states, **"And the great dragon was cast out, that old serpent, called the Devil, and Satan, which deceiveth the whole world: he was cast out into the earth, and his angels were cast out with him." (Rev 12:9).** The beasts of Revelation are satanically inspired agents on the earth which bring all of mankind into a counterfeit worship, which is in fact a form of Satanism.

Let's look at the first beast in more detail – it's like a leopard, with feet of a bear and the mouth of a lion. It has seven heads and ten horns. What on earth does this represent? We need to go to a parallel prophecy, again in the book of Daniel.

"And four great beasts came up from the sea, diverse one from another. The first _was_ like a lion, and had eagle's wings: I beheld till the wings thereof were plucked, and it was lifted up from the earth, and made stand upon the feet as a man, and a man's heart was given to it. And behold another beast, a second, like to a bear, and it raised up itself on one side, and _it had_ three ribs in the mouth of it between the teeth of it: and they said thus unto it, Arise, devour much flesh. After this I beheld, and lo another, like a leopard, which had upon the back of it four wings of a fowl; the beast had also four heads; and dominion was given to it. After this I saw in the night visions, and behold a fourth beast, dreadful and terrible, and strong exceedingly; and it had great iron teeth: it devoured and brake in pieces, and stamped the residue with the feet of it: and it _was_ diverse from all the beasts that _were_ before it; and it had ten horns. I considered the horns, and, behold, there came up among them another little horn, before whom there were three of the first horns plucked up by the roots: and, behold, in this horn _were_ eyes like the eyes of man, and a mouth speaking great things. (Dan 7:3-8)

Daniel Chapter 7 talks about four beasts coming out of the seas; prophetically seas can refer to tribes and peoples – these beasts are symbolic of ruling political systems. But we still don't have all the information we need to understand the beast of Revelation.

In Daniel Chapter 8 we see another prophecy about a ram with two horns and a goat with one mighty horn. These are explained in verses 20-22- **"The ram which thou sawest having two horns are the kings of Media and Persia. And the rough goat is the king of Grecia: and the great horn that is between his eyes is the first king. Now that being broken, whereas four stood up for it, four kingdoms shall stand up out of the nation, but not in his power." (Dan 8:20-22).**

From our understanding of history we can see that the rough goat with one great horn is Alexander the Great who defeated the Medo-Persian Empire, represented by the goat with two horns, to become the dominant power in the ancient world. The four nations that stand up after the great horn is broken are the four generals who divided the Alexander's Empire after his death. As we mentioned earlier, these were Lysimachus, Cassander, Seleucus, and Ptolemy. Lysimachus received Thrace and most of Asia Minor. Cassander obtained Macedonia and Greece. Ptolemy was given Egypt, Palestine, Cilicia, Petra, and Cyprus while Seleucus controlled the rest of Asia: Syria, Babylon, Persia, and India.

We can also see a parallel between these four generals and the four headed leopard – the third beast talked of in Daniel 7. Also notice the comparison between Alexander's lightening conquests and the speed of the leopard when hunting. If we make the connection that the ram with one horn equates to the four headed leopard then this represents the Empire of ancient Greece. This means that the goat with two horns which was defeated by the ram with one horn must also be represented by the earlier second beast – the bear which lost its dominion to the leopard. Now we can see that the Medo-Persian Empire can be represented by a bear.

As a side note, but well worth mentioning at this point, in our 20th century understanding the Bear represents the Soviet Union. We've mentioned earlier that the Persian crescent is an Iranian sponsored power block of Shia Muslims which stand opposed to the Arab Sunni Muslims (this article gives great background on this subject - http://www.globalpolitician.com/25046-iran). At the same time Russia is supporting a Syrian military build up with Iranian funding as discussed in this article - http://www2.debka.com/article.php?aid=1362. We can see that the Medo-Persian Empire of 530BCE is reforming in the 21st Century in the form of a Russian-Persian (Iran, Iraq, Syria and Lebanon) military cooperation pact.

Who are the first and last of these four beasts? Some have speculated that the first beast – the lion with eagle's wings represents the British/American alliance. But let's stay true to Bible prophecy and let the Bible provide the interpretation; another prophecy of Daniel, this time in chapter 2.

"Thou, O king, sawest, and behold a great image. This great image, whose brightness was excellent, stood before thee; and the form thereof was terrible. This image's head was of fine gold, his breast and his arms of silver, his belly and his thighs of brass, His legs of iron, his feet part of iron and part of clay. Thou sawest till that a stone was cut out without hands, which smote the image upon his feet that were of iron and clay, and brake them to pieces. Then was the iron, the clay, the brass, the silver, and the gold, broken to pieces together, and became like the chaff of the summer threshing floors; and the wind carried them away, that no place was found for them: and the stone that smote the image became a great mountain, and filled the whole earth. This is the dream; and we will tell the interpretation thereof before the king. Thou, O king, art a king of kings: for the God of heaven hath given thee a kingdom, power, and strength, and glory. And wheresoever the children of men dwell, the beasts of the field and the fowls of the heaven hath he given into thine hand, and hath made thee ruler over them all. Thou art this head of gold. And after thee shall arise another kingdom inferior to thee, and another third kingdom of brass, which shall bear rule over all the earth. And the fourth kingdom shall be strong as iron: forasmuch as iron breaketh in pieces and subdueth all things : and as iron that breaketh all these, shall it break

in pieces and bruise. **And whereas thou sawest the feet and toes, part of potters' clay, and part of iron, the kingdom shall be divided; but there shall be in it of the strength of the iron, forasmuch as thou sawest the iron mixed with miry clay. And as the toes of the feet were part of iron, and part of clay, so the kingdom shall be partly strong, and partly broken. And whereas thou sawest iron mixed with miry clay, they shall mingle themselves with the seed of men: but they shall not cleave one to another, even as iron is not mixed with clay. And in the days of these kings shall the God of heaven set up a kingdom, which shall never be destroyed: and the kingdom shall not be left to other people, but it shall break in pieces and consume all these kingdoms, and it shall stand for ever. Forasmuch as thou sawest that the stone was cut out of the mountain without hands, and that it brake in pieces the iron, the brass, the clay, the silver, and the gold; the great God hath made known to the king what shall come to pass hereafter: and the dream is certain, and the interpretation thereof sure."** (Dan 2:31-45)

Now this prophecy tells us of a great image of a man with a head of gold, chest of silver, belly and thighs of brass, legs of iron and toes of clay and iron. Daniel tells us that the head is Nebuchadnezzar, King of Babylon which will be followed by 3 inferior rulers. The final part of this statue will be toes made of a weak mixture of clay and iron. When this final political incarnation exists God will destroy the image and set up a kingdom that will never be destroyed, the world ruling government of Jesus.

If we notice the legs – they are made of iron. The fourth beast which came after the leopard (the Greek Empire) had great iron teeth. We know from our previous study that the Roman Empire emerged from the Seleucid Empire after Alexander the Great died. Also the Roman Empire was divided between the eastern empire centred in Constantinople and the western empire controlled from Rome; a clear parallel to the two legs of iron. The final conclusion we can draw from this is that the toes, which represent 10 kings, are not as strong as the original two legs of iron (as they are mixed with clay). This represents a weak political union consisting of many smaller political entities – sounds very much like the European Union don't you think? As we have seen before it is a final, weaker incarnation of the Roman Empire. The fourth beast is the end time manifestation of the Holy Roman Empire.

If we take the Bible literally the head of this statue, which must logically equate to the first beast rising from the sea, is the Babylonian Empire of King Nebuchadnezzar. And from correctly analysing these prophecies we can identify an unbroken line from Ancient Babylon down to the present European Union. The Roman Empire emerged from the Seleucid Empire after Alexander the Great died, which itself was derived from Medo-Persian Empire which had replaced the original Babylonian Empire of Nebuchadnezzar.

Again, another side note. I had originally thought that the resurgent, sabre rattling Russia was the King of the North. If you look at a map Moscow is directly due north of Jerusalem. But that would cause a problem with understanding this scripture about the King of the North – **"But tidings out of the east and out of the north shall trouble him: therefore he shall go forth with great fury to destroy, and utterly to make away many"**. (Dan

11:44). Why would the King of the North (Russia) be concerned about a military threat coming from Russia? Whereas, if the final incarnation of the King of the North is a German led militaristic European Union, then a threat from the North (Russia) and the East (China) – the 2 partners of the second seal of Revelation – would make more sense.

To summarise what the book of Daniel tells us about the beasts from the sea:

Order	Animal	Metal	Identification
1	Lion & eagles wings	Gold	Original Babylon
2	Bear	Silver	Medo-Persian empire – Russian Iranian alliance
3	Leopard	Bronze	Grecian Empire – European Union
4	Beast with iron teeth	Iron	Roman Empire – European Union

b. The Beast from the Earth

"And I beheld another beast coming up out of the earth; and he had two horns like a lamb, and he spake as a dragon. And he exerciseth all the power of the first beast before him, and causeth the earth and them which dwell therein to worship the first beast, whose deadly wound was healed. And he doeth great wonders, so that he maketh fire come down from heaven on the earth in the sight of men, and deceiveth them that dwell on the earth by the means of those miracles which he had power to do in the sight of the beast; saying to them that dwell on the earth, that they should make an image to the beast, which had the wound by a sword, and did live. And he had power to give life unto the image of the beast, that the image of the beast should both speak, and cause that as many as would not worship the image of the beast should be killed." (Rev 13:11-15).

This second beast causes the world to worship the first beast. This must be a religious figure. Also we notice that it has two horns "like a lamb" but speaks as a dragon. The true Lamb of God is Jesus, so this second beast a counterfeit form of Christianity that appears to be like Jesus, but actually teaches the things of the devil.

In Daniel Chapter 7 we discover this about the beast **"He shall speak pompous words against the Most High, shall persecute the saints of the Most High, and shall intend to change times and law. Then the saints shall be given into his hand for a time and times and half a time." (Dan 7:25)**

The persecution of the saints for time, times and half a time indicate that the person being spoken of is the political beast power who is ultimately revealed as the Antichrist. However, we know from the history of the Roman Empire that it was always manifest as a united politico-religious entity. In Roman times this power was vested in Caesar who was the political ruler and also considered to earthly manifestation of the sun god. By the time of Constantine this became an alliance between the political power of Rome and the (apostate) Christian Church. It was at the council of Nicaea in 325AD that the first ecumenical meeting of the various branches of the Christian church came together and agreed a common doctrine. This new doctrine also incorporated a great deal of the traditional Roman trappings of Emperor worship such was worshiping on the day of the sun (Sun-day), celebrating the feast/orgy of Saturnalia (25 December) and the spring fertility rite - the feast of Ishtar (Easter). Those who were not willing to abandon the Biblical teachings and doctrine of the Apostles (such as Sabbath worship and the annual Holy days) were ex-communicated and persecuted.

The Roman Church openly expresses it's willingness to change times and law (the Commandment requiring observance of the 7th day Sabbath):

James Cardinal Gibbons, *The Faith of our Fathers*, 88th ed., pp. 89. - *"But you may read the Bible from Genesis to Revelation, and you will not find a single line authorizing the sanctification of Sunday. The Scriptures enforce the religious observance of Saturday, a day which we never sanctify."*

Stephen Keenan, *A Doctrinal Catechism* 3rd ed., p. 174.

*"***Question***: Have you any other way of proving that the Church has power to institute festivals of precept?*

*"***Answer***: Had she not such power, she could not have done that in which all modern religionists agree with her-she could not have **substituted the observance of Sunday**, the first day of the week, for the observance of Saturday, the seventh day, **a change for which there is no Scriptural authority**."*
(http://biblelight.net/chalng.htm)

We see clear admission by the Roman Catholic Church's own doctrine that they "changed times and laws" in direct contravention of scriptural authority. There is further evidence as to the identity of the "beast from the earth" in Revelation chapter 17.

"Then one of the seven angels who had the seven bowls came and talked with me, saying to me, "Come, I will show you the judgment of the great harlot who sits on many waters, with whom the kings of the earth committed fornication, and the inhabitants of the earth were made drunk with the wine of her fornication." So he carried me away in the Spirit into the wilderness. And I saw a woman sitting on a scarlet beast which was full of names of blasphemy, having seven heads and ten horns. The woman was arrayed in purple and scarlet, and adorned with gold and precious stones and pearls, having in her hand a golden cup full of abominations and the filthiness of her fornication. And on her forehead a name was written: MYSTERY, BABYLON THE GREAT,

THE MOTHER OF HARLOTS AND OF THE ABOMINATIONS OF THE EARTH. I saw the woman, drunk with the blood of the saints and with the blood of the martyrs of Jesus. And when I saw her, I marveled with great amazement." (Rev 17:1-6)

Verse 3 tells us about the "great harlot who sits on many waters". This is referring to a false religious system (God equates false worship with spiritual whoredom) and sitting on many waters indicates that this false religious system has authority over many separate peoples and nations (represented by waters). The Babylonian mystery religion has been the source of all false Christian religions and in her final incarnation as the Roman Catholic Church, she sits as the mother of harlots, all the false churches that have been derived from the original apostate church established under Emperor Constantine including the Orthodox Church, the Catholic Church and the Protestant denominations. All these "daughter" churches will return to their mother under the final control of the beast when the entire world is made to worship him. Revelation chapter 17 gives us more information about the great harlot of Babylon:

But the angel said to me, "Why did you marvel? I will tell you the mystery of the woman and of the beast that carries her, which has the seven heads and the ten horns. The beast that you saw was, and is not, and will ascend out of the bottomless pit and go to perdition. And those who dwell on the earth will marvel, whose names are not written in the Book of Life from the foundation of the world, when they see the beast that was, and is not, and yet is. Here is the mind which has wisdom: The seven heads are seven mountains on which the woman sits. There are also seven kings. Five have fallen, one is, and the other has not yet come. And when he comes, he must continue a short time. And the beast that was, and is not, is himself also the eighth, and is of the seven, and is going to perdition. The ten horns which you saw are ten kings who have received no kingdom as yet, but they receive authority for one hour as kings with the beast. These are of one mind, and they will give their power and authority to the beast. These will make war with the Lamb, and the Lamb will overcome them, for He is Lord of lords and King of kings; and those who are with Him are called, chosen, and faithful." Then he said to me, "The waters which you saw, where the harlot sits, are peoples, multitudes, nations, and tongues. And the ten horns which you saw on the beast, these will hate the harlot, make her desolate and naked, eat her flesh and burn her with fire. For God has put it into their hearts to fulfil His purpose, to be of one mind, and to give their kingdom to the beast, until the words of God are fulfilled. And the woman whom you saw is that great city which reigns over the kings of the earth." (Rev 17:7-18)

"The seven heads are seven mountains on which the woman sits" can be interpreted that the false religion has control over 7 governments. But also this could be a literal clue that the seat of this false church is located in a place of 7 mountains (or hills). Ancient Rome was established on 7 hills with the Vatican hill, the site of today's Vatican City just North West of the city walls of ancient Rome. The State of the Vatican City is an independent state with its own elected monarchy, the Pope, which sends fully credentialed Ambassadors to virtually all countries of the earth as well as the

United Nations. You can see how The Roman Catholic church is the only religious entity that can be called "that great city which reigns over the kings of the earth". Also if we think back to the statement "arrayed in purple and scarlet, and adorned with gold and precious stones and pearls" think of the images we traditionally see coming out of the Vatican, how many purple and scarlet vestments adorned with gold, precious stones and pearls can you picture in those images. The "Beast from the earth" is the leader of the Roman Catholic Church, the Pope.

c. The Antichrist

In recent years there has been a great deal of speculation by prophecy watchers and sensationalism in the media about the identity of the Antichrist. So far they have all been proved wrong – the Antichrist is not Ronald Reagan, Bill Clinton, George Bush, Barak Obama, Vladimir Putin, Pope Benedict XVI or Mahmoud Ahmadinejad. Although some of these characters may have end times significance, they do not fit the criteria for the Antichrist.

In reality, the knowledge of the identity of the Antichrist is not critical to understanding end time events. And when he sets himself up as god and completes the abomination of desolation, there will be no doubt as to his identity. And the Bible talks of many anti-christs. The Apostle John wrote on this issue several times:

Little children, it is the last time: and as ye have heard that antichrist shall come, even now are there many antichrists; whereby we know that it is the last time. They went out from us, but they were not of us; for if they had been of us, they would no doubt have continued with us: but they went out, that they might be made manifest that they were not all of us. But ye have an unction from the Holy One, and ye know all things. I have not written unto you because ye know not the truth, but because ye know it, and that no lie is of the truth. Who is a liar but he that denieth that Jesus is the Christ? He is antichrist, that denieth the Father and the Son. Whosoever denieth the Son, the same hath not the Father: (1 Jn 2:18-23)

For many deceivers are entered into the world, who confess not that Jesus Christ is come in the flesh. This is a deceiver and an antichrist. (2 Jn 7)

Scripturally, an antichrist is anyone who denies that Jesus is the Son of God and came to earth in the flesh. This would include all non-Christian denominations and those Christian ones which deny His divinity, literal Sonship of God and earthly incarnation. This probably accounts for 70-75% of humanity.

When people ask who is the Antichrist? What they really want to know is who is the man whose number is 666? Let's look at what the Bible tells us: **"And that no man might buy or sell, save he that had the mark, or the name of the beast, or the number of his name. Here is wisdom. Let him that hath understanding count the number of the beast: for it is the number of a man; and his number is Six hundred threescore and six." (Rev 13:17-18)**

The one commonly referred to as the Antichrist, is in fact the beast from the sea who we have already discussed earlier. But what of this number 666 – can we gain any insight into who a potential candidate for this role might be? Well the scripture tells us that the number is of a man, of his name. How can a name be a number? There is a method of interpretation known as gematria. In Hebrew every letter has a specific numeric value, so using this system the name or title of a person can be calculated to a specific number. But to convert every persons name and title into Hebrew and then find the numerical value would be an impossible task. Can we narrow the field of possible contenders?

The prophet Daniel tells us: **"And after threescore and two weeks shall Messiah be cut off, but not for himself: and the people of the prince that shall come shall destroy the city and the sanctuary; and the end thereof shall be with a flood, and unto the end of the war desolations are determined." (Dan 9:26)**

After the Messiah is cut off (executed) the people of the prince who is to come will destroy the city. History clearly reports that Jerusalem was utterly destroyed by the Roman army in 70 AD. The beast power will have a leadership role in the final incarnation of the Holy Roman Empire and also be called a prince. This information helps us narrow the field dramatically. There are several Royal Families remaining in Europe, but none as prominent in the public eye as the British Royal family and the heir to the throne, Prince Charles.

א	ב	ג	ד	ה	ו	ז	ח	ט	י	כ	ך
Alef	Bet	Gimel	Dalet	He	Vav	Zayim	Chet	Tet	Yod	Kaf	Khaf
A	B/V	G	D	H	V	Z	Ch	T	Y	K	Kh
1	2	3	4	5	6	7	8	9	10	20	20

ל	מ	נ	ס	ע	פ	ף	צ	ק	ר	ש	ת
Lamed	Mem	Nun	Samech	Ayin	Peh	Feh	Tsadeh	Qof	Resh	Shin	Tav
L	M	N	S	-	P/F	F	Ts	Q	R	Sh	T
30	40	50	60	70	80	80	90	100	200	300	400

What is equally interesting is that using the English numbering gematria, derived from the Hebrew system we come up with the following equivalences:

A	B	C	D	E	F	G	H	I	J	K	L	M
1	2	3	4	5	6	7	8	9	10	20	30	40
N	O	P	Q	R	S	T	U	V	W	X	Y	Z
50	60	70	80	90	100	200	300	400	0	0	0	0

C	h	a	r	l	e	s				
3	8	1	90	30	5	100	=237			
P	r	i	n	c	e			o	f	
70	90	9	50	3	5	=227		60	6	=66
W	a	l	e	s						
0	1	30	5	100	=136					

237 + 227 + 66 + 136 = 666

Unfortunately I don't have the actual Hebrew script for "Charles, Prince of Wales" to give you as an example, but when we translate his official title, into Hebrew and use the Hebrew gematria, the number of this man is 666.

Statistically this is quite remarkable, not only does "Charles, Prince of Wales" work out to 666 in English script it also does the same in Hebrew script. If it was a million to one chance that this would occur in one language it's a 1,000,000,000,000 to 1 chance that it would occur in both Hebrew and English. But that's not all.

Prince Charles is an interfaith ecumenist – he has already stated that when he becomes King he will abandon his title as Head of the Church of England and Defender of the Faith and assume the title of *Defender of Faiths*. He already has an eye towards a one world religion, which is completely unscriptural and hearkens back to the blasphemy of Nimrod and the Tower of Babel, the source of the Babylonian mystery religion. (The Tower of Babel was built under Nimrod's authority to prevent the children of men from being scattered across all the earth in direct rebellion to God's instruction to be fruitful and multiply in all the earth).

Charles is one of the few people who can rightly claim the title of "Prince", as in "prince of the people to come". Also he is directly related to all the blood lines of the Royal Houses of Europe so assuming a leadership role within Europe would be natural. The British Royal family trace their lineage right back to the throne of King David of Judah, meaning Charles would also be acceptable to the Jews.

As we will study later in this book, if we think about the timing of the emergence of the beast power, it is after the time of Jacob's trouble, when Britain and America have been destroyed. That would also strengthen Prince Charles' claim as he would not pose any nationalistic threat to the countries who would be coming together under his authority as he would be a Prince without a Kingdom.

There is a great deal more information which points to Prince Charles as a very strong candidate for the end time Antichrist. Tim Cohen in his book, "The Antichrist and a cup of tea" gives an exhaustive analysis of this claim. Although I disagree with several of Tim's doctrinal statements, the investigative work he has put into his book is well worth reading.

One final player, who cannot qualify as the Antichrist, but nonetheless may have significant impact on end time events, is Tony Blair. He is the commensurate 21st century politician – a polished photogenic performer, a gifted communicator and extremely persuasive in the media. He held on to power as the British Prime Minster as long as possible, handing over to Gordon Brown a little over a year before the global economy crashed causing chaos in the British economy. He is the European Union's special envoy to the Middle East and he announced his conversion to Roman Catholicism after leaving office as Prime Minister, although a declared Anglican he had been covertly attending mass and taking communion while Prime Minister. He was also the first foreign statesman to meet President Obama – ahead of Gordon Brown the British Prime Minster and French President Nicolas Sarkozy.

Although Blair does not qualify as the Antichrist, he would be ideally placed within the European Union infrastructure and a high profile convert to the Roman Catholic Church to clear the path for Prince Charles to be accepted as the figurehead of the resurgent European Union after Britain and America are destroyed.

This all sounds highly far fetched – especially the statement about Britain and America being destroyed. What on earth is the rationale for making such an outlandish statement?

In chapter 4 – *"Where is the King of the West"* we'll discover the biblical justification for making these claims.

Chapter 4

Where is the King of the West?

In chapter 3 we identified the key players in end time prophecy, and as you can see the majority of present day political entities are represented – the Communist powers of Russia and China; the Muslim powers (both Shiite and Sunni); the resurgent European Union and even the Roman Catholic Church.

But there is one major player notable by his absence.

If I asked you to tell me the modern day identity of this Biblical figure, I'm 99.99% sure I know who you will instinctively say. Let's try it.

Which modern day identity do you think the Bible would describe as the King of the West?

I guess you said America. Was I right? I think just about everybody in the world acknowledges America as the only remaining global superpower, the driving force behind the world's economy and the undisputed leader of western capitalism.

If America has such a prominent place in the world today, why is it not mentioned as having a leading role in end time Bible prophecy?

Well America is clearly mentioned in Bible prophecy but it doesn't have any significant part in the end time activities. Please let me explain by starting with an unusual instruction Jesus gave to His disciples in Matthew Chapter 10 – **"These twelve Jesus sent forth, and commanded them, saying, go not into the way of the Gentiles, and into any city of the Samaritans enter ye not: But go rather to the lost sheep of the house of Israel."** (Mt 10:5-6) and later in Matthew Chapter 15 **"But he answered and said, I am not sent but unto the lost sheep of the house of Israel."** (Mt 15:24).

4.1   Are the Lost Ten Tribes of Israel Really Lost?

The northern ten tribes of Israel were carried away into captivity by the Assyrian kings between 740 and 722 BC. While the remaining tribe of Judah, Benjamin and part of the tribe of Levi were taken into captivity in Babylon between 605 and 581 BC. Approximately 70 years later, in 537 BC, these exiles from the tribe of Judah were allowed to return to their land. The lost 10 tribes of Israel have not returned to this day.

Most people believe that the Jews and the Israelites are the same people, but this is simply not true. Now, unless you have studied the Bible in some detail, you may not be aware that the Tribes of Israel and the Tribe of Judah are two separate groups. Let's look at Genesis chapter 35 to get some clarity on this. **"And Israel [Jacob] journeyed, and spread his tent beyond the tower of Edar. And it came to pass, when Israel dwelt in that land, that Reuben went and lay with Bilhah his father's concubine: and Israel heard it. Now the sons of Jacob were twelve: The sons of Leah; Reuben, Jacob's firstborn, and Simeon, and Levi, and Judah, and Issachar, and Zebulun: The sons of Rachel; Joseph, and Benjamin: And the sons of Bilhah, Rachel's handmaid; Dan, and Naphtali: And the sons of Zilpah, Leah's handmaid; Gad, and Asher: these are the sons of Jacob, which were born to him in Padanaram. And Jacob came unto Isaac his father unto Mamre, unto the city of Arbah, which is Hebron, where Abraham and Isaac sojourned. And the days of Isaac were an hundred and fourscore years. And Isaac gave up the ghost, and died, and was gathered unto his people, being old and full of days: and his sons Esau and Jacob buried him." (Ge 35:21-29).**

The 12 sons of Jacob are listed as – Reuben, Simeon, Levi, Judah, Issachar, Zebulun, Joseph, Benjamin, Dan, Napthali, Gad and Asher. Now the group of people we know as the Jews are the physical descendants of Judah, the 4th son of Jacob by his first wife Leah. The other 11 sons are all Israelites, but not Jews. Also Jacob (Israel), Isaac, and Abraham were neither Jews, nor Israelites; technically they are all Hebrews but not Israelites (Abraham's great-great-great grandfather was called Eber which is where the term Hebrew comes from).

Also notice in the beginning of that passage it says "and Israel journeyed" but later it refers to the same person as Jacob. This is quite common in the Old Testament – God changes the name of individuals when their character has changed. In this case Jacob (which means liar) was changed to Israel (Prince of God) as a result of over 20 years of being humbled at the hand of his uncle Laban.

The Bible clearly states that after the time of King David and King Solomon the northern ten tribes of Israel separated themselves from the authority of the King in Jerusalem and set up their own king. In fact there was so much animosity between these groups that there are recorded accounts in the Bible of Israel and Judah being at war with each other!

Read what the Bible says in the 2nd book of Chronicles Chapter 13 – "But Jeroboam caused an ambush to go around behind them; so they were in front of Judah, and the ambush *was* behind them. And when Judah looked around, to their surprise the battle line *was* at both front and rear; and they cried out to the LORD, and the priests sounded the trumpets. Then the men of Judah gave a shout; and as the men of Judah shouted, it happened that God struck Jeroboam and all Israel before Abijah and Judah. And the children of Israel fled before Judah, and God delivered them into their hand. Then Abijah and his people struck them with a great slaughter; so five hundred thousand choice men of Israel fell slain. Thus the children of Israel were subdued at that time; and the children of Judah prevailed, because they relied on the LORD God of their fathers. And Abijah pursued Jeroboam and took cities from him: Bethel with its villages, Jeshanah with its villages, and Ephrain with its villages. So Jeroboam did not recover strength again in the days of Abijah; and the LORD struck him, and he died". (2 Chr 13:13-20).

Five hundred thousand men of Israel were slain by the men of Judah in one battle! We see from this scripture that Israel and Judah were clearly 2 separate nations after the time of King Solomon.

Some 600 years after this battle, after the tribes of Israel had gone into the Assyrian captivity and lost their place in the land of Israel and after Judah had spent 70 years in the Babylonian captivity, but then returned to the land of Judah, Jesus instructed his disciples to go to the lost sheep of the tribes of Israel. There is no record that the disciples looked at Jesus as if He was stupid, or questioned Him about what He really meant by the instruction. They simply went on their way and returned later to report the results of their mission. It's a reasonable conclusion to think that at the time of Jesus the location of the lost tribes was known.

In fact, the ancient Jewish historian, Flavius Josephus, writing towards the end of the first century AD, makes this statement in his work *"Antiquities of the Jews"* (Book 11, Chapter 5, Section 2) *"The entire body of the people of Israel remained in that country, wherefore there are but two tribes in Asia and Europe subject to the Romans, while the ten tribes are beyond the Euphrates till now and are an immense multitude and not to be estimated by numbers"*.

We also get confirmation of this from the Bible. In the story of the Holy Spirit being poured out on the Apostles and them powerfully speaking in foreign languages on the day of Pentecost, the book of Acts Chapter 2 states – "And how is it that we hear, each in our own language in which we were born? Parthians and Medes and Elamites, those dwelling in Mesopotamia, Judea and Cappadocia, Pontus and Asia, Phrygia and Pamphylia, Egypt and the parts of Libya adjoining Cyrene, visitors from Rome, both Jews and proselytes, Cretans and Arabs—we hear them speaking in our own tongues the wonderful works of God." (Acts 2:8-11)

On the day of Pentecost, the festival the Old Testament calls the Feast of Weeks (which was one of the three pilgrimage feasts – when all the men were required to go to the temple and make an offering) Jerusalem was filled with men from other lands. Notice the first group this scripture mentions – Parthians, Medes, Elamites and those in Mesopotamia – these were all from the general area the Tribes of Israel were carried off to during the Assyrian captivity, the land beyond the Euphrates as Josephus indicated.

During the life of Jesus the lost tribes of Israel were known to be in the area formerly known as Assyria, which we would know as the area below the Caucasus Mountains. Over the following centuries these people migrated to the four corners of the earth as we will shortly demonstrate.

Let's look for another clue in the Bible as to the identity. In Genesis Chapter 49 we read this blessing given by Jacob to his son Dan, **"Dan shall judge his people as one of the tribes of Israel. Dan shall be a serpent by the way, a viper by the path, that bites the horse's heels so that its rider shall fall backward."** (Ge 49:16-17). This prophecy is commonly understood that the tribe of Dan would leave a trail of his progress across the globe. The Bible actually gives an account of this tribal characteristic in Judges Chapter 28 – **"And they called the name of the city Dan, after the name of Dan their father, who was born to Israel. However, the name of the city formerly was Laish".** (Jdg 28:29).

If I gave you another clue from the Hebrew language do you think you will be able to work out where the tribe of Dan resides today? Let's see.

In Hebrew the word for man or men is *iysh* (Strong's word H376 pronounced *eesh*). Where do you think we would find the men of the tribe of Dan today? How about the Dan-ish people who live in a place called Den-mark. The change from Dan to Den can easily be explained. In Hebrew only the consonants are written, so my name David would be written as Dvd. Now that's fine when the language is relatively simple, but as it becomes more complex the likelihood of error increases. Does Dvd mean David, dived or in today's language Digital Versatile Disk? To compensate vowel points are now added to let the reader know the correct pronunciation of the word. But before this started Dan would simply have been written DN. It could correctly be spoken as Dan, Den, Din, Don or Dun depending on the context.

The modern day nation of Denmark in northwest Europe is the place where the people of Dan have left their tribal mark. Remember the prophecy also said Dan would be like a snake – leaving a trail. In Judges Chapter 5 and verse 17 we also find out that the tribe of Dan were seafarers **"And why did Dan remain on ships?"** And if we look for the trail of the tribe of Dan we see north of the Caucasus mountains and into central Europe the rivers – *Do*N, *DN*ieper, *Do*Nets, *DN*iester, *Da*Nube, Dar*DaN*ielles, *Da*Nwina, Eri*Da*Nus (Rhine) and Rho*DaN*us (Rhone) all heading towards Scan*DiN*avia in north west Europe.

We can also identify a second (earlier) migration path through the Mediterranean. From the Holy land they settled *Da*Nai in Southern Greece, then through the Pillars of Hercules to the Iberian peninsula (remember the ancestor of Abraham called Eber). Then they travelled to Tuatha De *Da*Naan (Ireland), Scotland, Wales (Cymri) and South West England. Remember the scripture – "Dan shall judge his people" - did you know that in Gaelic the word for a judge is Dan?

This is just one example of how we can trace the movement of the Lost Ten Tribes of Israel from the Holy land to their present location today. Let's look at another example. About the time the Israelites were taken into captivity and apparently disappeared a new race emerged in the same location known as the Saka or Sacae – remember that Hebrew writing does not include vowels so Isaac would simply appear as SC and the race known as the sons of Isaac would be called the Sac-sons. Does this sound much like the Saxons who ended up settling in the south and east of England? In the Persian language these people were known as Scythians while in Greek they were called Cimmerians – and what is the old Welsh name for Wales – it is Cymri!

If you have never heard of the British Israelite understanding before this may seem farfetched. There are however numerous books written on the subject which go into far more detail than I am able to provide here. Many are freely available to download, just do a Google search "Britain and America in prophecy" and you'll find numerous articles and booklets on the subject. The book that gives one of the most scholarly treatments of this subject is "The Lost Ten Tribes of Israel – Found!" by Steven M. Collins. I don't think the book is in print at the moment but you can find used copies on Amazon from $20 to £40. Alternatively you could contact the publishers directly – CPA Book Publisher, PO Box 596, Boring, Oregon 97009 or call (503) 668 4977.

There have been many attempts to identify a specific tribe to a modern day nation. I'm not sure if I go along with the exactitude that many writers claim. Also some have used the understanding of British Israelism to promote racist and anti-Semitic doctrines, which I thoroughly reject (we must remember that the people who left Egypt were a "mixed multitude"). But I am convinced that the descendents of Joseph's sons Ephraim and Manasseh are the English speaking people of Britain, America, Canada, Australia, New Zealand and South Africa.

I don't have time to go into detailed proofs of all these witnesses to the present day location of the Israelites, so please do the research and prove this understanding for yourself. It's critical to understanding how the end time scenario will play out.

Here are a few other clues you should consider in your research:

- We've already learned that in Hebrew *iysh* means man or men. If I now tell you that *beriyth* (Strong's H1285) means covenant and is pronounced like *brit* we learn that the *brit-iysh* are the men of the covenant (look at Jeremiah Chapter 31 verse 33 - **But this shall be the covenant that I will make with the house of Israel; After those days, saith the LORD, I will put my law in their inward parts, and write it in their hearts; and will be their God, and they shall be my people.** The British (in Hebrew) are the people of the covenant!

- The book of Isaiah Chapter 49 talking of a time shortly after Jesus returns says this **"Surely these shall come from afar; look! Those from the north and the west"** (Is 49:12). If you get a world atlas and travel directly North West from Jerusalem – where do you arrive? In the British Isles!

- The Declaration of Arbroath (written on 6th April 1320) is considered by many to be the declaration of independence for the Scottish people. Read what it says – *"This nation having come from Scythia the Greater, through the Tuscan Sea, and the Hercules Pillars, and having for many ages taken its residence in Spain in the midst of a most fierce people, could never be brought in subjection by any people how barbarous soever; and having removed from these parts, above 1200 years after the coming of the Israelites out of Egypt, did by many victories and much toil obtain these parts in the West which they still possess, having expelled the British and entirely rooted out the Picts, notwithstanding the frequent assaults and invasions they met with from the Norwegians, Danes, and English; and these parts and possessions they have always retained free from all manner of servitude and subjection, as ancient Histories do witness.* In recognising their ancestry the Scots acknowledged that they travelled from Scythia, through the Gates of Hercules (the straight of Gibraltar), spent time in Spain (the Iberian or Eberian (Hebrew) peninsula) and they start their claim from the time 1200 years after the Israelites came out of Egypt (commonly dated as 1446 BC). This means the Scots moved out of Spain around 246 BC some 400-500 years after the Northern tribes were first taken into the Assyrian captivity.

- The order of service for the Coronation of Queen Elizabeth has in section 7 – The Anointing – the following passage – *"O Lord and heavenly Father, the exalter of the humble and the strength of thy chosen, who by anointing with Oil didst of old make and consecrate kings, priests, and prophets, to teach and govern thy people Israel: Bless and sanctify thy chosen servant ELIZABETH, who by our office and ministry is now to be anointed with this Oil"*. Later in the service it states *"Be thy Head anointed with holy Oil: as kings, priests, and prophets were anointed: And as Solomon was anointed king by Zadok the priest and Nathan the prophet, so be thou anointed, blessed, and consecrated Queen over the Peoples, whom the Lord thy God hath given thee to rule and govern"*. (http://www.oremus.org/liturgy/coronation/cor1953b.html).

- The Kings and Queens of Britain claim a Royal Lineage back to King Solomon, son of King David, King of Israel! Have a look at this article and you can trace the line from the present Monarch Queen Elizabeth II all the way back to King David.
(http://www.biblestudy.org/bibleref/queenadm.html)

4.2 Times of Blessing and Cursing

So, we've identified that America, Britain, our cousins in North West Europe and their descendents around the world are the physical descendents of the Northern Ten Tribes of Israel. But how does this account for the missing King of the West in end time prophecy?

To understand what is happening here we need to look at two more prophecies. First let's go back to Genesis Chapter 49, where we read about the blessing on Dan and this time we'll look at the blessing Jacob gave to Joseph. **"Joseph is a fruitful bough, a fruitful bough by a well; his branches run over the wall. The archers have bitterly grieved him, shot at him and hated him. But his bow remained in strength, and the arms of his hands were made strong by the hands of the Mighty God of Jacob (from there is the Shepherd, the Stone of Israel), by the God of your father who will help you, and by the Almighty who will bless you with blessings of heaven above, blessings of the deep that lies beneath, blessings of the breasts and of the womb. The blessings of your father have excelled the blessings of my ancestors, up to the utmost bound of the everlasting hills. They shall be on the head of Joseph, and on the crown of the head of him who was separate from his brothers."** (Ge 49:22-26).

As we can see the blessing on Joseph was that he (and his descendents) would be fruitful in his agriculture (boughs), natural resources – mines and fishing (deep), climate (heaven above) and people (breasts and womb). But also he shall be hated and shot at but that his military prowess would prevail.

If we look at the rise of the English speaking empire starting in 1805 at the battle of Trafalgar when Britain achieved naval dominance over the seas which subsequently allowed the land victory over Napoleon, the growth of the British Empire and the great wealth it produced, the constant wars between Britain and the other European powers up to the devastation of the First World War; and then the emergence of America as the natural successor of this economic, military and political might we can see how the prophetic blessing to Joseph has been fulfilled right up to the present day.

There is another blessing given to the children of Israel (throughout their generations i.e. for all time) which we can find in Deuteronomy Chapter 28. **"And it shall come to pass, if thou shalt hearken diligently unto the voice of the LORD thy God, to observe and to do all his commandments which I command thee this day, that the LORD thy God will set thee on high above all nations of the earth: And all these blessings shall come on thee, and overtake thee, if thou shalt hearken unto the voice of the LORD thy God. Blessed shalt thou be in the city, and blessed shalt thou be in the field. Blessed shall be the fruit of thy body, and the fruit of thy ground, and the fruit of thy cattle, the increase of thy kine, and the flocks of thy sheep. Blessed shall be thy basket and thy store. Blessed shalt thou be when thou comest in, and blessed shalt thou be when thou goest out. The LORD shall cause thine enemies that rise up against thee to be smitten before thy face: they shall come out against thee one way, and flee before thee seven ways. The LORD shall command the blessing upon thee in thy storehouses, and in all that thou settest thine hand unto; and he shall bless thee in the land which the LORD thy God giveth thee.**

The LORD shall establish thee an holy people unto himself, as he hath sworn unto thee, if thou shalt keep the commandments of the LORD thy God, and walk in his ways. And all people of the earth shall see that thou art called by the name of the LORD; and they shall be afraid of thee. And the LORD shall make thee plenteous in goods, in the fruit of thy body, and in the fruit of thy cattle, and in the fruit of thy ground, in the land which the LORD sware unto thy fathers to give thee. The LORD shall open unto thee his good treasure, the heaven to give the rain unto thy land in his season, and to bless all the work of thine hand: and thou shalt lend unto many nations, and thou shalt not borrow. And the LORD shall make thee the head, and not the tail; and thou shalt be above only, and thou shalt not be beneath; if that thou hearken unto the commandments of the LORD thy God, which I command thee this day, to observe and to do them: And thou shalt not go aside from any of the words which I command thee this day, to the right hand, or to the left, to go after other gods to serve them.". (Dt 28:1-14)

Again, we can see that these blessings have been richly fulfilled among the English speaking peoples and the inhabitants of North West Europe. Let's look at what God promised:

- **political power** – you shall be above all the nations of the earth ... make you the head and not the tail;

- **social power** – blessed in the city ... the fruit of your body

- **economic power** - blessed in your herds ... cattle and flocks ... basket and kneading bowl ... and your storehouses;

- **financial power** – you shall lend but not borrow;

- **military power** – your enemies defeated before you ... flee seven ways.

But unlike the earlier blessings given to Joseph, these are conditional. Here is the condition God set for us to receive these blessings – *"if you diligently obey the voice of the LORD your God, to observe carefully all His commandments which I command you today ... if you heed the commandments of the LORD your God, which I command you today, and are careful to observe them. So you shall not turn aside from any of the words which I command you this day, to the right or the left, to go after other gods to serve them"*.

During the 18th and 19th centuries some of the greatest missionary and evangelical movements came out of Britain and America and the God of the Bible was a central element of life in these leading Christian countries.

However today, Britain is an apostate and godless society and the secular left in America is fighting to remove any vestige of Christianity from the governmental structure with a zeal that would make any itinerant Bible thumping preacher proud.

With the recent election of Barak Obama as the President of the United States and the dominance the Democrat party has in Congress this process will speed up dramatically.

Unfortunately for us there is a second part to Deuteronomy Chapter 28. This is ominously called the "Cursing"; it goes on for a further 53 verses stating in explicit detail the curses God would pour out on the descendents of Israel if they turned away from Him.

Let's look at these in some detail to help us identify what signs to be looking out for. This is a long passage of scripture so I've taken each verse and identified it as present or future fulfilment in one of the 5 categories – political, social, economic, financial or military power.

4.3 Present Fulfilment

a. Political

[28] The LORD shall smite thee with madness, and blindness, and astonishment of heart.

When we look at the failure of our political institutions to understand and predict the rise of extremists who would do us harm – blind to the threat, astonished by their actions and madness in our attempts to negotiate with them - we see these curses being fulfilled.

b. Social

[16] Cursed shalt thou be in the city, … [18] Cursed shall be the fruit of thy body … [30] Thou shalt betroth a wife, and another man shall lie with her:

Marriage is the fundamental building block of successful society and as we abandon this institution to sexual immorality, cohabitation and one-parent families our social fabric continues to decay. One direct result of this is the increasing disaffection of our youth causing the increase in inner city crime.

c. Economic

[16] … cursed shalt thou be in the field. [17] Cursed shall be thy basket and thy store [18] and the fruit of thy land, the increase of thy kine (cattle), and the flocks of thy sheep. [22] The LORD shall smite thee … and with blasting, and with mildew … [23] And thy heaven that is over thy head shall be brass, and the earth that is under thee shall be iron.

The drought and failure of harvests (especially in the Prairies and Mid West), the collapse of bee colonies and the fisheries around the world, the large scale animal diseases (foot and mouth and mad cow disease) and the disruption to weather patterns, hurricanes and tornadoes all attest to this

d.   Financial

[30] **thou shalt build an house, and thou shalt not dwell therein:**
How well does this describe the collapse of the sub-prime mortgage market and it's knock on effect in global financial markets?

e.   Military

[19] **Cursed shalt thou be when thou comest in, and cursed shalt thou be when thou goest out.**

In days gone by the British and American military were the envy of the world. But since the 1950's, every time we have gone out to battle we have not won a decisive military campaign which has achieved it operational and political objectives (with the exception of the 1982 Falklands war) – Aden, Korea, Vietnam, Northern Ireland, Gulf War 1 and now Iraq and Afghanistan.

4.4   Future Fulfilment

a.   Political

[32] **Thy sons and thy daughters shall be given unto another people, and thine eyes shall look, and fail with longing for them all the day long: and there shall be no might in thine hand. ... [36] The LORD shall bring thee, and thy king which thou shalt set over thee, unto a nation which neither thou nor thy fathers have known; and there shalt thou serve other gods, wood and stone. [37] And thou shalt become an astonishment, a proverb, and a byword, among all nations whither the LORD shall lead thee. ... [41] Thou shalt beget sons and daughters, but thou shalt not enjoy them; for they shall go into captivity. ... [43] The stranger that is within thee shall get up above thee very high; and thou shalt come down very low. ... [48] Therefore shalt thou serve thine enemies which the LORD shall send against thee, in hunger, and in thirst, and in nakedness, and in want of all things : and he shall put a yoke of iron upon thy neck, until he have destroyed thee.**

As I write this [first edition], Barak Hussein Obama was announced the winner of the US presidential election – the king set up over them. The stranger is becoming more and more dominant due to our massive financial deficits and when America finally defaults on its debt this will ultimately lead to poverty, financial ruin and possibly even physical slavery of the people.

b.   Social

[20] The LORD shall send upon thee cursing, vexation, and rebuke, in all that thou settest thine hand unto for to do, until thou be destroyed, and until thou perish quickly; because of the wickedness of thy doings, whereby thou hast forsaken me. ... [21] The LORD shall make the pestilence cleave unto thee, until he have consumed thee from off the land, whither thou goest to possess it. [22] The LORD shall smite thee with a consumption, and with a fever, and with an inflammation, and with an extreme burning ...[26] And thy carcasses shall be meat unto all fowls of the air, and unto the beasts of the earth, and no man shall fray them away. [27] The LORD will smite thee with the botch of Egypt, and with the emerods, and with the scab, and with the itch, whereof thou canst not be healed. ... [35] The LORD shall smite thee in the knees, and in the legs, with a sore botch that cannot be healed, from the sole of thy foot unto the top of thy head. ... [59] Then the LORD will make thy plagues wonderful, and the plagues of thy seed, even great plagues, and of long continuance, and sore sicknesses, and of long continuance. [60] Moreover he will bring upon thee all the diseases of Egypt, which thou wast afraid of; and they shall cleave unto thee. [61] Also every sickness, and every plague, which is not written in the book of this law, them will the LORD bring upon thee, until thou be destroyed. ...

Every generation we are getting less and less healthy and more susceptible to drug resistant bacteria; MRSA is a major threat in our hospitals and the threat of Avian flu still hangs over us; the availability of affordable, effective health care is beyond the reach of growing numbers of our people and AIDS is a major health problem in our lands.

c.   Economic

[24] The LORD shall make the rain of thy land powder and dust: from heaven shall it come down upon thee, until thou be destroyed. ... [30] thou shalt plant a vineyard, and shalt not gather the grapes thereof. [31]Thine ox shall be slain before thine eyes, and thou shalt not eat thereof: thine ass shall be violently taken away from before thy face, and shall not be restored to thee: thy sheep shall be given unto thine enemies, and thou shalt have none to rescue them. ... [38]Thou shalt carry much seed out into the field, and shalt gather but little in; for the locust shall consume it. [39]Thou shalt plant vineyards, and dress them, but shalt neither drink of the wine, nor gather the grapes; for the worms shall eat them. [40]Thou shalt have olive trees throughout all thy coasts, but thou shalt not anoint thyself with the oil; for thine olive shall cast his fruit. ... [42] All thy trees and fruit of thy land shall the locust consume. ... [51]And he shall eat the fruit of thy cattle, and the fruit of thy land, until thou be destroyed: which also shall not leave thee either corn, wine, or oil, or the increase of thy kine, or flocks of thy sheep, until he have destroyed thee.

Every year more and more farmers go under because of high prices and low yields. This coupled with the threat from genetically modified crops, large scale disease outbreaks (foot and mouth, mad cow disease) and the collapse of the bee colonies all point to a time of immense famine in the land.

d.   Financial

[29] **And thou shalt grope at noonday, as the blind gropeth in darkness, and thou shalt not prosper in thy ways: and thou shalt be only oppressed and spoiled evermore, and no man shall save thee. ...[33] The fruit of thy land, and all thy labours, shall a nation which thou knowest not eat up; and thou shalt be only oppressed and crushed always: ... [44] He shall lend to thee, and thou shalt not lend to him: he shall be the head, and thou shalt be the tail.**

If you remember the panic and terror in the financial markets when the sub-prime market started to unravel; the groping ineffectiveness of financial regulators; the trillions of dollars of debt placed on us by governments frantic to prop up the banking system; the ballooning national and personal debt in the US and UK and the calls for a global financial regulator all point to the end of the US dollar as the reserve currency which would signal the death blow to the American economy.

e.   Military

[22] **The LORD shall smite thee ... and with the sword... and they shall pursue thee until thou perish ... [25] The LORD shall cause thee to be smitten before thine enemies: thou shalt go out one way against them, and flee seven ways before them: and shalt be removed into all the kingdoms of the earth. ... [45] Moreover all these curses shall come upon thee, and shall pursue thee, and overtake thee, till thou be destroyed; because thou hearkenedst not unto the voice of the LORD thy God, to keep his commandments and his statutes which he commanded thee: ... [49] The LORD shall bring a nation against thee from far, from the end of the earth, as swift as the eagle flieth; a nation whose tongue thou shalt not understand; [50]A nation of fierce countenance, which shall not regard the person of the old, nor shew favour to the young: ... [52] And he shall besiege thee in all thy gates, until thy high and fenced walls come down, wherein thou trustedst, throughout all thy land: and he shall besiege thee in all thy gates throughout all thy land, which the LORD thy God hath given thee. [53]And thou shalt eat the fruit of thine own body, the flesh of thy sons and of thy daughters, which the LORD thy God hath given thee, in the siege, and in the straitness, wherewith thine enemies shall distress thee: [54] So that the man that is tender among you, and very delicate, his eye shall be evil toward his brother, and toward the wife of his bosom, and toward the remnant of his children which he shall leave: [55] So that he will not give to any of them of the flesh of his children whom he shall eat: because he hath nothing left him in the siege, and in the straitness, wherewith thine enemies shall distress thee in all thy gates. [56] The tender and delicate woman among you, which would not adventure to set the sole of her foot upon the ground for delicateness and tenderness, her eye shall be evil toward the husband of her bosom, and toward her son, and toward her daughter, [57] And toward her young one that cometh out from between her feet, and toward**

her children which she shall bear: for she shall eat them for want of all things secretly in the siege and straitness, wherewith thine enemy shall distress thee in thy gates.

The final fulfilment of the military curse will result in the defeat and destruction of America, Britain and their allies. The death of young and old alike, social collapse and famine will be so severe that some will even turn to cannibalism of their own dead children!

The total destruction of the children of Israel will be so complete that only a small remnant will remain.

[62]And ye shall be left few in number, whereas ye were as the stars of heaven for multitude; because thou wouldest not obey the voice of the LORD thy God. [63]And it shall come to pass, that as the LORD rejoiced over you to do you good, and to multiply you; so the LORD will rejoice over you to destroy you, and to bring you to nought; and ye shall be plucked from off the land whither thou goest to possess it. [64]And the LORD shall scatter thee among all people, from the one end of the earth even unto the other; and there thou shalt serve other gods, which neither thou nor thy fathers have known, even wood and stone. [65]And among these nations shalt thou find no ease, neither shall the sole of thy foot have rest: but the LORD shall give thee there a trembling heart, and failing of eyes, and sorrow of mind: [66]And thy life shall hang in doubt before thee; and thou shalt fear day and night, and shalt have none assurance of thy life: [67]In the morning thou shalt say, would God it were even! and at even thou shalt say, would God it were morning! for the fear of thine heart wherewith thou shalt fear, and for the sight of thine eyes which thou shalt see. [68]And the LORD shall bring thee into Egypt again with ships, by the way whereof I spake unto thee, Thou shalt see it no more again: and there ye shall be sold unto your enemies for bondmen and bondwomen, and no man shall buy you.

And this remnant will be taken into a literal slavery, where their life is so worthless they live in dread morning and night. They will be removed from their homeland and dispersed through the nations until they are eventually brought into Egypt.

God is a God of justice and when He brought Israel out of Egypt, He killed the first born of the Egyptians in revenge for their policy of killing all the firstborn of the Israelites. He also allowed the Israelites to ransack the Egyptians for gold and silver, which was just compensation for their years of slavery when they were denied fair wages for their labour. It was pointed out to me that just as Britain and America grew their economic (and subsequent political) might on the backs of African slaves, so the justice of God will be done when the remnant of Britain and America go into slavery back into Egypt.

A level of destruction on a scale such as this is almost inconceivable for powerful nations such as America, Britain and the countries of Northwest Europe. But the Bible is explicit – our nations are going to be totally destroyed and the few who remain will be taken into slavery. Now, this is such a mind numbing concept that we have serious difficulty believing it, but Deuteronomy Chapter 28 is not the only witness. Let's look at another prophetic event which clearly parallels the description of God's cursing of our people.

4.5   The Time of Jacob's Trouble

The Prophet Jeremiah received this prophetic warning from God for the people of Israel and Judah. **"The word that came to Jeremiah from the LORD, saying, thus speaketh the LORD God of Israel, saying, Write thee all the words that I have spoken unto thee in a book. For, lo, the days come, saith the LORD, that I will bring again the captivity of my people Israel and Judah, saith the LORD: and I will cause them to return to the land that I gave to their fathers, and they shall possess it. And these are the words that the LORD spake concerning Israel and concerning Judah. For thus saith the LORD; We have heard a voice of trembling, of fear, and not of peace. Ask ye now, and see whether a man doth travail with child? wherefore do I see every man with his hands on his loins, as a woman in travail, and all faces are turned into paleness? Alas! for that day is great, so that none is like it: it is even the time of Jacob's trouble; but he shall be saved out of it. For it shall come to pass in that day, saith the LORD of hosts, that I will break his yoke from off thy neck, and will burst thy bonds, and strangers shall no more serve themselves of him: But they shall serve the LORD their God, and David their king, whom I will raise up unto them."** (Jer 30:1-9)

Some people try and dismiss this as talking about the first Israelite and Jewish captivities, but this cannot be as Jeremiah was written around 610BC which is *after* the Israelites were taken into the Assyrian captivity. Also read carefully what it says — "I will bring again the captivity of my people Israel and Judah" — Israel had already been taken into captivity; Judah was going into the Babylonian captivity for the first time, and God is saying He will take them *again* into captivity. Also notice that after God breaks the yoke of slavery from the neck of the remnant of Jacob they will serve God and King David who has been resurrected. This prophecy has not yet been fulfilled.

Others try and equate this to the Great Tribulation, but again that cannot be supported from scripture. The Bible states it is the time of *Jacob's* trouble, which indicates that this will fall on the descendents of the tribes of Israel (including Judah), whereas the Great Tribulation comes upon the whole world.

In the first edition of this book I mistakenly made the assertion that the "time" spoken of in relation to Jacob's trouble would be a one year period as the word "time" in Hebrew means one year. In Daniel's prophecy "time, times and half a time" this is correct. The word time is Strong's H4150 *mow'ed* which means appointed time or sacred season. In the prophetic interpretation this is taken to be a one year period (i.e. the period between appointed *mow'edim*). But in the case of "the time of Jacob's trouble" the Hebrew word is H6256 *'eth* which is interpreted as the time of an event or a specific occasion. Therefore it was incorrect to make the assertion that the time of Jacob's trouble will last for one year.

How long will the time of Jacob's trouble be?

Having looked at other examples of God's wrath being poured out I am now of the opinion that the time of Jacob's trouble will be an extremely short and violent event. The prophet Hosea states, "**They have dealt treacherously with the LORD, for they have begotten pagan children. Now a New Moon shall devour them and their heritage. Blow the ram's horn in Gibeah, the trumpet in Ramah! Cry aloud at Beth Aven, 'Look behind you, O Benjamin!' Ephraim shall be desolate in the day of rebuke; Among the tribes of Israel I make known what is sure". (Hos 5:7-9).** The statement about a new moon could indicate a one month period and this would tie in with the warning given in the New Testament. "**For when they say, "Peace and safety!" then sudden destruction comes upon them, as labor pains upon a pregnant woman. And they shall not escape". (1 Thes 5:3).** The sudden destruction spoken of in 1 Thessalonians makes more sense in relation to a catastrophic 30 day period rather than a drawn out 12 months of trouble.

But how could this possibly happen. Let's look again at the scripture above. We see that "men will hold their loins ... travail [labour] as with child ... and have faces turned pale". I believe the most likely cause of these symptoms comes from a massive dose of radiation, such as would be received in a nuclear war. The casualty develops Acute Radiation Sickness which has three main symptoms.

> 1) Hematologic syndrome (bone marrow) which is characterized by anorexia, malaise and haemorrhage.
> 2) Gastro Intestinal Syndrome is characterized by sever diarrhoea, dehydration and fever.
> 3) Cardiovascular/Central Nervous System syndrome resulting in confusion, severe nausea, diarrhoea, convulsions, coma and death (for more information visit –
> http://www.medterms.com/script/main/art.asp?articlekey=26759).

Would someone with internal haemorrhaging, severe diarrhoea and nausea, dehydration and convulsions be holding their stomach, appear as though they're having contractions and have pale faces? Yes they would.

The theory of a pre-emptive nuclear strike is given further support by the scripture we read in Hosea Chapter 8 "**They sacrifice flesh for the sacrifices of mine offerings, and eat it; but the LORD accepteth them not; now will he remember their iniquity, and visit their sins: they shall return to Egypt. For Israel hath forgotten his Maker, and buildeth temples; and Judah hath multiplied fenced cities: but I will send a fire upon his cities, and it shall devour the palaces thereof." (Hos 8:13-14).**

Again as we look closely at this verse we could interpret the sacrifice as being the return to sacrificial worship by the Jews on the temple mount, but that occurs after the time of Jacob's trouble, so I am more inclined to interpret that as the empty vain worship we see in the politically correct, materialistic churches of our present society.

We then read *"they shall return to Egypt"* which we also read in the cursing scripture. We know that Israel has forgotten his maker and Judah are fencing themselves in with the "security wall". Then God says he will "send fire on his cities and devour the palaces thereof". A pre-emptive nuclear strike would do exactly that! Massive firestorms would range at the centre of the strike and the sky scrapers and all the temples and palaces devoted to our false god, money, would come crashing down.

But there is far more to the punishment which will be placed on the cities of Israel. A nuclear strike on a typical city with a 15kT weapon would produce short term (in the first few weeks) fatalities in the range of 10-15%. The life time casualty rate would be higher due to long term radiation exposure and economic and social collapse coupled with famine caused by the "nuclear winter" but even eventual death toll tripled to say 30-45% it is still way short of the casualty rate the Bible foretells.

Amos Chapter 5 states, **"Hear this word which I take up against you, a lamentation, O house of Israel: The virgin of Israel has fallen; She will rise no more. She lies forsaken on her land; there is no one to raise her up. For thus says the Lord GOD: "The city that goes out by a thousand shall have a hundred left, and that which goes out by a hundred shall have ten left to the house of Israel."** **(Amos 5:1-2)** The Bible is clearly indicating that when the destruction of Israel comes, 90% of the population will die. There is no evidence of destruction on this scale before so it has to be an end time fulfilment.

But if nuclear war only results in a 45% fatality rate – where does the other 45% come from? Psalm 91 gives us another clue: **"You shall not be afraid of the terror by night, nor of the arrow that flies by day, nor of the pestilence that walks in darkness, nor of the destruction that lays waste at noonday. A thousand may fall at your side, and ten thousand at your right hand; but it shall not come near you. Only with your eyes shall you look, and see the reward of the wicked. Because you have made the LORD, who is my refuge, even the Most High, your dwelling place, no evil shall befall you, Nor shall any plague come near your dwelling; (Ps 91:5-10)**

In the passage even though ten thousand of the wicked fall at the right hand of a righteous person, notice that the *"pestilence ... [and] plague shall not come near your dwellings"*. In addition to the pre-emptive nuclear strike we are also going to suffer plague and pestilence – some of this may be through natural causes but I believe that there will also be biological and chemical attacks to follow after the nuclear strike. It is also interesting to note that in the cursing section of Deuteronomy Chapter 28 there is a siege which is so acute people turn to cannibalism.

How could this scenario play out? A massive coordinated pre-emptive nuclear strike from Russia and China (and now North Korean and possibly Iran) against the Israelitish nations followed by a physical blockade of all ports and airports during which time biological and chemical weapons are deployed against the survivors could easily create this scenario.

But the question is why would Russia and China want to do such a thing? As always, if you want to get to the truth of a matter – follow the money. America (primarily) and the western economies on a smaller scale have been extremely valuable for the Chinese when we were rampant consumers of every product and trinket they could manufacture.

The West got further and further into debt, the Chinese earned more and more foreign currency to fund their economic, social and military development and so the game was played for the last couple of decades and everyone was happy. However, now the west has stopped spending (because of the sub-prime/credit bubble burst) we are no longer fulfilling our side of the bargain – being willing consumers of Chinese goods. The money they had accumulated is becoming almost worthless and we are now all competing against them for a reducing supply of natural resources. Rather than being a favoured consumer we are now a direct competitor and have no further value to China.

Russia on the other hand was humiliated by the way Ronald Regan's administration outspent them to end the Cold War, so seeing America destroyed by their own profligate spending would be poetic justice. The recent Russian aggression against Georgia (and the oil pipeline which runs through their territory!) was poorly handled by NATO and the West. Also the expected return of Putin as the President (once his puppet caretaker has changed the Russian constitution to allow him to serve for a further 12 years) all point to increasing belligerence and military resurgence at a time when America is economically weakened, militarily exhausted and has politically lurched to one of the most leftist, pacifist governments ever.

Where is the King of the West in end time prophecy? The simple Biblical answer is that he has been totally destroyed by nuclear, biological and chemical weapons before the Great Tribulation begins. This concept is almost impossible for us to accept, but this is an exact parallel of the first destruction of Israel.

During this period the northern 10 tribes of Israel (who today we would recognise as the descendants of the Anglo Saxons) were take off into the Assyrian captivity. Some 70 years later the children of the tribe of Judah (plus Benjamin and some Levis) were carried away into the Babylonian captivity which Daniels speaks of. In the end time manifestation of this event, the Israelite nations (America, Britain and the English speaking nations) will be destroyed first and the survivors will be carried away into slavery. After this event is complete the Jews will be brought to the point of total destruction as the armies of the world surround Jerusalem period to the final battle of Armageddon.

The Bible indicates that there will be a 90% fatality rate during this period. But this also means that there is a 10% survival rate and anyone who has a working knowledge of the scriptures knows that the tithe (that which is holy and must be given to God) of the produce of the land is 10%. Out of all this destruction God will protect 10% of the people to be a blessing to Him for the purpose He has ordained for Israel. Let us make sure that we are doing everything He instructs us to do so that we will come under His protection and not His condemnation when the time of Jacob's trouble is poured out on our people.

We've discovered earlier that we are to be watching for the signs of the times, so if we're really going to understand the times that we are in, we need to understand about God's timing and the calendar He uses, which is very different from the secular calendars we use in the world at large.

In Chapter 5 we'll explore *"God's Divine Calendar"*.

Chapter 5

God's Divine Calendar

Before we learn about God's divine calendar, let's look at what a calendar is, why we have one, and how our present calendar was developed.

According to the Encarta English Dictionary a calendar is:

- a chart showing the days and months of the year, especially a particular year
- a system of calculating the days and months of the year and when the year begins and ends
- a timetable of events, usually covering a period of a year
- an official list of things to be done or considered

5.1   Defining the Biblical Calendar

The main purpose of a calendar is to allow different parties to coordinate activities to happen at mutually agreed points in the chronological system they are using. And as we can see from the dictionary definition, a typical calendar defines the year and its divisions; provides a timetable of events over the year and lists things to be done or considered. Based on this understanding we will soon see that the Bible provides a very specific calendar that God has ordained for His people to follow. But before we look at that, we need to understand where our present secular calendar came from.

In the world today we use the Gregorian calendar. Technically it is a solar arithmetical calendar which means that the rotation of the earth round the sun is the primary measure (of the year) and the months are based on an arithmetic formula. Because the period of rotation of the earth around the sun is not an exact number of days, leap years are introduced to correct the almost ¼ day error. The present calendar was introduced by Pope Gregory XIII in 1582 to replace the Julian calendar which was slightly too long. Following the Julian calendar meant that the timing of the vernal equinox, and hence the timing of Easter, was moving forward in the year. The rotation of the moon around the earth has no part in developing the Gregorian calendar, although the Catholic Church calculates the moons position separately to identify the timing of Easter. The names of the months are primarily named after Roman Emperors or pagan gods and the days of the week are named after pagan gods and goddesses.

Is the Gregorian calendar we follow in society the same as the calendar God revealed to us in the Bible? Let's look at a few scriptures to find out.

"And God said, Let there be lights in the firmament of the heaven to divide the day from the night; and let them be for signs, and for seasons, and for days, and years:" (Ge 1:14)

"He appointed the moon for seasons: the sun knoweth his going down". (Ps 104:19)

The first thing we learn about God's calendar is that it is based on both the sun and the moon. It is a solar-lunar calendar and it is the moon that defines the seasons, not the sun. Observing the equinox (equal day and night) and solstice (longest and shortest day) to define the seasons is using the sun not the moon and is unbiblical. God clearly tells us to use the moon for seasons.

"In the first month, on the fourteenth day of the month at even, ye shall eat unleavened bread, until the one and twentieth day of the month at even". (Ex 12:18)

"Observe the month of Abib, and keep the Passover unto the LORD thy God: for in the month of Abib the LORD thy God brought thee forth out of Egypt by night". (Dt 16:1)

How do we know when the year starts? According to the Bible the month in which we eat unleavened bread is to be the first month. And the Feast of Unleavened Bread is associated with the Passover (we'll discuss this in more detail later). In the book of Deuteronomy we are told to observe the month of Abib and keep the Passover. The month of Abib is the first month of the Biblical calendar. But when is it? We know that the Passover is observed in the spring – but why? Well, Abib comes from the Hebrew word for "tender" and is understood as meaning "young ears of barley". We are to observe the month of young ears of barley and keep the Passover. The first month of the year is when we can see young ears of barley (and as there is a dual harvest in the Holy land, which we don't have in northern climates, we take this observation from Israel).

What do we take as the beginning of the month? Unfortunately the Bible does not give explicit instructions here which means we have to do some analysis, which is more complex than I need to go into for this book. In summary, there are three main understandings as to what constitutes the beginning of the month – the astronomical conjunction of the sun, moon and earth; the first observed crescent of the moon or the full moon (this is an exceedingly small minority). I discount the observed crescent of the moon for three main reasons – it is a very subjective assessment and can be weather dependant; it raises issues as to where the observation should be taken from (Jerusalem or anywhere around the world) and the crescent moon is a highly pagan symbol which is not mentioned at all in the Bible, but was a common pagan symbol used in Babylon during the period of the Jewish captivity. The Biblically correct timing of the new moon is the astronomical conjunction. Also by following this method of starting the month we can know exactly when the new month starts anywhere in the world, it is not at all subjective (the conjunctions can be calculated years ahead if need be) and the appointed feast days and heavenly signs, such as solar and lunar eclipses all occur at the same time which has great symbolic meaning as you will find out later.

We have found a biblical definition for the year, seasons and months. But what about days and weeks?

"And God said, Let there be light: and there was light. And God saw the light, that it was good: and God divided the light from the darkness. And God called the light Day, and the darkness he called Night. And the evening and the morning were the first day". (Ge 1:3-5)

"Jesus answered, Are there not twelve hours in the day? If any man walk in the day, he stumbleth not, because he seeth the light of this world. But if a man walk in the night, he stumbleth, because there is no light in him." (Jn 11:9-10)

The Biblical day is the period of light and the night is the period of darkness. Technically day is from dawn (the first visible light) to dusk (the last visible light). The day is also divided into 12 hours - this is a bit difficult for us to understand but before the invention of clocks and watches the length of the hour varied to fit into the length of the light portion of the day.

What about the week?

"Thus the heavens and the earth were finished, and all the host of them. And on the seventh day God ended his work which he had made; and he rested on the seventh day from all his work which he had made. And God blessed the seventh day, and sanctified it: because that in it he had rested from all his work which God created and made." (Ge 2:1-3)

"See, for that the LORD hath given you the Sabbath, therefore he giveth you on the sixth day the bread of two days; abide ye every man in his place, let no man go out of his place on the seventh day. So the people rested on the seventh day. And the house of Israel called the name thereof Manna: and it was like coriander seed, white; and the taste of it was like wafers made with honey. (Ex 16:29-31)

The week is the only division of time which is not defined by the relative movement of the earth, moon and sun. The 7 day week was specifically instituted by God. He rested on the seventh day and sanctified it. He then went to the trouble of emphasizing this day as a sanctified (holy or set apart) day by using the miracle of providing manna every day (except the Sabbath) for forty years in the wilderness. Before the acceptance of Christianity as the official religion of Rome and eventually the global administration of the British Empire, there were several variations of the week based on time divisions of other than 7 days. The ancient Egyptians used a 10 day week (as did the French revolutionary calendar). The Mayans used 13 and 20 day weeks, the pre-Christian Lithuanians a 9 day week and the Soviet Union a 5 and 6 day week, only moving to a 7 day week in 1940.

The Bible clearly gives us the first requirement for a calendar - *a system of calculating the days and months of the year and when the year begins and ends.* What does it tell us about the second requirement - *a timetable of events, usually covering a period of a year?*

5.2 Identifying God's Appointments

Well as you would expect, the major appointments God has for His divine calendar are clearly laid out in the Bible. In fact the book of Leviticus, Chapter 23 explains every one of these appointments. The first of the feasts of God is the weekly Sabbath.

And the LORD spake unto Moses, saying, speak unto the children of Israel, and say unto them, concerning the feasts of the LORD, which ye shall proclaim to be holy convocations, even these are my feasts. Six days shall work be done: but the seventh day is the Sabbath of rest, an holy convocation; ye shall do no work therein: it is the Sabbath of the LORD in all your dwellings.

Next the Lord tells us to observe the Passover and the Feast of Unleavened Bread, which as we learned identify the beginning of the Biblical year. These festivals are commonly grouped into a period we call the spring Holy days.

These are the feasts of the LORD, even holy convocations, which ye shall proclaim in their seasons. In the fourteenth day of the first month at even is the LORD'S Passover. And on the fifteenth day of the same month is the feast of unleavened bread unto the LORD: seven days ye must eat unleavened bread. In the first day ye shall have an holy convocation: ye shall do no servile work therein. But ye shall offer an offering made by fire unto the LORD seven days: in the seventh day is an holy convocation: ye shall do no servile work therein.

Next we learn about a celebration called the Feast of Firstfruits which happens on the day after the weekly Sabbath during the Feast of Unleavened Bread.

And the LORD spake unto Moses, saying, speak unto the children of Israel, and say unto them, When ye be come into the land which I give unto you, and shall reap the harvest thereof, then ye shall bring a sheaf of the firstfruits of your harvest unto the priest: and he shall wave the sheaf before the LORD, to be accepted for you: on the morrow after the Sabbath the priest shall wave it. And ye shall offer that day when ye wave the sheaf an he lamb without blemish of the first year for

a burnt offering unto the LORD. And the meat offering thereof shall be two tenth deals of fine flour mingled with oil, an offering made by fire unto the LORD for a sweet savour: and the drink offering thereof shall be of wine, the fourth part of an hin. And ye shall eat neither bread, nor parched corn, nor green ears, until the selfsame day that ye have brought an offering unto your God: it shall be a statute for ever throughout your generations in all your dwellings.

Starting on the day of the Feast of Firstfruits we are told to complete seven weeks and count to the fiftieth day, this is the day of Pentecost (50 count) in the New Testament calendar and usually occurs between mid May and mid June.

And ye shall count unto you from the morrow after the Sabbath, from the day that ye brought the sheaf of the wave offering; seven Sabbaths shall be complete: even unto the morrow after the seventh Sabbath shall ye number fifty days; and ye shall offer a new meat offering unto the LORD. Ye shall bring out of your habitations two wave loaves of two tenth deals: they shall be of fine flour; they shall be baken with leaven; they are the firstfruits unto the LORD. And ye shall offer with the bread seven lambs without blemish of the first year, and one young bullock, and two rams: they shall be for a burnt offering unto the LORD, with their meat offering, and their drink offerings, even an offering made by fire, of sweet savour unto the LORD. Then ye shall sacrifice one kid of the goats for a sin offering, and two lambs of the first year for a sacrifice of peace offerings. And the priest shall wave them with the bread of the firstfruits for a wave offering before the LORD, with the two lambs: they shall be holy to the LORD for the priest. And ye shall proclaim on the selfsame day, that it may be an holy convocation unto you: ye shall do no servile work therein: it shall be a statute for ever in all your dwellings throughout your generations. And when ye reap the harvest of your land, thou shalt not make clean riddance of the corners of thy field when thou reapest, neither shalt thou gather any gleaning of thy harvest: thou shalt leave them unto the poor, and to the stranger: I am the LORD your God.

Then we come to the end of the agricultural year with the main harvest and the celebration we call the autumn (or Fall for our North American cousins) Holy days. These start with the Day of Trumpets.

And the LORD spake unto Moses, saying, speak unto the children of Israel, saying, In the seventh month, in the first day of the month, shall ye have a Sabbath, a memorial of blowing of trumpets, an holy convocation. Ye shall do no servile work therein: but ye shall offer an offering made by fire unto the LORD.

Followed by the Day of Atonement, this is the only day in the whole of the Biblical calendar we are instructed to fast.

And the LORD spake unto Moses, saying, also on the tenth day of this seventh month there shall be a day of atonement: it shall be an holy convocation unto you; and ye shall afflict your souls, and offer an offering made by fire unto the LORD. And ye shall do no work in that same day: for it is

a day of atonement, to make an atonement for you before the LORD your God. For whatsoever soul it be that shall not be afflicted in that same day, he shall be cut off from among his people. And whatsoever soul it be that doeth any work in that same day, the same soul will I destroy from among his people. Ye shall do no manner of work: it shall be a statute for ever throughout your generations in all your dwellings. It shall be unto you a Sabbath of rest, and ye shall afflict your souls: in the ninth day of the month at even, from even unto even, shall ye celebrate your Sabbath.

Next we are told to observe the Feast of Tabernacles for seven days. And there is an additional Feast, called the Eighth day, which many erroneously include with the feast of Tabernacles.

And the LORD spake unto Moses, saying, speak unto the children of Israel, saying, the fifteenth day of this seventh month shall be the feast of tabernacles for seven days unto the LORD. On the first day shall be an holy convocation: ye shall do no servile work therein. Seven days ye shall offer an offering made by fire unto the LORD: on the eighth day shall be an holy convocation unto you; and ye shall offer an offering made by fire unto the LORD: it is a solemn assembly; and ye shall do no servile work therein. These are the feasts of the LORD, which ye shall proclaim to be holy convocations, to offer an offering made by fire unto the LORD, a burnt offering, and a meat offering, a sacrifice, and drink offerings, every thing upon his day: (Lev 23:1-37)

If you were brought up in a mainstream church like I was you've probably never heard about these feasts, with the possible exception of Passover and Pentecost. But I'm sure you won't have observed them as God instructed us to. You may have been in church on Pentecost Sunday, but this will have been more by good luck than good judgement and I doubt if your minister waved two loaves of leavened bread as an offering!

What's the big deal about these Old Testament ceremonies? Surely there's no need for the New Testament church to keep them. We need to focus on Jesus' sacrifice and not get bogged down with all this Jewish tradition, don't we? I agree that we should avoid Jewish and Rabbinic traditions, especially when they lead us away from the true word of God, but let's understand what these festivals really are. In Hebrew they are called *Moadim* or appointments. And these are specific appointments which God has decreed for all of the children of Israel (not just the Jews). If you remember the purposes of a calendar - *is to allow different parties to coordinate activities to happen at mutually agreed points in the chronological system they are using.* For an appointment to be effective all parties have to turn up at the correct time and place. If God tells us these are His appointed times, His divine appointments with mankind, it doesn't do us much good to turn up on the wrong days. I mean just think about it – if you had an appointment for a job interview next Tuesday, and you decided to turn up on Thursday – do you think you would get the job? Of course not! And if we want to get into an intimate relationship with the God of Love who is declared to us in the pages of the Bible, we need to start doing what He tells us to do. And observing all His feast days is central to this relationship with Him. Exodus chapter 31 and verse 13 states, **"Speak also to the children of Israel, saying: 'Surely My Sabbaths you shall keep, for it is a sign between Me and you throughout your generations, that you may know that I am the LORD who sanctifies you."** (Ex 31:13) Observing the Weekly and Annual Sabbaths is the sign between God and His people that He has sanctified us (set us apart) and this sign applies throughout all the generations of the children of Israel.

Also it might surprise you to learn that every one of these feasts point to a specific aspect of Jesus' ministry. Jesus has spiritually completed every one of these required sacrifices. During His first coming He observed every one of these annual Holy days and became the literal fulfilment of four out of eight of them. In the very near future He will literally fulfil the remaining four at His second coming. There is so much depth and richness associated with the Feasts of God and the ministry of Jesus that you could write a book just on the feasts, in fact you could write a separate book on the meaning and depth of each individual feast. But that's not our purpose here. However, you do need to have a working knowledge of the physical and spiritual meaning of each of God's feast days to be able to understand the timing of end time events and the countdown to the second coming of Jesus.

In the next few pages, we're going to take a very brief look at each of the annual Holy days to discover how they point us to Jesus, how they have been fulfilled and how they are going to be fulfilled and most important for us in terms of the intent of this book – when they are going to be fulfilled.

a.   Passover

"Speak ye unto all the congregation of Israel, saying, In the tenth day of this month they shall take to them every man a lamb, according to the house of their fathers, a lamb for an house: ... Your lamb shall be without blemish, a male of the first year: ye shall take it out from the sheep, or from the goats: And ye shall keep it up until the fourteenth day of the same month: and the whole assembly of the congregation of Israel shall kill it in the evening. And they shall take of the blood, and strike it on the two side posts and on the upper door post of the houses, wherein they shall eat it ... And the blood shall be to you for a token upon the houses where ye are : and when I see the blood, I will pass over you, and the plague shall not be upon you to destroy you , when I smite the land of Egypt." (Ex 12:3-13)

The Passover lamb was a male lamb, without blemish selected on the 10th day of the month. It was to be kept until the 14th day and killed in the evening (this is the period towards the end of the day, the temple tradition was that the evening sacrifice was conducted at 3:00 pm). The blood was a symbol so that God would not destroy the Israelites as He was going to do the Egyptians.

How does this point to Jesus?

Then Jesus six days before the Passover came to Bethany, where Lazarus was which had been dead, whom he raised from the dead. There they made him a supper; and Martha served: but Lazarus was one of them that sat at the table with him. ... On the next day much people that were come to the feast, when they heard that Jesus was coming to Jerusalem, took branches of palm trees, and went forth to meet him, and cried, Hosanna: Blessed is the King of Israel that cometh in the name of the Lord. (Jn 12:1-12)

Before we can correctly analyze this statement we need to understand the biblical definition of a day is the period from sunset to sunset. Although the Passover lamb is killed on the 14th day, it is actually not eaten until after sunset, which is the evening of the 15th day, six days before Passover would be the 9th day. Jesus then had supper with Lazarus and Martha (the evening of the 10th day) and on the next day – the daylight portion of the 10th – the people chose Him as the King of Israel. Jesus fulfilled the first requirement of the Passover – being selected on the 10th day.

"And it was about the sixth hour, and there was a darkness over all the earth until the ninth hour. And the sun was darkened, and the veil of the temple was rent in the midst. And when Jesus had cried with a loud voice, he said, Father, into thy hands I commend my spirit: and having said thus, he gave up the ghost". (Lk 23:44-46)

Remember the biblical day consists of 12 hours starting at first light (around 6:00 am at that time of year in Jerusalem) the 6th hour would be noon and the 9th hour 3:00pm. Jesus died on the cross at the exact time of the evening sacrifice of the lamb in the temple.

The Jews therefore, because it was the preparation, that the bodies should not remain upon the cross on the Sabbath day, (for that Sabbath day was an high day,) besought Pilate that their legs might be broken, and that they might be taken away. Then came the soldiers, and brake the legs of the first, and of the other which was crucified with him. But when they came to Jesus, and saw that he was dead already, they brake not his legs: But one of the soldiers with a spear pierced his side, and forthwith came there out blood and water. And he that saw it bare record, and his record is true: and he knoweth that he saith true, that ye might believe. For these things were done, that the scripture should be fulfilled, a bone of him shall not be broken. And again another scripture saith, they shall look on him whom they pierced. (Jn 19:31-37)

This scripture from the Book of John gives us several more details about the death of Jesus. Firstly it was a preparation day (the day before the Sabbath); second it was a High Sabbath (annual Holy day) in this case the Feast of Unleavened bread; we can tell that Jesus died on the 14th as the scripture required of the Passover sacrifice. Also we are told that His blood was poured out, also required of the Passover Lamb and not a bone was broken. This in fulfilment of the Passover instruction in Exodus chapter 12 verse 46 – **"In one house shall it be eaten; thou shalt not carry forth ought of the flesh abroad**

out of the house; neither shall ye break a bone thereof." (Ex 12:46) We also see that He fulfilled another prophecy "they shall look on Him who they pierced".

Not only did the crucifixion fulfil the requirement for the Passover sacrifice it also completed numerous other Messianic prophecies. By some estimates Jesus fulfilled over 300 prophecies in His lifetime and 30 on the day of His death. Have a look at Psalm 22 to see how eerily accurate this prophetic song is about Jesus death.

Another principle we need to understand when looking at Biblical prophecy is that of *"let the Bible interpret the Bible"* the closer we stay to the word, the less likely we are to be deceived. We do have to look to present day media to observe the signs, but as far as discerning Biblical intent we should stay with the Bible. In that light we see that the Bible also produces an additional witness that Jesus was the Passover – **"Purge out therefore the old leaven, that ye may be a new lump, as ye are unleavened. For even Christ our Passover is sacrificed for us: Therefore let us keep the feast, not with old leaven, neither with the leaven of malice and wickedness; but with the unleavened bread of sincerity and truth." (1 Cor 5:7-9).** This scripture from the First letter to the Corinthians (a newly founded gentile church) clearly states that Christ was our Passover [lamb] sacrificed for us. But notice, it immediately goes on to tell them to *"keep the feast ... with the unleavened bread of sincerity and truth"*. If the feasts are just for the Jews, why is Paul giving this instruction to a gentile New Testament church?

And this requirement to eat unleavened bread is continued today in the Jewish tradition of the Seder meal. This meal is eaten after sunset on the 14th day of Abib. It is rife with Jewish tradition, much relating to the Biblical requirement to retell the Passover story and some of which is pagan corruption that has unfortunately been included in the service. Typically the service is read in Hebrew with a parallel translation in the native tongue of the attendees.

At one part in the service a piece of unleavened bread, called matza, is broken and a piece is wrapped in a napkin and hidden to be discovered later. In a restaurant setting this would be a stylized discovery, while in an orthodox Jewish home this may include a hunt around the house by the children to find the hidden piece of matza. If you haven't seen a matza before it is usually baked in a square and because of the importance of making sure that it doesn't rise in any way while it is being baked it is rolled and pricked at very close intervals. When baked, matzot (plural) have a striped appearance with holes about every centimetre across its length and breadth.

Now, what is really interesting is the piece of matza which is hidden is called the "Afikomen". It is used in both the Hebrew and native translations of the service, but it is actually derived from a Greek word (aphikomen) meaning "I arrive" or "I come". Here we see in the Jewish Seder meal a clear commemoration of the death, burial and resurrection of Jesus. The matza represents His body which was scourged for us – "by His stripes we are healed" and pierced on the cross. He was broken off from His people (the matza broken), buried (the matza wrapped in linen as His body was and hidden) and then resurrected (the matza is found again and unwrapped – just as his grave clothes were unwrapped). Even though most of them do not know what they are doing, every year Jews commemorate the death, burial and resurrection of Jesus at the Seder meal!

We see that Jesus spiritually and physically fulfilled the requirements of the Passover sacrifice on the exact day and hour God had ordained through His annual feast days. (We will look at an even more amazing prophetic fulfilment later in this chapter when we decipher Daniel's seventy week prophecy!)

b.   The Feast of Unleavened Bread

"And this day shall be unto you for a memorial; and ye shall keep it a feast to the LORD throughout your generations; ye shall keep it a feast by an ordinance for ever. Seven days shall ye eat unleavened bread; even the first day ye shall put away leaven out of your houses: for whosoever eateth leavened bread from the first day until the seventh day, that soul shall be cut off from Israel. And in the first day there shall be an holy convocation, and in the seventh day there shall be an holy convocation to you; no manner of work shall be done in them, save that which every man must eat, that only may be done of you. And ye shall observe the feast of unleavened bread; for in this selfsame day have I brought your armies out of the land of Egypt: therefore shall ye observe this day in your generations by an ordinance for ever. In the first month , on the fourteenth day of the month at even, ye shall eat unleavened bread, until the one and twentieth day of the month at even. Seven days shall there be no leaven found in your houses: for whosoever eateth that which is leavened, even that soul shall be cut off from the congregation of Israel, whether he be a stranger, or born in the land. Ye shall eat nothing leavened; in all your habitations shall ye eat unleavened bread." (Ex 12:14-20)

We are told to keep this feast throughout our generations for ever. We are to eat unleavened bread from evening on the 14th day (the time when the Passover lamb was sacrificed) to evening on the 21st day. What does this represent and how did Jesus fulfil this festival?

Matthew Chapter 16 gives us the definition of spiritual leaven – **"Then Jesus said unto them, take heed and beware of the leaven of the Pharisees and of the Sadducees. And they reasoned among themselves, saying, It is because we have taken no bread. Which when Jesus perceived, he said unto them, O ye of little faith, why reason ye among yourselves, because ye have brought no bread? Do ye not yet understand, neither remember the five loaves of the five thousand, and how many baskets ye took up? Neither the seven loaves of the four thousand, and how many baskets ye took up? How is it that ye do not understand that I spake it not to you concerning bread, that ye should beware of the leaven of the Pharisees and of the Sadducees? Then understood they how that he bade them not beware of the leaven of bread, but of the doctrine of the Pharisees and of the Sadducees". (Mt 16:6-12)**

Spiritual leavening is the pride and conceit that goes along with false religious doctrines. And if we recall Jesus was merciful and forgiving to all sinners – except the religious elite of His day who he repeatedly called hypocrites and vipers! Remember the warning in the first letter to the Corinthians **"Knowledge puffeth up, but charity edifieth." (1 Cor 8:1)** – or to put it another way – knowledge puffs up (our ego) but love builds (our brethren).

What is the lesson for us from this Feast of Unleavened Bread? Remember what we read earlier **"Your glorying is not good. Know ye not that a little leaven leaveneth the whole lump? Purge out therefore the old leaven, that ye may be a new lump, as ye are unleavened. For even Christ our Passover is sacrificed for us: therefore let us keep the feast, not with old leaven, neither with the leaven of malice and wickedness; but with the unleavened bread of sincerity and truth." (1 Cor 5:6-9)** We are to purge out the conceit and hypocrisy of false doctrine and after we accept Jesus as our Passover sacrifice we must change our attitude from malice and wickedness and humble ourselves by taking sincerity and truth into our lives.

But how did Jesus fulfil this instruction? In two ways – firstly He brought the Commandments from being an external set of rules and regulations which the scribes and Pharisees used to justify their own self-righteousness, to an internal attitude – a humble way of life which is the model all who follow Jesus should strive to achieve – **"Ye have heard that it was said by them of old time, Thou shalt not kill; and whosoever shall kill shall be in danger of the judgment: But I say unto you, that whosoever is angry with his brother without a cause shall be in danger of the judgment: and whosoever shall say to his brother, Raca, shall be in danger of the council: but whosoever shall say, thou fool, shall be in danger of hell fire. Therefore if thou bring thy gift to the altar, and there rememberest that thy brother hath ought against thee; leave there thy gift before the altar, and go thy way; first be reconciled to thy brother, and then come and offer thy gift. Agree with thine adversary quickly, whiles thou art in the way with him; lest at any time the adversary deliver thee to the judge, and the judge deliver thee to the officer, and thou be cast into prison. Verily I say unto thee, thou shalt by no means come out thence, till thou hast paid the uttermost farthing. Ye have heard that it was said by them of old time, thou shalt not commit adultery: but I say unto you, That whosoever looketh on a woman to lust after her hath committed adultery with her already in his heart." (Mt 5:21-28)**

And secondly, He lived a perfect sinless live as an example of living a life without leaven that we should follow:

For He made Him who knew no sin to be sin for us, that we might become the righteousness of God in Him. (2 Cor 5:21)

For we do not have a High Priest who cannot sympathize with our weaknesses, but was in all points tempted as we are, yet without sin. (Heb 4:15)

For to this you were called, because Christ also suffered for us, leaving us an example, that you should follow His steps: "Who committed no sin, nor was deceit found in His mouth" (1 Pet 2:21-22)

And you know that He was manifested to take away our sins, and in Him there is no sin." (1 Jn 3:5)

Again we see that spiritually and physically Jesus fulfilled the requirements of the Feast of Unleavened Bread.

c.   The Feast of Firstfruits

This is a feast that is frequently overlooked in Christian and Messianic circles alike – it is also one which had the most explicit record of its fulfilment by Jesus. Let's start by looking at the requirements for this feast.

Speak unto the children of Israel, and say unto them, when ye be come into the land which I give unto you, and shall reap the harvest thereof, then ye shall bring a sheaf of the firstfruits of your harvest unto the priest: and he shall wave the sheaf before the LORD, to be accepted for you: on the morrow after the Sabbath the priest shall wave it. And ye shall offer that day when ye wave the sheaf an he lamb without blemish of the first year for a burnt offering unto the LORD. And the meat offering thereof shall be two tenth deals of fine flour mingled with oil, an offering made by fire unto the LORD for a sweet savour: and the drink offering thereof shall be of wine, the fourth part of an hin. And ye shall eat neither bread, nor parched corn, nor green ears, until the selfsame day that ye have brought an offering unto your God: it shall be a statute for ever throughout your generations in all your dwellings. (Lev 23:10-14)

This festival requires that on the day after the Sabbath, the priest shall wave the sheaf of the firstfruits before the Lord. The first question is which Sabbath are we talking about? That's easy to identify – notice that *"ye shall eat neither bread, nor parched grain, nor green ears ..."* and as we have already seen green ears relates to the month of Abib and the main festival "The Feast of Unleavened Bread" so the Sabbath being identified here is the weekly Sabbath observed in the week long festival of the Feast of Unleavened Bread.

What is meant by the firstfruits? The Hebrew word is re'shiyth (Strong's H7225) which means "first, beginning, best, chief, choice part". All of these statements could easily point to Jesus. In fact, the Bible explicitly states that Jesus is the firstfruit – "But now is Christ risen from the dead, and become the firstfruits of them that slept. For since by man came death, by man came also the resurrection of the dead. For as in Adam all die, even so in Christ shall all be made alive. But every man in his own order: Christ the firstfruits; afterward they that are Christ's at his coming." (1 Cor 15:20-23)

The Bible clearly identifies that Jesus is the firstfruit, but how did he fulfil the requirements of this festival? The main part of this festival is presenting the firstfruit offering to the Lord by waving the sheaf (the wavesheaf offering). As you will see Jesus did exactly that.

In the Gospel of John, Chapter 20, we read, **"Jesus saith unto her, Touch me not; for I am not yet ascended to my Father: but go to my brethren, and say unto them, I ascend unto my Father, and your Father; and to my God, and your God. Mary Magdalene came and told the disciples that she had seen the Lord, and that he had spoken these things unto her. Then the same day at evening, being the first day of the week, when the doors were shut where the disciples were assembled for fear of the Jews, came Jesus and stood in the midst, and saith unto them, Peace be unto you. And when he had so said, he shewed unto them his hands and his side. Then were the disciples glad, when they saw the Lord"**. (Jn 20:17-20)

At the beginning of this chapter we read that it was the first day of the week, i.e. Sunday, and that Mary had gone to the grave and found the stone rolled away. Then Jesus appeared to her and told Mary not to touch Him because he had not yet ascended to His Father. Then we read that later that day at evening Jesus appeared to the disciples and showed them His hands and side. First thing on Sunday morning (the day after the Sabbath) Mary was not allowed to touch Him because being human she was sinful and would have profaned Him (remember that the lamb which accompanies the wavesheaf offering has to be without blemish). At some time during that day He ascended to present Himself to His Father, as he stated to Mary, and as is required of the wavesheaf offering. Towards the end of the day He appeared to the disciples, this time he gave them no warning about touching Him, so He must have already ascended completing the sacrificial requirement, and showed them His hands and side.

Immediately after His resurrection, Jesus spiritually and physically fulfilled the requirements of the Feast of Firstfruits on the exact day and hour God had ordained through His annual feast days.

d.   The Day of Pentecost

The Day of Pentecost is also known as the Feast of Weeks in the Old Testament because we are instructed to count the days for seven weeks until we come to the fiftieth day, which is were we get the term Pentecost (Greek for 50 count).

And ye shall count unto you from the morrow after the Sabbath, from the day that ye brought the sheaf of the wave offering; seven Sabbaths shall be complete: Even unto the morrow after the seventh Sabbath shall ye number fifty days; and ye shall offer a new meat offering unto the LORD. Ye shall bring out of your habitations two wave loaves of two tenth deals: they shall be of fine flour; they shall be baken with leaven; they are the firstfruits unto the LORD. (Lev 23:15-17)

Notice that the timing for this feast starts on the Feast of Firstfruits, so if we have not been observing this feast, how will we be able to correctly identify the Day of Pentecost?

Also this is the only feast where the offering is baked with leaven. Notice that two wave loaves are to be offered as the firstfruits to the Lord. Now leaven symbolizes sin (specifically the self-righteousness of the Pharisees) but on this occasion this symbolically sinful offering is acceptable to the Lord. Also note that these two loaves are called the firstfruits to the Lord and we know that Jesus was identified as the first of the firstfruits, but who do these two loaves represent?

As we have read earlier, **"But now is Christ risen from the dead, and become the firstfruits of them that slept. For since by man came death, by man came also the resurrection of the dead. For as in Adam all die, even so in Christ shall all be made alive. But every man in his own order: Christ the firstfruits; afterward they that are Christ's at his coming".** (1 Cor 15:20-23) Those who belong to Messiah at His return also are numbered in the firstfruits. But who are these people?

The physical nation of Israel were called God's chosen people and similarly the members of the New Testament church were chosen by God, **"But we are bound to give thanks alway to God for you, brethren beloved of the Lord, because God hath from the beginning chosen you to salvation through sanctification of the Spirit and belief of the truth: Whereunto he called you by our gospel, to the obtaining of the glory of our Lord Jesus Christ. Therefore, brethren, stand fast, and hold the traditions which ye have been taught, whether by word, or our epistle." (2 Thes 2:13-15)**

Neither physical Israel or the members of the New Testament Church were without sin, and not all the people who were in these groups were truly repentant and true to God, but God accepted them even in their sin, which is what the two wave loaves represent.

There are further similarities between Israel in the wilderness and the New Testament Church. The journey through the wilderness to receiving the Ten Commandments at Mt Sinai was around 50 days, in fact Jewish tradition states that the Law, a great blessing on Israel, was given on the Feast of Weeks. Similarly the account in the Book of Acts Chapter 2 clearly states that the blessing of the Holy Spirit was poured out on the Church on the Day of Pentecost. Also if you read the detailed description of these two events you will notice great similarities – both groups were told to wait for the Lord, there were great sounds and noises and fire in the sky accompanying both events.

But how can we say that Jesus has fulfilled this feast? Remember Jesus is called the Word and at Mt Sinai the children of Israel actually heard the Word of God spoken to them in the Ten Commandments. And in the New Testament example, John chapter 16 tells us, **"Nevertheless I tell you the truth; It is expedient for you that I go away: for if I go not away, the Comforter will not come unto you; but if I depart, I will send him unto you". (Jn 16:7).** The "comforter" is a name for the Holy Spirit, so Jesus is clearly stating that

He would send the Holy Spirit, which is of God as we know that God is Spirit, just as He gave the Word on Mt Sinai.

Jesus spiritually and physically fulfilled the requirements of the Feast of Weeks/Day of Pentecost for both the Old and New Testament assemblies on the exact day and hour God had ordained through His annual feast days.

e.   The Feast of Trumpets

"And the LORD spake unto Moses, saying, Speak unto the children of Israel, saying, In the seventh month, in the first day of the month, shall ye have a Sabbath, a memorial of blowing of trumpets, an holy convocation. Ye shall do no servile work therein: but ye shall offer an offering made by fire unto the LORD. (Lev 23:23-25)

There is a break of approximately 3 ½ months between the end of the spring Holy days and the start of the Autumn holy days, when on the first day of the seventh month we celebrate the Feast of Trumpets. What does this feast represent?

There are two types of trumpet identified in the Bible – silver trumpets – similar to what we would see blown at a royal pageant and the shofar - the ram's horn. These two trumpets are used for different reasons and they have a different symbolism for us. The book of Number chapter 10 gives us the first indication.

"And the LORD spake unto Moses, saying, Make thee two trumpets of silver; of a whole piece shalt thou make them: that thou mayest use them for the calling of the assembly, and for the journeying of the camps. And when they shall blow with them, all the assembly shall assemble themselves to thee at the door of the tabernacle of the congregation. And if they blow but with one trumpet, then the princes, which are heads of the thousands of Israel, shall gather themselves unto thee. When ye blow an alarm, then the camps that lie on the east parts shall go forward. When ye blow an alarm the second time, then the camps that lie on the south side shall take their journey: they shall blow an alarm for their journeys. But when the congregation is to be gathered together, ye shall blow, but ye shall not sound an alarm. And the sons of Aaron, the priests, shall blow with the trumpets; and they shall be to you for an ordinance for ever throughout your generations. And if ye go to war in your land against the enemy that oppresseth you, then ye shall blow an alarm with the trumpets; and ye shall be remembered before the LORD your God, and ye shall be saved from your enemies. Also in the day of your gladness, and in your solemn days, and in the beginnings of your months, ye shall blow with the trumpets over your burnt offerings, and over the sacrifices of your peace offerings; that they may be to you for a memorial before your God: I am the LORD your God. (Nu 10:1-10)

The silver trumpets had four mains functions:

- To call the assembly of Israel to the tabernacle of meeting

- To move the camp of Israel on their journey to the promised land
- To sound the alarm in times of war and call upon God's help
- To announce the beginning of months and feast days of God

But what about the shofar – the ram's horn trumpet? The first time we hear of this is in the book of Exodus as God is preparing to deliver the Ten Commandments to Israel.

And it came to pass on the third day in the morning, that there were thunders and lightnings, and a thick cloud upon the mount, and the voice of the trumpet exceeding loud; so that all the people that was in the camp trembled. And Moses brought forth the people out of the camp to meet with God; and they stood at the nether part of the mount. And Mount Sinai was altogether on a smoke, because the LORD descended upon it in fire: and the smoke thereof ascended as the smoke of a furnace, and the whole mount quaked greatly. And when the voice of the trumpet [shofar] sounded long and waxed louder and louder, Moses spake, and God answered him by a voice. (Ex 19:16-19)

On this occasion the trumpets were sounded to announce to the people the imminent arrival of God to speak directly to the children of Israel. And after the long sounding of the shofar in heaven God spoke to Moses and His voice was heard throughout the camp.

In the book of Leviticus we read, **"Then shalt thou cause the trumpet of the jubilee to sound on the tenth day of the seventh month, in the day of atonement shall ye make the trumpet sound throughout all your land." (Lev 25:9)** Jubilee actually means "loud of sound" in Hebrew. And the Jubilee was the year when all debts were forgiven, people returned to their original homes and great rejoicing was experienced throughout all the land.

The prophet Ezekiel gives us another indication of the use of the Shofar, in Chapter 33 of his book it states: **Again the word of the LORD came unto me, saying, Son of man, speak to the children of thy people, and say unto them, When I bring the sword upon a land, if the people of the land take a man of their coasts, and set him for their watchman: If when he seeth the sword come upon the land, he blow the trumpet, and warn the people; Then whosoever heareth the sound of the trumpet, and taketh not warning; if the sword come, and take him away, his blood shall be upon his own head. He heard the sound of the trumpet, and took not warning; his blood shall be upon him. But he that taketh warning shall deliver his soul. (Ezk 33:1-5)**

In this case, God is prophetically warning the people that when they hear the shofar war is coming to their land and they must take heed of the warning. If they do obey the warning they will be delivered from the destruction to come but if they don't take note of the warning they will die in the battle which engulfs their land.

And the prophet Joel makes a direct connection between the sounding of the shofar and the coming of the Day of the Lord. **"Blow ye the trumpet in Zion, and sound an alarm in my holy mountain: let all the inhabitants of the land tremble: for the day of the LORD cometh, for it is nigh at hand;" (Joel 2:1-2)**

And this prophetic connection to the day of the Lord is taken up in the Gospel of Matthew. **"Immediately after the tribulation of those days shall the sun be darkened, and the moon shall not give her light, and the stars shall fall from heaven, and the powers of the heavens shall be shaken: And then shall appear the sign of the Son of man in heaven: and then shall all the tribes of the earth mourn, and they shall see the Son of man coming in the clouds of heaven with power and great glory. And he shall send his angels with a great sound of a trumpet, and they shall gather together his elect from the four winds, from one end of heaven to the other."** (Mt 24:29-31)

On this occasion, after the people of the earth see the sign of His return in the clouds, the sound of the heavenly trumpet will indicate the gathering of the elect.

There is more information provided about this in Paul's first letter to the Corinthians. **"In a moment, in the twinkling of an eye, at the last trump: for the trumpet shall sound, and the dead shall be raised incorruptible, and we shall be changed."** (1 Cor 15:52) We see here that the heavenly trumpet will announce the resurrection of the saints at the end of this age.

Finally, and probably the most well known of the trumpet scriptures, the book of Revelation talks of the seven angels who sound the seven trumpets.

And the seven angels which had the seven trumpets prepared themselves to sound. The first angel sounded, and there followed hail and fire mingled with blood, and they were cast upon the earth: and the third part of trees was burnt up, and all green grass was burnt up. And the second angel sounded, and as it were a great mountain burning with fire was cast into the sea: and the third part of the sea became blood; And the third part of the creatures which were in the sea, and had life, died; and the third part of the ships were destroyed. And the third angel sounded, and there fell a great star from heaven, burning as it were a lamp, and it fell upon the third part of the rivers, and upon the fountains of waters; And the name of the star is called Wormwood: and the third part of the waters became wormwood; and many men died of the waters, because they were made bitter. And the fourth angel sounded, and the third part of the sun was smitten, and the third part of the moon, and the third part of the stars; so as the third part of them was darkened, and the day shone not for a third part of it, and the night likewise. And I beheld, and heard an angel flying through the midst of heaven, saying with a loud voice, Woe, woe, woe, to the inhabiters of the earth by reason of the other voices of the trumpet of the three angels, which are yet to sound! (Rev 8:6-13)

As we read through the book of Revelation we see that the 5th trumpet heralds 5 months of torment by demons with scorpion like powers; the 6th trumpet paves the way for the 200 million man army to cross the Euphrates for the final battle of Armageddon. And the 7th trumpet announces a great voice from heaven which declares that Jesus has come to reclaim the world. There is an interesting parallel to the sounding of the 7th trumpet and the delivering of the Ten Commandments.

When the Ten Commandments were delivered, the trumpet sound grew progressively stronger until finally all the people had assembled to hear the very voice of God coming out from a sound of great thunder. Many people are aware of the seven seals of Revelation, the seven trumpets and the seven bowls of wrath, but in Revelation chapter 10 we are told that there are also seven thunders, which John was told to seal up and not write down. Many people believe these thunders to be the voice of God pronouncing His final judgement on the world.

We can also see that this feast day has been fulfilled spiritually in that Jesus came to bring the good news of the Gospel of the Kingdom of God, He acted as the herald to pronounce the word. But it has not yet been physically fulfilled in the way the Bible tells us these final trumpets will be heard on the earth.

f.   The Day of Atonement

And the LORD spake unto Moses, saying, Also on the tenth day of this seventh month there shall be a day of atonement: it shall be an holy convocation unto you; and ye shall afflict your souls, and offer an offering made by fire unto the LORD. And ye shall do no work in that same day: for it is a day of atonement, to make an atonement for you before the LORD your God. For whatsoever soul it be that shall not be afflicted in that same day, he shall be cut off from among his people. And whatsoever soul it be that doeth any work in that same day, the same soul will I destroy from among his people. Ye shall do no manner of work: it shall be a statute for ever throughout your generations in all your dwellings. It shall be unto you a Sabbath of rest, and ye shall afflict your souls: in the ninth day of the month at even, from even unto even, shall ye celebrate your Sabbath. (Lev 23:26-32)

Nine days after the celebration of the Feast of Trumpets we are told to observe the Day of Atonement. This is a Holy day, a Sabbath rest and we are told to afflict our souls.

But what does it mean to afflict our souls? And why do we do it? The traditional understanding is that we are to fast (no food or water) from sunset on the 9th day until sunset on the 10th day of the 7th month. The purpose of this is to show us how frail we are without the blessings (of food and water) which God provides. It also signifies that we are humbling ourselves before God as an act of repentance so that we can once again be "at-one" with Him.

If we look at the sacrificial requirements of this day we can see that Jesus has fulfilled the spiritual aspects of this Holy day. Let's look at the Book of Leviticus to find out more about this.

And he shall take of the congregation of the children of Israel two kids of the goats for a sin offering, and one ram for a burnt offering. And Aaron shall offer his bullock of the sin offering, which is for himself, and make an atonement for himself, and for his house. And he shall take the

two goats, and present them before the LORD at the door of the tabernacle of the congregation. And Aaron shall cast lots upon the two goats; one lot for the LORD, and the other lot for the scapegoat. And Aaron shall bring the goat upon which the LORD'S lot fell, and offer him for a sin offering. But the goat, on which the lot fell to be the scapegoat, shall be presented alive before the LORD, to make an atonement with him, and to let him go for a scapegoat into the wilderness. (Lev 16:5-10)

Here we see that two goats were selected by the people (just as Jesus had been selected by the people before the Passover). One goat is for the sin offering the other is selected by God to perform the duty of the scapegoat. We know that Jesus died for our sins, so we can see that He spiritually has performed this sacrificial requirement. But what of the scapegoat? We'll discuss that in a minute.

And Aaron shall bring the bullock of the sin offering, which is for himself, and shall make an atonement for himself, and for his house, and shall kill the bullock of the sin offering which is for himself: And he shall take a censer full of burning coals of fire from off the altar before the LORD, and his hands full of sweet incense beaten small, and bring it within the vail: And he shall put the incense upon the fire before the LORD, that the cloud of the incense may cover the mercy seat that is upon the testimony, that he die not: And he shall take of the blood of the bullock, and sprinkle it with his finger upon the mercy seat eastward; and before the mercy seat shall he sprinkle of the blood with his finger seven times. Then shall he kill the goat of the sin offering, that is for the people, and bring his blood within the vail, and do with that blood as he did with the blood of the bullock, and sprinkle it upon the mercy seat, and before the mercy seat: And he shall make an atonement for the holy place , because of the uncleanness of the children of Israel, and because of their transgressions in all their sins: and so shall he do for the tabernacle of the congregation, that remaineth among them in the midst of their uncleanness. And there shall be no man in the tabernacle of the congregation when he goeth in to make an atonement in the holy place , until he come out, and have made an atonement for himself, and for his household, and for all the congregation of Israel. And he shall go out unto the altar that is before the LORD, and make an atonement for it; and shall take of the blood of the bullock, and of the blood of the goat, and put it upon the horns of the altar round about. And he shall sprinkle of the blood upon it with his finger seven times, and cleanse it, and hallow it from the uncleanness of the children of Israel. (Lev 16:11-19)

In this part of the atonement ceremony, the high priest sprinkles the blood of the bullock on the mercy seat and the altar. This is to make atonement for himself. Then he takes the blood of the goat selected as the sin offering and makes atonement for the sins of the children of Israel. Now there are numerous sacrificial offerings required by God for the Levitical form of worship. But on this occasion something very unique happens.

The high priest sprinkles the blood of the bull and the goat on the mercy seat. The mercy seat is the location of the very presence of God on earth. It is in the holiest of holies, behind the second veil where no one is allowed to enter. Since the death of Aarons two sons for offering profane fire before God, no one had been allowed into the holiest of holies. Only the high priest on the Day of Atonement is allowed into the very presence of God. And this ceremony was not undertaken lightly. Jewish tradition was that a rope was tied around the thigh of the high priest and if the priests who were waiting outside the tabernacle could no longer hear him moving around, they assumed that he had been killed by God for profane behaviour and pulled his body out.

If we think back to the crucifixion of Jesus we read in Mark's gospel account: **And Jesus cried with a loud voice, and gave up the ghost. And the veil of the temple was rent in twain from the top to the bottom. (Mk 15:37-38)** At the moment of the sacrificial death of Jesus, the veil which was separating man from the presence of God was torn in two. Just as the atoning blood offered by the high priest allowed him to come into the presence of God on behalf of the children of Israel, so the blood of Jesus, our High Priest, allowed all of spiritual Israel to be reconciled, to become at-one with the Father and come into the presence of God.

And when he hath made an end of reconciling the holy place , and the tabernacle of the congregation, and the altar, he shall bring the live goat: And Aaron shall lay both his hands upon the head of the live goat, and confess over him all the iniquities of the children of Israel, and all their transgressions in all their sins, putting them upon the head of the goat, and shall send him away by the hand of a fit man into the wilderness: And the goat shall bear upon him all their iniquities unto a land not inhabited: and he shall let go the goat in the wilderness. (Lev 16:20-22)

Some commentators suggest that this second goat the "scapegoat", is representative of Satan the devil, who has sin placed on his head where it belongs before he is bound for a thousand years. But this is a misunderstanding of the scripture for several reasons. Firstly there is no other holy day which includes any representation of Satan in the ceremony, and why would God include this when we are explicitly instructed to have nothing to do with demons and false gods? Secondly, the sin does not belong on Satan's head – it belongs firmly and squarely on our heads, it is our sin and we deserve the punishment for this sin, which is death. Satan fills the world with confusion, deceit and temptation, but we are the ones who chose to sin when we could have, or indeed should have, chosen to withstand the devil and holdfast to our faith and not sin. By accepting this false doctrine, we are trying to find an excuse or a let out clause for our own sin. The first step to redemption is the acknowledgement that we are responsible for our own sin, which must then be followed by repentance for the sins we have committed.

Finally, the Bible gives us a very clear statement as to who fulfils the function of carrying the sins of mankind. In the gospel of John we read **"The next day John seeth Jesus coming unto him, and saith, Behold the Lamb of God, which taketh away the sin of the world." (Jn 1:29)** Jesus is clearly the one who takes away the sin of the world. And we can actually tell when this sin was placed upon His head. Remember after the crucifixion a good man, Joseph of Arimathea, took His body and placed it in the tomb (the wilderness of death).

Another indication that Jesus fulfilled the requirement of the scapegoat comes from the Jewish customs of tying a red cord around the horns of the scapegoat and a similar cord to the door of the temple. It was considered an extremely bad omen for the scapegoat to wander back into the camp, the custom was that the goat was thrown off a cliff. When the scapegoat died the cord on the door of the temple turned white, indicating that God had accepted the sacrifice. However, on Yom Kippur (the Day of Atonement) in 31 AD the red cord did not turn white for the first time in almost 1500 years. This was the same year that Jesus died on the cross to take away the sins of the world as the perfect sacrifice chosen by God and bring an end to the sacrificial form of worship.

We can see that Jesus has fulfilled the spiritual requirements of this Holy day. But what of the physical fulfilment?

There is another major event which occurs on the Day of Atonement, but only once every 49 years. In the book of Leviticus we read, **"Then shalt thou cause the trumpet of the jubilee to sound on the tenth day of the seventh month, in the Day of Atonement shall ye make the trumpet sound throughout all your land. And ye shall hallow the fiftieth year, and proclaim liberty throughout all the land unto all the inhabitants thereof: it shall be a jubilee unto you; and ye shall return every man unto his possession, and ye shall return every man unto his family. (Lev 25:9-10)**

Nine days after the feast of trumpets another trumpet sounds, this time on the Day of Atonement and it announces the beginning of the year of Jubilee. This was a time of great rejoicing in Israel, people returned to their tribal homes, debts were forgiven and liberty was given to bondsmen and debtors.

We have already learned of the seven trumpets of the book of Revelation, **"And the seventh angel sounded; and there were great voices in heaven, saying, The kingdoms of this world are become the kingdoms of our Lord, and of his Christ; and he shall reign for ever and ever".** **(Rev 11:15)** When the seventh angel sounds the final trumpet, the earth will return to its rightful owner, as it was intended from the time of the Garden of Eden. Also in the letter to the Corinthians we read, **"In a moment, in the twinkling of an eye, at the last trump: for the trumpet shall sound, and the dead shall be raised incorruptible, and we shall be changed."** **(1 Cor 15:52)** At this time all the saints of God who are the firstfruits will be resurrected along with those who are alive and be taken up in the clouds as "born again" spirit beings to meet Jesus, to be at-one with Him.

Also we know from the book of Revelation that after the seventh trumpet sounds the "seven bowls of the wrath of the Lord" are poured out upon the earth. This will bring affliction on all those who are alive and remain in rebellion against God. This affliction poured out by God is the cosmic equivalent of the affliction that we are to bring on ourselves during the fast on the Day of Atonement.

Obviously this has not yet happened, nor have we experience the resurrection of the dead, so we can safely state that the physical fulfilment of this Holy Day has not yet occurred.

g.   The Feast of Tabernacles

And the LORD spake unto Moses, saying, Speak unto the children of Israel, saying, The fifteenth day of this seventh month shall be the feast of tabernacles for seven days unto the LORD. On the first day shall be an holy convocation: ye shall do no servile work therein. Seven days ye shall offer an offering made by fire unto the LORD: on the eighth day shall be an holy convocation unto you; and ye shall offer an offering made by fire unto the LORD: it is a solemn assembly; and ye shall do no servile work therein. (Lev 23:33-36)

The Feast of Tabernacles occurs just 5 days after the Day of Atonement. It starts with a High Sabbath, a holy convocation, and consists of 7 days of sacrifice and offerings to the Lord. But what does this represent? If we read on in the book of Leviticus Chapter 33 we will find out more about the symbolism of this feast.

Also in the fifteenth day of the seventh month, when ye have gathered in the fruit of the land, ye shall keep a feast unto the LORD seven days: on the first day shall be a Sabbath, and on the eighth day shall be a Sabbath. And ye shall take you on the first day the boughs of goodly trees, branches of palm trees, and the boughs of thick trees, and willows of the brook; and ye shall rejoice before the LORD your God seven days. And ye shall keep it a feast unto the LORD seven days in the year. It shall be a statute for ever in your generations: ye shall celebrate it in the seventh month. Ye shall dwell in booths seven days; all that are Israelites born shall dwell in booths: That your generations may know that I made the children of Israel to dwell in booths, when I brought them out of the land of Egypt: I am the LORD your God. (Lev 23:39-43)

We learn from this scripture that the children of Israel were to dwell in booths made of the boughs of trees. And the word tabernacle actually means a booth, tent or temporary dwelling. It was also to be a time of rejoicing and remembrance that God had brought Israel out of the bondage of slavery in Egypt and the temporary dwelling reminds us of the 40 years journey through the wilderness on the way to the Promised Land. But does this feast have any relevance to us today? Absolutely it does for three reasons.

The prophet Zechariah tells us, **"Behold, the day of the LORD cometh, and thy spoil shall be divided in the midst of thee. For I will gather all nations against Jerusalem to battle; and the city shall be taken, and the houses rifled, and the women ravished; and half of the city shall go forth into captivity, and the residue of the people shall not be cut off from the city. Then shall the LORD go forth, and fight against those nations, as when he fought in the day of battle. ... And it shall come to pass, that every one that is left of all the nations which came against Jerusalem shall** even go up from year to year to worship the King, the LORD of hosts, and to keep the feast of tabernacles. And it shall be, that whoso will not come up of all the families of the earth unto Jerusalem to worship the King, the LORD of hosts, even upon them shall be no rain. And if the family of Egypt go not up, and come not, that have no rain; there shall be the plague, wherewith the LORD will smite the heathen that come not up to keep the feast of tabernacles. This shall be the punishment of Egypt, and the punishment of all nations that come not up to keep the feast of tabernacles. (Zec 14:1-4, 16-19)

At the beginning of that scripture we see that the period Zechariah is talking about is the "Day of the Lord" this is the cataclysmic event discussed in great detail throughout the Book of Revelation. It is the period immediately before the return of Jesus to rule the earth. But notice the second part of the scripture. Everyone is required to come to Jerusalem to worship Jesus and keep the Feast of Tabernacles. In fact, for those people who refuse to come up and worship Him there will be no rain and plagues will be poured out on them. In answer to the question is keeping the feast important? Yes it is! Ancient Israel was required to keep it; it is a statute forever and after the return of Jesus all the nations of the earth will be required to keep it.

What does it actually signify? The book of Hebrews gives us a better understanding.

By faith Abraham, when he was called to go out into a place which he should after receive for an inheritance, obeyed; and he went out, not knowing whither he went. By faith he sojourned in the land of promise, as in a strange country, dwelling in tabernacles with Isaac and Jacob, the heirs with him of the same promise: For he looked for a city which hath foundations, whose builder and maker is God. Through faith also Sara herself received strength to conceive seed, and was delivered of a child when she was past age, because she judged him faithful who had promised. Therefore sprang there even of one, and him as good as dead, so many as the stars of the sky in multitude, and as the sand which is by the sea shore innumerable. These all died in faith, not having received the promises, but having seen them afar off, and were persuaded of them, and embraced them, and confessed that they were strangers and pilgrims on the earth. For they that say such things declare plainly that they seek a country. And truly, if they had been mindful of that country from whence they came out, they might have had opportunity to have returned. But now they desire a better country, that is, an heavenly: wherefore God is not ashamed to be called their God: for he hath prepared for them a city. (Heb 11:8-16)

Abraham's journey of faith, when he left his own country to follow the instructions of the Lord, was spent entirely in tabernacles. And this state of remaining in a temporary dwelling signified that he was a pilgrim, wandering the earth looking forward to coming to his permanent home. And that is the state God's people are to have, an understanding that this physical world is temporary, an illusion compared to the great blessings we shall receive when His kingdom is established on the earth. We are literally just passing through and must not get distracted by the carnal and materialistic cares of this world. God's people are to be focusing on the kingdom yet to come.

Abraham died in faith having not yet received the promise of the Lord but knowing that there would be a place for him in the city that God has created, New Jerusalem, which will come to earth after the thousand years that Satan is bound. The 1,000 years of rest while Satan is bound is often called the millennial Sabbath and this seven day period of rejoicing symbolizes that period. The Feast of Tabernacles is the seventh of the Lord's feasts – a Sabbath feast, it lasts seven days which is God's number of completeness and it indicates the completion of the age of man. During this period, those who are raised up at the first resurrection will receive their reward and the 144,000 will be working with Jesus to return the world to the state it was intended to be in from the beginning – a perfect Garden of Eden environment.

The final understanding we obtain from studying the Feast of Tabernacles relates to the life of Jesus. At the beginning of the Gospel of John, we read: **In the beginning was the Word, and the Word was with God, and the Word was God. The same was in the beginning with God. All things were made by him; and without him was not any thing made that was made. In him was life; and the life was the light of men. And the light shineth in darkness; and the darkness comprehended it not. There was a man sent from God, whose name was John. The same came for a witness, to bear witness of the Light, that all men through him might believe. He was not that Light, but was sent to bear witness of that Light. That was the true Light, which lighteth every man that cometh into the world. He was in the world, and the world was made by him, and the world knew him not. He came unto his own, and his own received him not. But as many as received him, to them gave he power to become the sons of God, even to them that believe on his name: Which were born, not of blood, nor of the will of the flesh, nor of the will of man, but of God. And the Word was made flesh, and dwelt among us, (and we beheld his glory, the glory as of the only begotten of the Father,) full of grace and truth. (Jn 1:1-14)**

This passage is discussing the pre-incarnate form of Jesus the Logos, or Word, of God. But notice the final sentence, "and the Word was made flesh and dwelt among us". The word translated as *dwelt* is Strong's G4637 which means "to live in a tabernacle". What this scripture is saying is that Jesus put on this temporary dwelling of a human body to be with us on earth and just as when he finished this temporary assignment on earth He returned to the Father, so the people of faith who are pilgrims on this temporary journey will also come to the Father when their journey ends.

There is also another very significant understanding that this scripture brings us to. In the Gospel of Luke we learn about Jesus' birth and we are told: **Now there were in the same country shepherds living out in the fields, keeping watch over their flock by night. And behold, an angel of the Lord stood before them, and the glory of the Lord shone around them, and they were greatly afraid. Then the angel said to them, Do not be afraid, for behold, I bring you good tidings of great joy which will be to all people. For there is born to you this day in the city of David a Saviour, who is Christ the Lord. And this will be the sign to you: You will find a Babe wrapped in swaddling cloths, lying in a manger. (Lk 2:8-12)**

You've probably heard this scripture dozens of times – it is the traditional scripture used to begin the nativity services in churches around the world at Christmas time. There is one major problem using it in this context. In the land of Israel the flocks are brought down from the hills in September or October to their winter dwellings because the weather is too cold for them. The shepherds could not possibly be out in the fields on 25th December! What time of year is this?

The previous chapter in Luke gives us a very detailed account of the time of Mary's conception and the birth of Jesus, but it takes a bit of detective work to come up with the answer. Let's first list the clues from Luke Chapter 1 to help us identify this timing.

There was in the days of Herod, the king of Judea, a certain priest named Zacharias, of the division of Abijah. His wife was of the daughters of Aaron, and her name was Elizabeth. (Lk 1:5)

So it was, that while he was serving as priest before God in the order of his division, (Lk 1:8)

Zacharias was a priest of the order of Abijah, his wife is Elizabeth and he was serving in the temple in the order of his division. The priests were organized into 24 divisions each serving for a one week period twice a year with all the priests serving at the time of the Feast of Unleavened Bread and the Feast of Tabernacles. The division of Abijah was the 8th of the 24 divisions (see 1 Chr 24:10). The Feast of Unleavened Bread falls between mid March and mid April and the Feast of Tabernacles between mid September and mid October. To simplify things we'll use the mid point of 1 April and 1 October. So, if we count eight weeks on from these dates, Zacharias would have had this meeting with the angel Gabriel around either 1 June or 1 December.

But the angel said to him, "Do not be afraid, Zacharias, for your prayer is heard; and your wife Elizabeth will bear you a son, and you shall call his name John. (Lk 1:13)

And so it was, as soon as the days of his service were completed, that he departed to his own house. Now after those days his wife Elizabeth conceived; and she hid herself five months, saying, (Lk 1:23-24)

Zacharias had a divine message that Elizabeth would bear a son and soon after his service was finished he went home and Elizabeth conceived (mid June or mid December).

Now in the sixth month the angel Gabriel was sent by God to a city of Galilee named Nazareth, to a virgin betrothed to a man whose name was Joseph, of the house of David. The virgin's name was Mary. (Lk 1:26-27)

"Now indeed, Elizabeth your relative has also conceived a son in her old age; and this is now the sixth month for her who was called barren. (Lk 1:36)

The Angel visited Mary when Elizabeth was six months pregnant, this would have been in mid December or mid June.

Now Mary arose in those days and went into the hill country with haste, to a city of Judah and entered the house of Zacharias and greeted Elizabeth. (Lk 1:39-40)

And it came to pass, that, when Elisabeth heard the salutation of Mary, the babe leaped in her womb; and Elisabeth was filled with the Holy Ghost: And she spake out with a loud voice, and said, Blessed art thou among women, and blessed is the fruit of thy womb. (Lk 1:41-42)

Mary visited Elizabeth shortly after her meeting with the Angel and the baby in Elizabeth's womb (John the Baptist) leaped for joy. We know that Mary had conceived by late June or late December, which means she would have delivered Jesus, nine months later in either late September or late March.

Jesus' ministry started around his 30th birthday (Lk 3:23) and it lasted 1½, 2½ or 3½ years depending on which commentary you are reading. We know he was executed at Passover, in March/April so if He was 31, 2, 3 and ½ years old when he died, He must have been born in September or October – not December as is erroneously believed by the majority of people. This timing agrees with the evidence we presented earlier. And some people who have studied this believe that Jesus was actually born on the first day of the Feast of Tabernacles. This means that John was giving us another clue when he told us that Jesus "tabernacled" among us.

In this case we see that Jesus has fulfilled a physical manifestation of "tabernacling" among us as an example as the "first of the firstfruits". Also he has given us the spiritual understanding of this period, but the ultimate, millennial fulfilment of this festival for all of humanity has not yet occurred.

h. The Eighth Day

The Eighth Day is probably the least understood of all the Feasts of YHWH. Many people regard it as the final day of the Feast of Tabernacles, but this is not correct. Let's look again at what we are told in the Book of Leviticus.

And the LORD spake unto Moses, saying, Speak unto the children of Israel, saying, The fifteenth day of this seventh month shall be the feast of tabernacles for seven days unto the LORD. On the first day shall be an holy convocation: ye shall do no servile work therein. Seven days ye shall offer an offering made by fire unto the LORD: on the eighth day shall be an holy convocation unto you;

and ye shall offer an offering made by fire unto the LORD: it is a solemn assembly; and ye shall do no servile work therein. (Lev 23:33-36)

The Feast of Tabernacles starts with a holy convocation and lasts for seven days. It then says *"on the eighth day shall be a holy convocation unto you"*, so this "Eighth Day" is a separate feast. But what does it signify?

In Hebrew the Feats of Tabernacles is known as Sukkot (the plural of Sukkah meaning a booth or hut) and the Eighth Day is called Shemini Atzeret (meaning Eighth of Assembly). This doesn't give us much of a clue. But there is another name for this day Simchat Torah (meaning rejoicing with Torah) and this is the day the Torah scrolls are rewound for the annual cycle of reading to begin over again. And if we think about the weekly Sabbath, the eighth day (the day after the Sabbath) is the beginning of the new weekly cycle, the first day of the new week.

Also if we recall the counting to Pentecost – seven Sabbaths are completed and the day after the Sabbath, the eight day of the seventh week, is the Feast of Weeks or Pentecost. The Old Testament commemoration was celebrating the completion of the spring barley harvest and the looking forward to the main autumn wheat harvest. The New Testament understanding is the pouring out of the Holy Spirit on the Church. Both of these symbolize the end of one cycle and the looking forward to the next – barley to wheat harvest and physical to spiritual covenants.

There is another major event in the custom of Israel which centres around the Eighth Day and that is the act of circumcision (Lev 12:3). Only when a male is circumcised are they considered to be full members of the Tribe of Israel and eligible to participate in the rites and blessings of Israel, as we read in the Book of Exodus Chapter 12: **"And when a stranger shall sojourn with thee, and will keep the Passover to the LORD, let all his males be circumcised, and then let him come near and keep it; and he shall be as one that is born in the land: for no uncircumcised person shall eat thereof." (Ex 12:48)**. And just as physical Israel were required to be physically circumcised we, as members of the spiritual Israel must also be circumcised, not in the flesh, but in our hearts!

Can we now gain a better understanding of the meaning behind this Eighth Day festival? It seems to indicate the beginning of a new cycle – first day of the new week, rewinding of the Torah scrolls and entry into the Tribe of Israel. But does this match what we know of end time prophecy? Absolutely! Let's look at the Book of Revelation to find out more.

And I saw an angel come down from heaven, having the key of the bottomless pit and a great chain in his hand. And he laid hold on the dragon, that old serpent, which is the Devil, and Satan, and bound him a thousand years, And cast him into the bottomless pit, and shut him up, and set a seal upon him, that he should deceive the nations no more, till the thousand years should be fulfilled: and after that he must be loosed a little season. And I saw thrones, and they sat upon them, and judgment was given unto them: and I saw the souls of them that were beheaded for the

witness of Jesus, and for the word of God, and which had not worshipped the beast, neither his image, neither had received his mark upon their foreheads, or in their hands; and they lived and reigned with Christ a thousand years. But the rest of the dead lived not again until the thousand years were finished. This is the first resurrection. Blessed and holy is he that hath part in the first resurrection: on such the second death hath no power, but they shall be priests of God and of Christ, and shall reign with him a thousand years. (Rev 20:1-6)

Here we see that Satan is bound for 1000 years to *"deceive the nations no more"*. Also the firstfruits who come up in the first resurrection will reign with Christ as Kings and Priests for 1000 years. During this 1000 period, the earth is ruled by Jesus with the 144,000 administering His law throughout the whole earth. This period of peace is symbolized by the Feast of Tabernacles – a period of rejoicing with Jesus, a 1000 year Sabbath rest for creation. The book of Romans Chapter 8 gives us a better understanding of this period.

For the earnest expectation of the creature waiteth for the manifestation of the sons of God. For the creature was made subject to vanity, not willingly, but by reason of him who hath subjected the same in hope, Because the creature itself also shall be delivered from the bondage of corruption into the glorious liberty of the children of God. For we know that the whole creation groaneth and travaileth in pain together until now. And not only they, but ourselves also, which have the firstfruits of the Spirit, even we ourselves groan within ourselves, waiting for the adoption, to wit , the redemption of our body. (Ro 8:19-23)

This 1000 year period is when all the physical creation is released from the bondage of corruption and brought back to the state God originally intended for it – the Garden of Eden. But what happens after the physical creation is released from corruption?

And when the thousand years are expired, Satan shall be loosed out of his prison, And shall go out to deceive the nations which are in the four quarters of the earth, Gog and Magog, to gather them together to battle: the number of whom is as the sand of the sea. And they went up on the breadth of the earth, and compassed the camp of the saints about, and the beloved city: and fire came down from God out of heaven, and devoured them. And the devil that deceived them was cast into the lake of fire and brimstone, where the beast and the false prophet are, and shall be tormented day and night for ever and ever. And I saw a great white throne, and him that sat on it, from whose face the earth and the heaven fled away; and there was found no place for them. And I saw the dead, small and great, stand before God; and the books were opened: and another book was opened, which is the book of life: and the dead were judged out of those things which were written in the books, according to their works. And the sea gave up the dead which were in it; and death and hell delivered up the dead which were in them: and they were judged every man according to their works. And death and hell were cast into the lake of fire. This is the second death. And whosoever was not found written in the book of life was cast into the lake of fire. (Rev 20:7-15)

We see that yet again Satan deceives mankind, but this time final judgement is passed on him by being cast into the lake of fire and destroyed. Now with the earth in this utopian state – all of creation as it was intended to be (like the Garden of Eden) and Satan the devil no longer able to deceive and corrupt mankind – all of humankind who have ever lived are resurrected and given the opportunity to understand God's ways and accept Him. Those who still refuse to repent at the end of this period are finally destroyed in the lake of fire.

(A quick side note – there is massive confusion about the resurrections, judgement and the lake of fire, if you would like to understand what the Bible really says on this, please contact me david@spiritandtruthrevival.org and I'll send you out a booklet explaining the complete process of God's judgement).

And I saw a new heaven and a new earth: for the first heaven and the first earth were passed away; and there was no more sea. And I John saw the holy city, New Jerusalem, coming down from God out of heaven, prepared as a bride adorned for her husband. And I heard a great voice out of heaven saying, Behold, the tabernacle of God is with men, and he will dwell with them, and they shall be his people, and God himself shall be with them, and be their God. And God shall wipe away all tears from their eyes; and there shall be no more death, neither sorrow, nor crying, neither shall there be any more pain: for the former things are passed away. And he that sat upon the throne said, Behold, I make all things new. And he said unto me, Write: for these words are true and faithful. And he said unto me, It is done. I am Alpha and Omega, the beginning and the end. I will give unto him that is athirst of the fountain of the water of life freely. He that overcometh shall inherit all things; and I will be his God, and he shall be my son. (Rev 21:1-7)

In this passage from the Book of Revelation we see the culmination of God's plan for us. At the end of the period of judgement, the physical heaven and earth pass away and God Himself will come and live among us (tabernacle with us) in a new spiritual creation where death no longer exists. Everyone who accepts Him become a spirit born son of God the Father. In fact if you read this literally we become full members of the family of God alongside our older brother Jesus! Again we see here the Eighth Day concept of endings and new beginnings – Alpha and Omega.

The Eighth Day festival points us directly to the plan of God for the Salvation of all mankind and a new beginning as spiritual members of the God family in a new heaven and a new earth after the 7 festivals of the physical cycle are complete.

We also are told that Jesus was circumcised on the eighth day of His physical life as is required by the Levitical law (Lk 2:21). If He was born on the first day of the Feast of Tabernacles He would have been circumcised on the Feast of the Eighth Day, when He would have been fully accepted into the tribe of Israel. Again He is giving us an example with His physical life, partly fulfilling the physical requirement, to reveal the spiritual understanding and show us the way for all humanity to follow in His path.

5.3   Sabbath and Jubilee Years

There is one final cycle in God's calendar that we need to be aware of to fully understand the end time countdown. Just as God defined the weekly Sabbath based on a seven day cycle, He also defined an annual Sabbath based on a seven year cycle.

And the LORD spake unto Moses in mount Sinai, saying, Speak unto the children of Israel, and say unto them, When ye come into the land which I give you, then shall the land keep a Sabbath unto the LORD. Six years thou shalt sow thy field, and six years thou shalt prune thy vineyard, and gather in the fruit thereof; But in the seventh year shall be a Sabbath of rest unto the land, a Sabbath for the LORD: thou shalt neither sow thy field, nor prune thy vineyard. That which groweth of its own accord of thy harvest thou shalt not reap, neither gather the grapes of thy vine undressed: for it is a year of rest unto the land. And the Sabbath of the land shall be meat for you; for thee, and for thy servant, and for thy maid, and for thy hired servant, and for thy stranger that sojourneth with thee, And for thy cattle, and for the beast that are in thy land, shall all the increase thereof be meat. (Lev 25:1-7)

We can see that just as God ordained a day of rest for man, He provided a year of rest for the earth. Unfortunately we have become so disconnected from nature and the wonders of creation that we often can't recognize the Biblical lessons which would be so obvious if we had retained our agricultural experience. In the days before high intensity, chemically based farming, leaving fields fallow (resting) was a common practice to improve the overall yield of the land. In this passage God is instructing Israel that good stewardship of the land required a year of rest every seven years. This Sabbath year was also good for the people. The majority of people would be involved in some form of farming to produce the basic foodstuff needed for their families and in the seventh year they were forbidden from farming. This would be a year of very light activity where they could spend the time rebuilding and repairing – their homes, their equipment and probably more importantly their friendships, family ties and relationships. Just imagine what your life would be like if every seventh year you were free from your labours!

According to the Jewish website chabad.org the Sabbath year is from 13 September 2007 to 29 September 2008, the year 5768 in the Jewish calendar. But the Jewish civil New Year is celebrated 6 months before the Biblical New Year (in the 7th month as opposed to the first month. While Biblically the Sabbath year runs from spring to spring which means the actual Sabbath year is 6 April 2008 (Nisan 1, 5768) 25 March 2009 (29 Adar 5769) and the next one after that is 21 March 2015 to 9 March 2016.

Just as the weekly Sabbath cycle points to the annual Sabbath cycle, the 50 day count to Pentecost has an annual equivalent. This is called the Jubilee year and is explained in this passage from the Book of Leviticus.

And thou shalt number seven Sabbaths of years unto thee, seven times seven years; and the space of the seven Sabbaths of years shall be unto thee forty and nine years. Then shalt thou cause the trumpet of the jubile to sound on the tenth day of the seventh month, in the day of atonement shall ye make the trumpet sound throughout all your land. And ye shall hallow the fiftieth year, and proclaim liberty throughout all the land unto all the inhabitants thereof: it shall be a jubile unto you; and ye shall return every man unto his possession, and ye shall return every man unto his family. A jubile shall that fiftieth year be unto you: ye shall not sow, neither reap that which groweth of itself in it, nor gather the grapes in it of thy vine undressed. For it is the jubile; it shall be holy unto you: ye shall eat the increase thereof out of the field. In the year of this jubile ye shall return every man unto his possession. (Lev 25:8-13)

We are to count seven Sabbaths of years and on the Day of Atonement of the 49th year the shofar is sounded and the Jubilee commences. This would be a time of great rejoicing because all the people of Israel were to return to their ancestral homes, property which had been sold off was returned, debts were forgiven and everyone was given the opportunity to make a fresh start, uninhibited by the poor decision they, or their families, had made in the previous 50 years.

Can you see the parallels between the Jubilee and the Eighth Day? At the end of the cycle of seven Sabbath years we enter in to a time of rest, restitution and release. After the seven annual feasts conclude with the seven days of the Feast of Tabernacles we come to the Eighth Day a time of rest and renewal with the Lord.

And just as with the Day of Pentecost, the fiftieth day of counting, when the covenant was changed from a physical blessing on the Tribes of Israel to a spiritual blessing, the out pouring of the Holy Spirit onto the members of the New Testament church, so also the Jubilee points to a future period when we will come to the next stage of human development. The firstfruits will come up in the first resurrection, not as physical beings with an indwelling of the Holy Spirit, but as sanctified spirit beings, just as Jesus now is, capable of manifesting in physical form to complete their ministry on the earth.

Now that we have a clearer understanding of the appointments God has established with mankind and revealed to us through the words of His Holy Bible, let us look at the evidence God has provided us to indicate that He is paying attention to His calendar and, in fact, is extremely punctual in all of His appointments with mankind.

In Chapter 6, *"God's Punctuality"*, we'll look at a number of prophetic events which were fulfilled to the very day that God indicated through His servants the prophets.

Chapter 6

God's Punctuality

If we study the Bible carefully we find that God is extremely punctual in fulfilling His promises. As we saw in the previous chapter, the Holy Days which have been fulfilled so far have been completed on the exact day God declared they would be. And this example of prophetic fulfilment is seen is several areas of the Bible. Let's start by looking at the Exodus and Daniel's 70 week prophecy.

6.1   The Exodus and Daniel's 70 week prophecy

The book of Exodus states, **"Now the sojourning of the children of Israel, who dwelt in Egypt, was four hundred and thirty years. And it came to pass at the end of the four hundred and thirty years, even the selfsame day it came to pass, that all the hosts of the LORD went out from the land of Egypt." (Ex 12:40-41)**

What's so significant about this? How does this tell us about God's punctuality?

God prophesied to Abraham in the book of Genesis **"And he said unto Abram, Know of a surety that thy seed shall be a stranger in a land that is not theirs, and shall serve them; and they shall afflict them four hundred years; And also that nation, whom they shall serve, will I judge: and afterward shall they come out with great substance. (Ge 15:13-14)**

The Bible tells us that the children of Israel came out of Egypt with great abundance after they pillaged the Egyptians. But don't we have a contradiction between the 400 and 430 year time scales?

On face value we do, but let's look closer. In Exodus it says, the sojourn of the children of Israel was 430 years. The fact that they dwelt in Egypt is a sub clause. And in Genesis we see that it is Abraham's seed who would be afflicted 400 years. Who is Abraham's seed? Isaac, who became Abraham's official heir after Ishmael was cast out, and this event occurred 30 years after Abraham had started his journey into Caanan. We can see that God's chosen people, which started with Abraham being called out of Haran, spent 430 dwelling (sojourning) in the land and that Abraham's descendents, starting with Isaac were afflicted for 400 years. The beginning and the end of this period both occurred on Feast days. The end is on the Feast of Unleavened bread, the day after Passover and the beginning on the day of the great feast for Isaac (Ge 21:8-10).

There is also a unique symmetry in this chronology. The time from Abraham's entry into Caanan to Jacob entering Egypt was 215 years. And the time from Israel (Jacob) entering Egypt to the Exodus was also 215 years.

A detailed account of this chronology can be found at this website http://creationontheweb.com/images/pdfs/tj/j21_1/j21_1_67-68.pdf.

Another common chronology is that of Daniel's 70 week prophecy. Let's first look at what the scripture says. **Seventy weeks are determined upon thy people and upon thy holy city, to finish the transgression, and to make an end of sins, and to make reconciliation for iniquity, and to bring in everlasting righteousness, and to seal up the vision and prophecy, and to anoint the most Holy. Know therefore and understand, that from the going forth of the commandment to restore and to build Jerusalem unto the Messiah the Prince shall be seven weeks, and threescore and two weeks: the street shall be built again, and the wall, even in troublous times. And after threescore and two weeks shall Messiah be cut off, but not for himself: and the people of the prince that shall come shall destroy the city and the sanctuary; and the end thereof shall be with a flood, and unto the end of the war desolations are determined. And he shall confirm the covenant with many for one week: and in the midst of the week he shall cause the sacrifice and the oblation to cease, and for the overspreading of abominations he shall make it desolate, even until the consummation, and that determined shall be poured upon the desolate. (Da 9:24-27)**

From this prophecy we can see:

- 70 weeks are determined to make reconciliation, bring righteousness, seal prophecy and anoint the most Holy.
- From the commandment to restore Jerusalem until Messiah the prince there shall be seven weeks and 62 weeks.
- After 62 weeks Messiah shall be cut off.

The most common interpretation of this prophecy starts in the book of Ezra chapter 7. **Some of the children of Israel, the priests, the Levites, the singers, the gatekeepers, and the Nethinim came up to Jerusalem in the seventh year of King Artaxerxes. … This is a copy of the letter that King Artaxerxes gave Ezra the priest, the scribe, expert in the words of the commandments of the LORD, and of His statutes to Israel:** *Artaxerxes, king of kings, To Ezra the priest, a scribe of the Law of the God of heaven: Perfect peace, and so forth. I issue a decree that all those of the people of Israel and the priests and Levites in my realm, who volunteer to go up to Jerusalem, may go with you."* **(Ez 7:7, 12-14)**

History tells us that Artaxerxes reigned from 464-424 BC. The Jewish civil calendar celebrates New Year in the autumn so the seventh year of his reign would be September 458BC to September 457BC.

7 + 62 weeks = 69 weeks = 483 days and in bible prophecy there are two ways of interpreting dates – literally the days are exactly as counted or prophetically using what is what is known as "the day for a year principle". In this case we know that

nothing significant happened in the first 483 days after the decree was given so let's use the day for a year principle.

457BC + 483 +1 (because there is no year 0) = 27. The prophetic fulfilment of this prophecy must occur after September 27AD. Does the Bible give us any clue as to what may have happened at this time?

The Gospel of Luke gives us this information: **Now in the fifteenth year of the reign of Tiberius Caesar, Pontius Pilate being governor of Judea, Herod being tetrarch of Galilee, his brother Philip tetrarch of Iturea and the region of Trachonitis, and Lysanias tetrarch of Abilene, while Annas and Caiaphas were high priests, the word of God came to John the son of Zacharias in the wilderness. … When all the people were baptized, it came to pass that Jesus also was baptized; and while He prayed, the heaven was opened. And the Holy Spirit descended in bodily form like a dove upon Him, and a voice came from heaven which said, "You are My beloved Son; in You I am well pleased." Now Jesus Himself began His ministry at about thirty years of age,"** (Lk 3:1-2, 21-23)

According to Kenneth F. Doig in his book, *New Testament Chronology,* Pontius Pilate took over as Governor of Judea in September 27 AD and Tiberius Caesar became Emperor of Rome on 19 August 14AD. When Luke states that it was in the 15th year of the reign of Tiberius we are brought to a period from the 19th August 28 AD to 18 August 29 AD when using the Julian calendar. But this gives a wide margin of error for the revealing of Messiah (from September 27AD to August 28AD). However, Luke was a Greek and he was writing to a fellow Greek, Theophilus and the Greeks did not use the Julian calendar. They used a Syro-Macedonian calendar which beagn with the month of Dios, typically occurring in October. Also they used inclusive reckoning which means that the year in which a king or emperor starts his reign is considered as to be the first full year of the reign. According to the Syro-Macedonian calendar the first year of the reign of Tiberius Caesar (which contains the Julian date of 19 August 14AD) would be the period 25 October 13AD to 14 October 14 AD. Counting forward 15 years from October 13AD, we come to October 27AD.

We can see that we now have three dates September 27AD from the decree of Artaxerxes, September 27AD from the beginning of the rule of Pontius Pilate and October 27 AD from the 15th year of Tiberius Caesar. All these dates point to the beginning of Jesus' ministry as being September/October 27AD.

We can see that after the 69 prophetic weeks are fulfilled in September 27AD, Jesus was baptized by John to begin his ministry in or around October 27AD. This baptism was His anointing which is what Messiah actually means – the anointed one.

It's also interesting to note that Luke says Jesus was about 30 years old when he started His ministry. In Numbers chapter four we are told that a man must be thirty years old to serve in the tabernacle. Jesus began His ministry immediately after His 30th birthday, which was at the Feast of Tabernacles, the annual Biblical festival in the autumn. This fact also gives us another witness to the accuracy of these dates.

We know He started his ministry in late 27AD at age 30 and we know that He died at Passover. But what year? Traditionally we have believed that His ministry lasted 3 ½ years and this is based on the scripture from Daniel - **And he shall confirm the covenant with many for one week: and in the midst of the week he shall cause the sacrifice and the oblation to cease, and for the overspreading of abominations he shall make it desolate, even until the consummation, and that determined shall be poured upon the desolate. (Dan 9:27)**

This is usually read that he (Jesus) would confirm the covenant with many (through His earthly ministry) and in the middle of the week (after 3 ½ years) cause sacrifice and the oblation to cease (through His death on the cross as the perfect sacrifice). But is this the correct understanding? Let's look at the larger context of this passage which starts with – **"and the people of the prince that shall come shall destroy the city and the sanctuary; and the end thereof shall be with a flood, and unto the end of the war desolations are determined".** Now this cannot possibly be talking about Jesus as He neither destroyed the city nor the sanctuary and the temple sacrificial system continued for another 40 years after His death, until 70 AD when the Roman army destroyed the holy temple and sacked Jerusalem.

If Jesus ministry wasn't 3½ years how long was it?

As always let's turn to the Bible for our answer. The Gospel of John talks about Jesus observing 3 Passovers. John chapter 2 tells us that after the wedding at Cana in Galilee Jesus travelled to Jerusalem. He went into the temple to overturn the tables of the money lenders, around the time of Passover. Then Jesus travelled to Judea (Chapter 3) and returned to Cana of Galilee via Samaria (Chapter 4). In chapter 5 we are told that there was a feast of the Jews and Jesus went to Jerusalem. This was probably one of the pilgrimage feasts Pentecost or Tabernacles. In chapter 6 we read that He went over the Sea of Galilee and the feast of Passover was near. This must be a different Passover from the one in Chapter 2 as He'd done all that travelling and celebrated another feast in between. He then taught in the synagogue in Capernaum and in chapter 7 we are told the Feast of Tabernacles was near. In chapter 10 we hear of the Feast of Dedication and that it was winter when Jesus was in the Temple. And then He went to Bethany (2 miles from Jerusalem) and on to Ephraim. Finally in Chapter 12 we are told it was 6 days before the Passover that He made His triumphal entry into Jerusalem.

How long would this take?

Passover in 28 AD was on 29 March and Passover in 30 AD was on 5 April, so it actually took just over two years to cover three Passovers. If we add 6 months from the time of His baptism in October 27 AD to Passover in March 28AD, we find this His ministry lasted only 2 ½ years!

Does this knowledge help us validate these prophetic dates? Again it does. Passover, 14th Nisan in 30 AD was on the Julian date of 5 April. And if you look at the calendar for that year we find that the 5 April 30AD was a Wednesday. But doesn't this pose a problem because we've always believed that Jesus was crucified on Good Friday?

No it doesn't. In the Gospel of Matthew, Jesus tells us this – **"Then some of the scribes and Pharisees answered, saying, "Teacher, we want to see a sign from You." But He answered and said to them, "An evil and adulterous generation seeks after a sign, and no sign will be given to it except the sign of the prophet Jonah. For as Jonah was three days and three nights in the belly of the great fish, so will the Son of Man be three days and three nights in the heart of the earth." (Mt 12:38-40)**

Jesus said he would be in the ground three days AND three nights. We know he died late in the afternoon. If this was on Good Friday, three days and three nights takes us to late afternoon on MONDAY, not Sunday as most people have been taught. But the Bible tells us He was risen early on the first day of the week (Sunday) so he must have come out of the grave late afternoon on the Sabbath. If we take three days and three nights off late afternoon on the Sabbath we come to late afternoon on Wednesday, which fits the date we have identified for Passover in 30 AD.

Does this statement not contradict the Gospel of John? **"Therefore, because it was the Preparation Day, that the bodies should not remain on the cross on the Sabbath (for that Sabbath was a high day), the Jews asked Pilate that their legs might be broken, and that they might be taken away." (Jn 19:31)**

If we read the scriptures carefully it doesn't. It says He was crucified on the preparation day which is the day before the Sabbath. And this is why so many believe that Jesus died on a Friday. But read the rest of the verse – *for the Sabbath was a high day*. It was not the weekly Sabbath but one of the annual Holy days we are talking about. Knowing what we do about the events at the time of His death, do the scriptures support a Wednesday crucifixion?

Again, they do! In the Gospel of Mark we are told that the Sabbath being past the women bought spices to anoint Him. And in the Gospel of Luke we are told the women returned and prepared spices and fragrant oils, then rested on the Sabbath day. How can they have bought spices after the Sabbath and at the same time prepared spices and then rested on the Sabbath? Here's how.

- Jesus was crucified on Wednesday afternoon and hurriedly taken off the cross before sunset when the Holy day started.
- Thursday was the first day of the Feast of Unleavened bread – an annual Sabbath and High day.
- On Friday (after the annual Sabbath) the women went out, bought spices and prepared the oil.
- They then rested on the weekly Sabbath (Saturday).
- And went to the tomb early on the Sunday morning and found that He was already risen.

Again, by allowing the scripture to interpret scripture we have a clear explanation of the clear, literal fulfilment of Biblical prophecy.

6.2 Duality of Prophecy

There is a recurring theme throughout the Bible of the dual nature of events and prophecies. We can see this duality in numerous events such as:

- The first coming of Jesus and the suffering Messiah and His second coming as the conquering King
- The story of Abraham being commanded to sacrifice his son Isaac gave us the statement that God would provide for Himself a lamb, which He did with the ram caught in the thicket. But this prophetic statement was also fulfilled with the life and death of Jesus and the lamb who takes away the sins of the world.
- Paul tells us of the first man (Adam) becoming a living being and the last man (Jesus) a life giving spirit.
- The tribes of Israel were to be physically circumcised to enter in to the covenant with God. Christians are required to have a circumcised heart to enter in to a spiritual relationship with God.
- Jesus indicated that John the Baptist had fulfilled the prophetic role of Elijah for His first coming, but another Elijah figure was to come before His second coming.
- Jesus spoke of those who are in Judea fleeing to the hills when they see Jerusalem surrounded by armies – this occurred in 70 AD when the Roman army sacked Jerusalem and destroyed the temple. And it will be fulfilled again just before His second coming.
- In 167 BC Antiochus Epiphanies desecrated the Jewish temple by setting up a statue of Zeus for people to worship and sacrificing a pig on the altar. This is called the abomination of desolation. But Jesus also spoke of this happening again before His second coming.

Now when we explore the scriptures looking for future prophecies we must be extremely careful and honest with ourselves not to read into the scriptures our own perceptions of the possible fulfilment. In some cases the prophecies are completely fulfilled and by trying to shoe horn them into our pet theory about what might happen is at best misleading and at worst deceitful. Also there may be occasions when we understand that a prophecy has an end time application but we can't see where it fits. Again we need to acknowledge the prophecy, try and place it in the prophetic timeline as best we can, but also be open and honest and clearly state that this particular event is our "best guess". Remember the scrolls of Daniel were sealed up to the end of time so any prophetic analysis of them carried out in the past could well be wrong. We must not be afraid to discard long held beliefs that no longer fit the evidence we are now seeing.

We must also be scrupulously honest about allowing our own prejudice and preconceptions to colour our understanding of prophecy and the development of the prophetic timeline. In all cases, the safest option is to rely on the adage – let the Bible interpret the Bible - and if we're not sure about the specific detail or application of a prophetic understanding we must say so. Finally, there will be gaps between specific prophetic events while at the same time we will see current world events coming together, and in this case it's fine to include the world event to round out the overall picture, but again we must be absolutely honest that we are basing our statement on logic rather than prophecy.

All that being understood, let's go back to Daniel's prophecy which was sealed until the end of time.

6.3   Daniel's 70 week prophecy – taking another look

If you recall Daniel's 70 week prophecy, it talked about a 7 week period, 62 weeks and 1 final week. And in the beginning of this chapter we saw how the 69 week prophecy was accurately fulfilled with the 483 year period from the issuing of the decree in 457 BC by Artaxerxes to Ezra the scribe to the baptism of Jesus in 27 AD. But is there a dual fulfilment of this prophecy?

Why did Daniel talk about 7 weeks and 62 weeks? Why didn't he just say there would be 69 weeks? Let's look again at this prophecy and see if there is a dual fulfilment.

Seventy weeks are determined upon thy people and upon thy holy city, to finish the transgression, and to make an end of sins, and to make reconciliation for iniquity, and to bring in everlasting righteousness, and to seal up the vision and prophecy, and to anoint the most Holy.

Has this prophecy been totally fulfilled? Have transgressions and sins ended? Have all people been reconciled to God? Do we have everlasting righteousness on the earth? Obviously not – we are far from it. Obviously there must be a dual fulfilment of this prophecy. Let's look at the next couple of verses.

Know therefore and understand, that from the going forth of the commandment to restore and to build Jerusalem unto the Messiah the Prince shall be seven weeks, and threescore and two weeks: the street shall be built again, and the wall, even in troublous times.

We found the first commandment to restore Jerusalem, but is there a modern day example of when Jerusalem was restored? Obviously it's not happening today, with all the talk of a Palestinian homeland and the division of Jerusalem it's unlikely that we'll see a restoration of Jerusalem before the second coming of Jesus. But, there has been an event in recent history that could fulfil this requirement to restore Jerusalem. On the 7th June 1967, the third day of the 6 day war, control of Jerusalem was restored to the Jews for the first time in almost 1900 years when the Jordanian troops were forced back from the west bank over the river Jordan.

Using this as our starting point can we identify any literal fulfilments? Seven literal weeks later and 62 weeks later nothing of any significance affecting Jerusalem was reported. What about the year for a day principle? Seven weeks equates to 49 years which would bring us to 7 June 2016. This equates to 1 Sivan 5776 in the Hebrew calendar, but other than it is the first of the month, there doesn't appear to be anything significant about the date.

There is another way we can look at the prophetic years. If you recall the story of Noah, we are told that the waters prevailed on the earth for 150 days. Also we learn that there were 5 months between Noah entering the ark and it coming to rest on Mt Ararat, which indicates that the Bible talks about a 30 day month.

"In the six hundredth year of Noah's life, in the second month, the seventeenth day of the month, the same day were all the fountains of the great deep broken up, and the windows of heaven were opened". (Ge 7:11)

" …and Noah only remained alive , and they that were with him in the ark. And the waters prevailed upon the earth an hundred and fifty days". (Ge 7:23-24)

"And the ark rested in the seventh month, on the seventeenth day of the month, upon the mountains of Ararat". (Ge 8:4)

Also in the Book of revelation we are told of several periods – time, time and half a time, forty two months and 1260 days. Now a time is one year, so time, times and half a time is 3½ years which is also 42 months. And 42 months of 30 days works out to be 1260 days! Prophetically we can see that God uses a 360 day year as well as a literal solar year. As a side note it's interesting that all ancient cultures were aware of a 360 day year and this is where we come up with 360 degrees in a circle. There is speculation that before the great flood the earth may have been rotating in a perfect 360 day orbit around the sun and the moon had an exact 30 day orbit around the earth. As I said it's speculation, but it does give some credence to using the 360 day year in our prophetic calculations.

What do 7 prophetic weeks work out to in literal days using a 360 day year? The answer is 17,640 days. Let's add this to the date we have identified for the restoration of Jerusalem to Jewish control. There are 207 days from 7 June to 31 December and adding all the days (remembering the leap years) from 1 January 1968 to 31 December 2014 gives us 17,167 days. This means we need an extra 266 days in 2015 to bring us to the prophetic count of 17,640. (207 + 17167 + 266 = 17640).

	0	1	2	3	4	5	6	7	8	9	
1960								207	366	365	938
1970	365	365	366	365	365	365	366	365	365	365	3652
1980	366	365	365	365	366	365	365	365	366	365	3653
1990	365	365	366	365	365	365	366	365	365	365	3652
2000	366	365	365	365	366	365	365	365	366	365	3653
2010	365	365	366	365	365	266					2092

And counting 266 days into 2015 brings us to 23 September. This doesn't sound like a particularly special date in the Gregorian calendar. What about in the Hebrew calendar? 23 September 2015 is 10 Tishrei 5776 which is a far more interesting date. Tishrei is the seventh month of the Hebrew calendar and if we read our Bibles the 10th day of the seventh month is the Day of Atonement. It is the day our sins are forgiven and we become "At-One" with God.

This sounds like a possible fulfilment of Daniel's statement – "**to finish the transgression, and to make an end of sins, and to make reconciliation for iniquity, and to bring in everlasting righteousness, and to seal up the vision and prophecy, and to anoint the most Holy.**" (**Da 9:24**)

The Day of Atonement is one of the annual holy days, so we can expect it to happen every year. Is there anything else that makes this year special? Remember in chapter 5 we talked about the Sabbath and Jubilee years? Well the year, 2008-2009 was a Sabbath year, which means that the next Sabbath year will be seven years from that date. It is going to start in March 2015 and complete in March 2016. And logically if we're looking for completion of 7 weeks the cycle of 7 x seven years would naturally finish in a Sabbath year.

Also we discovered that the Sabbath year cycle points to the Jubilee year. And when does the Jubilee year start? The Jubilee is announced by sounding the shofar on the Day of Atonement in the 7th cycle of Sabbath years. According to Hebrew scholars, the next Jubilee year starts on the 10 Tishrei 5776, which is 23 September 2015!

An interesting observation from this is that Jerusalem was restored to Jewish control in a Jubilee year, which makes perfect sense when we understand that the purpose of the jubilee was for the tribes of Israel to return to their ancestral homes and Judah's tribal land includes Jerusalem!

From our prophetic countdown from the restoration of Jerusalem on 7 June 1967 we come exactly to the Day of Atonement 2015, which is also the start of the Jubilee year. Do you remember how Jesus started His ministry? After He had been tempted by the devil He went to Nazareth and read from the scroll of Isaiah, and half way through the verse He stopped and said "Today this scripture is fulfilled in your hearing". This is what Jesus read "**The Spirit of the Lord GOD is upon me; because the LORD hath anointed me to preach good tidings unto the meek; he hath sent me to bind up the broken hearted, to** proclaim liberty to the captives, and the opening of the prison to them that are bound;   To proclaim the acceptable year of the LORD, (Is 61-2a)

And we know that in the earthly ministry of His first coming He preached the Gospel to the meek, comforted the broken hearted, freed those who were sick and demon possessed and proclaimed the Kingdom of God. But look how the rest of the passage in Isaiah continues "and the day of vengeance of our God; to comfort all that mourn; to appoint unto them that mourn in Zion, to give unto them beauty for ashes, the oil of joy for mourning, the garment of praise for the spirit of heaviness; that they might be called trees of righteousness, the planting of the LORD, that he might be glorified. And they shall build the old wastes, they shall raise up the former desolations, and they shall repair the waste cities, the desolations of many generations. (Is 61:2b-4)

If Jesus' first ministry proclaimed the acceptable year of the Lord, His second coming starts with a day of vengeance and goes on to comforting those who mourn and rebuilding and repairing the desolations. There are significant parallels between this statement and the events of the Book of Revelation – the destruction of the 7 seals and trumpet plagues, the bowls of wrath of the Lord followed by the 1,000 year reign when the earth is renewed and the earth is prepared for receiving the New Jerusalem.

We've seen that a dual fulfilment of the prophetic 7 weeks of Daniel's 70 week prophecy points to the Day of Atonement in a Jubilee year. This is all very interesting and exciting information, which certainly gives us a prophetic date to consider. But is this enough evidence to say that Jesus will return on 23 September 2015? No it's not!

We must establish all things by two or three witnesses. Are there any other witnesses we can look for to support this prophetic date?

Revelation Chapter 6 tells us "I looked when He opened the sixth seal, and behold, there was a great earthquake; and the sun became black as sackcloth of hair, and the moon became like blood. (Rev 6:12). What astronomical phenomena could cause the moon to turn to blood and the sun to appear as sackcloth? Obviously a lunar and a solar eclipse would create this appearance. Is it possible to predict when lunar and solar eclipses occur? Yes, in fact it's very easy and NASA has done all the hard work for us!

6.4   It's not rocket science but NASA gives us a clue

When 4 total solar eclipses (blood moons) occur together it's called a tetrad and if we look at the NASA predictions for eclipses in 2014 and 2015 we find:

Date	Eclipse Type	Saros	Eclipse Duration	Geographic Region of Eclipse Visibility
2014 Apr 15	Total	122	03h35m	Aus., Pacific, Americas
2014 Oct 08	Total	127	03h20m	Asia, Aus., Pacific, Americas

Date	Eclipse Type	Saros	Eclipse Duration	Geographic Region of Eclipse Visibility
2015 Apr 04	Total	132	03h30m	Asia, Aus., Pacific, Americas
2015 Sep 28	Total	137	03h21m	Pacific, Americas, Europe, Africa, Asia

Total lunar eclipses on 4 April and 28 Sep 2015, and in the Hebrew calendar these dates are 15 Nisan and 15 Tishrei respectively. We know these dates more commonly as Passover and the Feast of Tabernacles. Similarly 15 April and 8 October 2014 are 15 Nisan and 14 Tishrei, Passover and Erev Sukkot, the Eve of the Feast of Tabernacles. We can see that in 2014 a blood moon occurs at Passover and Tabernacles and the same again in 2015.

But how common is it for the Tetrad (4 consecutive blood moons) to fall on Biblical holy days? Well there are no more this century. There were six tetrads in the 1500's but none fell on Holy Days; there were none in the 1600's, 1700's or 1800's. In fact there have been a total of only 16 tetrads over the last 4,000 years that fall on Biblical Holydays, eight before and eight after the birth of Christ.

But in the 20th century 4 blood moons occurred in 1967 and 1968 – when Israel regained control of Jerusalem and 1949-50 the year after the modern state of Israel was established.

Date	Gregorian	Hebrew	Holy Day	Event
1949	13 April	14 Nisan	Erev Pesach/Eve of Passover	Israel
1949	7 October	14 Tishrei	Erev Sukkot/ Eve of Tabernacles	established in 1948
1950	2 April	15 Nisan	Pesach/First day of Unleavened bread	
1950	26 September	15 Tishrei	Sukkot/Feast of Tabernacles	
1967	24 April	14 Nisan	Erev Pesach/Eve of Passover	Israel
1967	18 October	14 Tishrei	Erev Sukkot/Eve of Tabernacles	regains
1968	13 April	15 Nisan	Pesach/First day of Unleavened bread	control of Jerusalem
1968	6 October	15 Tishrei	Sukkot/Feast of Tabernacles	
2014	15 April	15 Nisan	Pesach/First day of Unleavened bread	Year of preparation
2014	8 October	14 Tishrei	Erev Sukkot/Eve of Tabernacles	
2015	4 April	15 Nisan	Pesach/First day of Unleavened bread	2nd Coming of Jesus
2015	28 September	15 Tishrei	Sukkot/Feast of Tabernacles	
21c	Tetrads occur in 2032-33, 43-44, 61-62, 72-73 but not on Holy Days.			

If we look at these dates carefully we see that 1949-50 tetrad was 1-2 years after the establishment of Israel; the 1967-68 tetrad was the year of the restoration of Jerusalem and the year after and the 2014-15 tetrad is the year before and year of the possible return of Jesus. We can see that God has been drawing our attention to the tetrad blood moons and His holy days.

Does NASA give us any clue about solar eclipses? There are two solar eclipses in 2015 on 20 March and 13 September. In the Hebrew Calendar these dates are 29 Adar, which is the eve of 1 Nisan, the first day of the Biblical year and 29 Elul, which is the eve of 1 Tishrei – the Feast of Trumpets! Again let's look at the solar eclipses around the Tetrads in 1949-50, 1967-68 and 2014-2015.

Date	Gregorian	Hebrew	Holy Day	Event
1949	No solar eclipses			
1950	18 March	29 Adar	Eve of the Biblical year	Israel established in 1948
1950	12 September	1 Tishrei	The Feast of Trumpets	
1967	9 May	29 Nisan	No Biblical significance	Israel regains control of Jerusalem
1967	2 November	29 Tishrei	No Biblical significance	
1968	28 March	28 Adar	No Biblical significance	
1968	22 September	29 Elul	Eve of the Feast of Trumpets	
2014	29 April	29 Nisan	No Biblical significance	Year of preparation
2014	23 October	29 Tishrei	No Biblical significance	
2015	20 March	29 Adar	Eve of the Biblical year	2nd Coming of Jesus?
2015	13 September	29 Elul	Eve of the Feast of Trumpets	
21st C	Eclipses occur in 2032-33, 43-44, 61-62, 72-73 but none fall on Holy Days.			

We see in the 1949-50 Tetrad there were two solar eclipses with Biblical significance – 18 March 1950 (29 Adar) the Eve of the Biblical New Year and 12 September (1 Tishrei) the Feast of Trumpets. In the 1967-68 Tetrad there was one solar eclipse with Biblical significance – 22 September 1968 (29 Elul) the Eve of the Feast of Trumpets. But when we look to the 2014-15 Tetrad, there are two solar eclipses with biblical significance – 20 March (29 Adar) Eve of the Biblical New Year and 13 September (29 Elul) the Eve of the Feast of Trumpets!

Again we see that God is using signs in the heavens, this time solar eclipses, to point us to the Holy days in 2015.

6.5   Defining the prophetic anchor point

Now let's put all the information we have together into a single coherent form and see what we can identify.

Date	Greg'n	Hebrew	Holy Day	Event
2014	15 Apr	15 Nisan	Pesach/First day of Unleavened bread	Lunar Eclipse
2014	8 Oct	14 Tishrei	Erev Sukkot/Eve of Tabernacles	Lunar Eclipse
2015	20 Mar	29 Adar	Eve of first day of the Biblical year	Total Solar
2015	4 Apr	15 Nisan	Pesach/First day of Unleavened bread	Lunar Eclipse
2015	13 Sep	29 Elul	Eve of the Feast of Trumpets	Partial Solar
2015	23 Sep	10 Tishrei	Yom Kippur/The Day of Atonement – the 17,640 day countdown from the restoration of Jerusalem on 7 June 1967 completes. The Jubilee year starts.	
2015	28 Sep	15 Tishrei	Sukkot/Feast of Tabernacles	Lunar Eclipse

When we represent this data graphically we get this, remarkable information:

Year	2014		2015				
Date	15 Apr	8 Oct	20 Mar	4 Apr	13 Sep	23 Sep	28 Sep
Eclipse						Prophetic 49 years completes 7 Jun 67 – Jerusalem restored.	
Event	Passover	Feast of Tabernacles	Biblical New Year	Passover	Feast of Trumpets	Day of Atonement	Feast of Tabernacles
Notes	The preparation year for the following Sabbath year in 2015.		The Sabbath year starts in 2015 and the Jubilee year starts at the sounding of the shofar on the Day of Atonement in 2015. This sounding of the shofar would be the final trump after the Day of Trumpets and would signify the resurrection of the dead.				

The solar/lunar eclipse combinations in the spring and autumn of 2015 also point to the 6th seal of revelation **"I looked when He opened the sixth seal, and behold, there was a great earthquake; and the sun became black as sackcloth of hair, and the moon became like blood"** (Rev 6:12) and the end time prophecy of Joel **"The sun shall be turned into darkness, and the moon into blood, before the coming of the great and awesome day of the LORD"** (Joel 2:31). But there is room for interpretation in these two events so for the purpose of developing the time line I will use the Day of Atonement, 23 September 2015, as the prophetic anchor point for establishing the "End Time Countdown".

There are three other solar eclipses worth mentioning and these occurred on 1 August 2008, 22 July 2009 and 11 July 2010. When we convert these dates to the Hebrew calendar we come to 29 Tammuz (the Eve of 1 Av) or 1 Av. What's so significant about 1 Av? This is the beginning of the nine days of mourning leading up to the Jewish fast known as Tisha b'Av. This day is remembered for "the five calamities" — the destruction of the first and second temples (586 BC and 70 AD); the delivering of the false report of the promised land by the 12 spies; the failure of the bar Kobah revolt (135 AD) and the razing of Jerusalem (136 AD).

Also more modern associations with this fast include expulsion of Jews from England in 1290 AD; the Alhambra decree of 1492 AD expelling Jews from Spain took effect in 7th Av; the deportation of Jews from the Warsaw ghetto started on the eve of Tisha b'Av in 1942. And bringing this day of mourning right up to present day, Jewish settlers were expelled from Gush Katif on the day after Tisha b'Av in 2005. This is a day signifying great destruction and loss of their homeland for the children of Israel, so we will also be using these dates in the end time countdown to give us markers for potential prophetic fulfilment.

Having established a prophetic "anchor point" we now need to search the scriptures to find all the end time prophetic information we need to piece together the jigsaw puzzle of these end time events. But before we do this there are some assumptions which I have made in developing the end time chronology and these are discussed in Chapter 7.

Chapter 7

Development of the Timeline

7.1 Assumptions

For the purpose of developing the end time countdown, I have made the following assumptions in creating the model:

- The Bible should be taken literally word for word, unless there is obvious indication that the scripture is allegorical.

- Every statement must be assessed in the wider context of the passage to avoid misinterpretation.

- No single statement can be taken as evidentiary proof, two or three witnesses or high levels of corroborating evidence are required to declare a statement absolute.

- The chronology within and specific passage is linear, there is no reason to believe that the author is jumping forward and backward in time, unless there is an explicit statement to indicate that a time shift has occurred.

- Some statements are parenthetical, what some call inset chapters, these can normally be identified by taking the whole statement in context and seeing where the context changes.

- Scriptural statement should be prioritised as follows:

  - Explicit statements (i.e. only Noah, his three sons and their wives entered the ark)
  - Implicit statements (i.e. therefore no one else entered the ark)
  - Implied statements (i.e. all those outside the ark must have drowned when the earth flooded)

7.2   Prophetic Biblical Timings

We have already spent a great deal of time looking at various prophetic dates and indicators, but to make sure that the timing in the checklist is as open, and free from personal bias as is possible, I will use the following criteria for dates and times:

- All dates will be given as both Gregorian dates and Hebrew dates to allow for comparison and identification of Biblically significant events.

- The New Year shall be considered to the Biblical New Year 1 Nisan (where reference to the Jewish civil New Year (1 Tishrei) is appropriate it will be clearly identified.

- When dealing with prophetic statements of time they will be assessed as literal periods of time (hours, days, weeks, months and years). If this does not help with the analysis prophetic periods will be considered using the day for a year principle and the prophetic 360 day year based on twelve 30 day months.

There are a number of references to a "woman in labour" in relation to the end times and although this can give us a vivid impression of the pain people will suffer in the end there is also a prophetic interpretation which is helpful in developing the timeline. Just as a woman in labour experiences contractions which start gently and increase in frequency and intensity as the time for birth draws near. The end times signs will follow the same pattern. As we get closer to the end the intensity of signs will increase as will their frequency. This helps address one of the potential problems with understanding the end time events.

There are four seals clearly identified in the book of Revelation – false religion, war, famine and death. But these events have been with us since before the earthly ministry of Jesus and this has caused some to propose that the seals have been opening since His earthly ministry and have just been growing in intensity. I don't believe that this is the case as the analogy of a seal is something that is brittle – it is intact, complete and sealed, or the seal is broken and open. I believe it is a more honest interpretation to identify that events will be getting worse as the end time approaches until a point when the seal is finally opened and the full climax of the event is unleashed upon the earth and all humankind.

7.3   Planning basis

As I have stated before the purpose of this book and the Armageddon countdown checklist is not to be a complete, exhaustive theological commentary of end time scriptures. Rather it is meant to be a practical guide to help you discern the signs so that you can monitor world events and prepare yourself – spiritually, mentally, emotionally and physically for what you know will come next in the countdown.

In the original version of this book, I used the principle of "worst case credible scenario" for developing the time line. Using this approach where I had two possible credible start dates for an event, I chose the earliest. My reasoning was that I wanted to give people the maximum possible time to prepare themselves because if they were ready for the first date, they would also be ready for any date which occurred after that time.

I now realise that this approach was a mistake for three main reasons. Firstly I have no authority to be seen to be trying to influence the hand of God in the execution of His divine plan. Secondly, it paints an unduly pessimistic picture for end time events, time is short but not that short. Several events which were identified in the 2008 edition as potentially occurring in 2009 have not come to pass and this gives critics an obvious vehicle to attack the time line which could still be valid but just not meeting the worst case criteria. Finally, the sequence of events leading to the end of the age will be horrific for us all to witness and experience. And human nature being what it is always prefers to "shoot the messenger" rather than face up to the message. By discrediting events which have been sequenced based on worst case planning gives immediate cause to dismiss the whole message when in fact, the sequence could still be correct, it is just the indexing (by date) of the event which is in error. In this second edition I have adopted a different method for presenting possible dates in the end time countdown.

With the level of understanding we currently have about world events and potential scenarios that could fulfil a specific prophetic requirement there is going to be a level of interpretation required. And this is especially true when trying to identify dates to accompany events in the end time sequence. In this first edition I have used date ranges to index the sequence. That way I can show the earliest and latest possible dates which will still serve to give people warning and time to prepare themselves, while at the same time maintaining the integrity of the time line so that it cannot be immediately dismissed when the first possible earliest date does not occur.

Also to make it absolutely clear where I made interpretations, interpolations and assumptions I have rated every point on the time line for the quality of the data. I have indicated this in a column marked QA – Quality Assessment. This is based on a 4 level scale from A (absolute certainty) to D (highly inferred). To create this scale I have assessed the definition of the event, the expected date the event will occur and the level of correlation between the event and the date. This is shown in the following table.

Quality	Event Definition	Expected Date	Correlation
A	Clearly defined	Explicitly identified	Direct correlation between event and date
B	Clearly defined	Explicitly identified	Inferred correlation
C	Clearly defined	Inferred or assumed	Inferred correlation
D	Details inferred from sources	Inferred or assumed	Inferred correlation

Finally, as I have said several times now – do not blindly believe what I present in the next Chapter. Prove all things, work out your own salvation with fear and trembling, and if you believe that the Bible indicates there are errors or inaccuracies in this book, please let me know I'd be pleased to discuss them with you. Please feel free to contact me directly at david@spiritandtruthrevival.org.

So let's look at the end time chronology in Chapter 8 "Armageddon 2015 Countdown Checklist".

Chapter 8

Armageddon 2015 Countdown Checklist

This checklist provides the "bare bones" of the end time chronology. I have provided the analysis information for each event in the time line in Chapter 9 – the event justification. Each event is given a 4 digit index number representing the 2 digit year and sequence – I have left space in the sequence for adding additional information as it becomes available – event 6710 refers to the restoration of Jerusalem to Jewish control in 1967.

I have provided the Gregorian date so that the prophetic event can easily be index against the modern calendar and the Hebrew date so that we can see where these events fall in relation to God's predetermined Holy days. As I have stated earlier, where a date cannot be absolutely defined I have provided, what I believe to be, the credible range of dates during which the event could occur.

My intention is to keep the time line updated and as new information comes available I'll be refining the chronology and posting updates through the internet at www.Armageddon2015.com.

Year	Gregorian Date	Hebrew Date	Event	Event Index	Q A
1967	7 June	28 Iyyar	**Control of Jerusalem regained by Israel** – historical fact.	6710	A
2008	29 Sep	29 Elul 5768	**Possible start of Daniels 70th week** - divine intervention on the eve of the Feast of Trumpets and Jewish civil New Year causes financial markets to crash.	0810	A
	In Progress	NA	**Economic Collapse of western economies** – will continue through to the beginning of the Time of Jacob's trouble.	0820	A
	27 December	30 Kislev 5769	**Israel commences operations against Hamas in Gaza**	0830	A
2009	25 March	29 Adar 5769	**2008/2009 Sabbatical Year Ends**	0910	A
	26 March	1 Nisan 5769	**70th Week of Daniel begins** – Beast power confirms a covenant with many. Start of confederacy against Israel.	0920	C
	22 July	1 Av 5769	**Total Solar Eclipse**	0955	A
2010	11 July	29 Tammuz 5770	**Total Solar Eclipse**	1010	A
	No later than 30 November 2010		**Israel attacks Iranian nuclear facilities** – Israel cannot allow Iran to create operational nuclear weapons.	1020	C

Year	Gregorian Date	Hebrew Date	Event	Event Index	Q A
	Response to event 1020		**Hezbollah attacks Israel with WMD** – Weapons of Mass Destruction consisting of biological and chemical warhead rockets from Syria and Lebanon	1030	C
	Response to event 1030		**Israel invokes the "Samson Option"** - uses tactical nuclear weapons against Syria. Damascus is destroyed in one night.	1040	C
	Present date to early 2011		**1st Seal of Revelation** – White horse with bow and crown set to conquer. Sunni Muslim's Messiah the 12th Imam (or Mahdi)	1050	C
2011	Response to event 1040		**2nd Seal of Revelation** opened– Red horse with great sword to take peace from the earth - China and Russia pre-emptive nuclear strike against Israelite nations	1100	C
	Results from event 1100		**Time of Jacobs Trouble** short period (possibly no longer than 1 month) leading to total destruction of Israelite nations – US, UK, Canada, Australia, NZ, NW Europe. NATO loses World War 3 – 90% of Israelites die.	1110	C
	After event 1110 and no later than 30 September 2011		**3rd Seal of Revelation** – Global Famine – direct result of WW3 and harvest failures after destruction of major food producing nations	1120	C

Year	Gregorian Date	Hebrew Date	Event	Event Index	Q A
	After event 1120		**4th Seal of Revelation – Widespread Death** – global population weakened by famine and breakdown in social infrastructure	1130	C
	Resulting from event 1130		**Calls for world peace by increasing mandate of the UN -** One World Government – Beast Power/Antichrist emerges as global saviour. Resulting from WW3 and global famine	1140	C
2012	27 January	3 Shevat 5772	**Prophetic 1335 Days of Revelation starts**	1210	A
			Temple sacrifice starts in Jerusalem	1220	C
	12 March	18 Adar 1 5772	**Prophetic 1290 Days of Revelation starts – Abomination of Desolation.** Temple Sacrifice ceases – those in Judea instructed to flee to the mountains	1230	A
	24 March	1 Nisan 5772	**4th (Middle) Year of Daniel's 70th week starts**	1240	A

Year	Gregorian Date	Hebrew Date	Event	Event Index	Q A
	11 April	19 Nisan 5772	**Prophetic 1260 Days of Revelations starts** - 2 Witnesses commence ministry. Woman (Church) fed in wilderness. Holy people scattered, holy city trampled underfoot, Beast power has authority.	1250	A
			5th Seal of Revelation – The Great Tribulation begins – persecution against those who remain faithful to Jesus.	1260	A
2014	15 April	15 Nisan 5774	**Total Lunar Eclipse Blood Moon** (on Passover)	1410	A
	8 October	14 Tishrei 5774	**Total Lunar Eclipse Blood Moon** (Eve of the First Day of Feast of Tabernacles)	1420	A
2015	20 March	29 Adar 1 5775	**Total Solar Eclipse Sackcloth Sun** (on the eve of the first day of Biblical New Year)	1505	A
	4 April	15 Nisan 5775	**Total Lunar Eclipse Blood Moon** (on Passover)	1510	A
			6th Seal of Revelation Opened – Sun turned to sackcloth and moon to blood.	1512	A
	After event 1512		**144,000 sealed on their foreheads**	1516	B
	5 April	16 Nisan 5775	**7th Seal of Revelation Opened** – **7 trumpets plagues** Silence in Heaven for ½ an hour.	1520	B
			1st Trumpet Plague – Hail and Fire kill vegetation	1522	B
			2nd Trumpet Plague – Burning Mountain falls into sea	1524	B

Year	Gregorian Date	Hebrew Date	Event	Event Index	Q A
			3rd Trumpet Plague - Wormwood	1526	B
			4th Trumpet Plague – 1/3 of sun, stars and moon struck	1528	B
			5th Trumpet Plague, the 1st Woe – demonic spirits (like locusts) torment mankind like scorpions for 5 months.	1530	B
	2 September	18 Elul 5775	**5th Trumpet plague ends**	1535	B
	3 September	19 Elul 5775	**6th Trumpet Plague** 200 million man army released 1/3 of mankind killed	1540	B
	13 September	29 Elul 5775	**Partial Solar Eclipse Sun Darkened** (on the eve of the Feast of Trumpets)	1550	A
	Between 14 -19 September	1-6 Tishrei 5776	**7 Thunders from God** – Sign of the Son of man appears in the heavens	1555	C
2015	20 September	7 Tishrei 5776	**2 Witnesses killed** in Jerusalem	1560	A
	23 September	10 Tishrei 5776	**Prophetic Anchor Point** – 17,640 Days from Jerusalem being restored on 7 June 1967 (7/6/67)	1565	A
			Day of Atonement - Jubilee year starts with sound of shofar. Final Trump Sounds - Elect are resurrected and taken up into clouds to meet Jesus	1566	A
			The First Resurrection	1570	C
			7 Bowls of God's Wrath poured out	1572	C
			Judah accepts the Messiah	1574	C
	24 September	11 Tishrei 5776	**Wedding Supper of the Lamb**	1576	C

Year	Gregorian Date	Hebrew Date	Event	Event Index	Q A
	26 September	13 Tishrei 5776	**Jesus makes war against the Kings of the earth**	1578	C
	27 September	14 Tishrei 5776	**Satan Bound for 1,000 years**	1580	C
	28 September	15 Tishrei 5776	**Total Lunar Eclipse Blood Moon** (on First Day of the Feast of Tabernacles)	1585	A
			Millennial Sabbath begins – the 1,000 year reign of Jesus over the earth	1590	C
3015	Unknown		**Gog Magog War** – Satan causes one final rebellion against God	3010	C
			Satan is destroyed in the lake of fire	3020	C
			God creates New Heaven and Earth	3030	C
After 3015	Unknown		**Resurrection of all of humanity and the Great White Throne Judgement**	3040	C

Chapter 9

Event Analysis and Justification

Index No.	6710	Event	Israel Regains Control of Jerusalem		
Date	7 Jun 1967	Hebrew	28 Iyyar 5727	Scripture	Dan 9:25
Event Defined		Explicit Date	Direct Correlation		Assessed Quality
Yes		Yes	Yes		A
Discussion	This is historical fact. See chapter 2 for the prophetic understanding of this event and the start of the 17,640 day count of Daniel's prophetic 7 week period from restoring Jerusalem to the return of Messiah. http://www.virtualjerusalem.com/jeisholidays/JerusalemDay/1967.htm.				

Index No.	0810	Event	Warning of Daniel's 70th week		
Date	29 Sep 2008	Hebrew	29 Elul 5678	Scripture	Ex 32:4
Event Defined		Explicit Date	Direct Correlation		Assessed Quality
No		Yes	No		D
Discussion	On the eve of the Feast of Trumpets (which symbolises announcing the calling of God to His people) and Jewish Civil New Year (the first day of the seventh Biblical month) the global financial markets crashed. God's number for completion is 7 and on the eve of the first day of the seventh month the Dow fell 777.7 points, which was 7% of the market value as a result of the failure to agree the $700 Billion bailout package. Is this just coincidence?				

On the eve of the Feast of Trumpets (which symbolises announcing the calling of God to His people) and Jewish Civil New Year (the first day of the seventh Biblical month) the global financial markets crashed. God's number for completion is 7 and on the eve of the first day of the seventh month the Dow fell 777.7 points, which was 7% of the market value as a result of the failure to agree the $700 Billion bailout package. Is this just coincidence?

I don't think so. YHWH, the God of the Bible, attacks the false gods of the people before recovering Israel. Remember the plagues on the Egyptians; they were all against the false gods of that area. What is the false god Israel created for itself? The golden calf and what is the statue on Wall St - a bronze charging bull! **And he received them at their hand, and fashioned it with a graving tool, after he had made it a molten calf: and they said, These be thy gods, O Israel, which brought thee up out of the land of Egypt. (Ex 32:4)** Jesus warned us about serving God and Mammon and I believe that this is a divine warning for Israelites to turn back to their God or face the consequences.

(I don't define this as the beginning of Daniel's 70th week as the first day of the Biblical year is 1 Nisan in the spring, not 1 Tishrei - the Jewish civil New Year which is in the fall).

Index No.	0820	Event	**Economic Collapse of US & UK economies**		
Date	In Progress		Hebrew	NA	Scripture	Deut 28:43-44
Event Defined		Explicit Date		Direct Correlation		Assessed Quality
Yes		No		No		C

Discussion	**The stranger that is within thee shall get up above thee very high; and thou shalt come down very low. He shall lend to thee, and thou shalt not lend to him: he shall be the head, and thou shalt be the tail. (Dt 28:43-44)** The economic collapse will continue through to he beginning of the time of Jacob's Trouble. Nouriel Roubini is the Economics Professor who predicted the US housing market crash. His analysis of the 2009 prospects for the banks and financial markets does not paint a pretty picture - http://www.rgemonitor.com/roubini-monitor.

And even though the governments of the world have poured trillions of taxpayers' money into the banks to try and prevent the global economic collapse the contagion continues. Now the future existence of the Euro is being threatened due to the failure of the Greek economy and the growing risks identified with Portugal, Spain, Ireland and Britain. All that has been achieved with the various bailout and economic stimulus packages is an ever expanding bubble which when it bursts, as all bubbles inevitably do, will collapse the economic system of the developed world. |

Index No.	0830	Event	**Israel commence operations against Hamas in Gaza**		
Date	27 Dec 2008		Hebrew	30 Kislev 5769	Scripture	NA
Event Clearly Defined		Explicit Date		Direct Correlation	Assessed Quality
Yes		Yes		Yes	A
Discussion	This is in retaliation for the continued rocket attacks fired on Israel by Hamas from Gaza. Initially I thought it was possibly a preparatory operation to avoid fighting on two fronts after attacking Iranian nuclear facilities or a feint to provoke Iran into action to justify the attack on their nuclear facilities. The Gaza operation has now completed but Israel is no safer than before and the rhetoric and genocidal intentions of Iran are becoming more pronounced every day.				

Index No.	0910	Event	**2008/2009 Sabbatical Year Ends**		
Date	25 Mar 2009		Hebrew	29 Adar	Scripture	Lev 25:1-7
Event Defined		Explicit Date		Direct Correlation	Assessed Quality
Yes		Yes		Yes	A
Discussion	As we have already discussed in Chapter 5, God defines every 7th year as a Sabbath year, a period when we should give the land rest. Unfortunately throughout history Israel has been extremely unfaithful in observing the Sabbatical year, so there is some disagreement about when the Sabbath years actually occur. This website gives a well researched article into the timing of the Jubilee years - http://www.fivedoves.com/letters/aug2006/Jubilee.pdf. From this information it can be seen that Tishrei 2015 is the start of the 52nd Jubilee. We've already learned that the Jubilee starts on the Day of Atonement in a Sabbath year. 2015 is a Sabbath year and the Biblical New Year is 1 Nisan (March/April on the Gregorian calendar). If March 2015 is the start of a Sabbath year, March 2008 is the start of the previous Sabbath year which ends one year later on 29 Adar (March 2009).				

Index No.	0920	Event	**70th Week of Daniel begins**		
Date	26 Mar 2009	Hebrew	1 Nisan	Scripture	Dan 9:24-27 Ps 83
Event Clearly Defined		Explicit Date	Direct Correlation		Assessed Quality
Yes		Yes	Yes		A

Discussion	In Chapter 6 we identified that the first 69 weeks of Daniels 70 week prophecy were fulfilled at the time Jesus commenced his earthly ministry in 27AD. Based on the second fulfilment of 7 week element of Daniel's prophecy we came to the date of 23 September 2015 for Messiah the Prince. We have also identified that this is a Sabbatical year and God's cycle of 7 always finishes with a Sabbath. Counting back 6 years to the beginning of the 7 year cycle brings us to 1 Nisan in 2009 as the start of the 70th week of Daniel's prophecy.

Dan 9:27 tells us **"And he shall confirm the covenant with many for one week: and in the midst of the week he shall cause the sacrifice and the oblation to cease, and for the overspreading of abominations he shall make *it* desolate, even until the consummation, and that determined shall be poured upon the desolate."**

Ps 83:3-5 states **"They have taken crafty counsel against thy people, and consulted against thy hidden ones. They have said, Come, and let us cut them off from being a nation; that the name of Israel may be no more in remembrance. For they have consulted together with one consent: they are confederate against thee:"**

At the beginning of the 70th week the beast power confirms a covenant with many. Although there was no obvious grand proclamation against Israel in March 2009, the Goldstone commission was established by the UN on 3 April 2009 (one week from the start of the prophetic 70th week) to investigate alleged Israeli atrocities and war crimes committed during the Gaza operation. The commission was criticised from its inception as biased against Israel as the resolution explicitly limited the mission to investigate Israel only and made no mention of any atrocities committed by Hamas, or even the years of mortar attacks against Israeli civilians.

The report was also widely critical of Israel, but itself was criticised by many groups in the west. The organization UN Watch said: "*no one has ever disputed that the Arab-controlled Human Rights Council deliberately selected individuals who had made up their mind well in* |

<table>
<tr><td></td><td colspan="5">advance - not only that Israel was guilty, but that a democratic state with an imperfect but respected legal system should be considered the same as, or worse than, a terrorist group". (Haviv Rettig Gur, <u>Lawyers, watchdog allege Goldstone bias</u>, Jerusalem Post, 14-09-2009)

Although not conclusive of an overt confederacy against Israel there is certainly growing evidence of institutional bias against Israel by numerous UN commissions.</td></tr>
</table>

Index No.	0930	Event	**Total Solar Eclipse**		
Date	22 Jul 2009	Hebrew	1 Av	Scripture	NA
Event Defined		Explicit Date		Direct Correlation	Assessed Quality
Yes		Yes		Yes	A
Discussion		A total solar eclipse occurred (http://eclipse.gsfc.nasa.gov/solar.html) 1 Aug 2008 and on 22 Jul 2009. The next will occur on 11 Jul 2010. Using the Hebrew calendar each total eclipse falls on 1 Av. In chapter 6 we discussed the fast of Tisha b'Av (the Ninth of Av) – the mourning for the destruction of the first and second temples. This period has always been considered a period of bad fortune for Israel and lamenting starts on the 1st of Av and continues through to the fast on the 9th. In 2008 the Russian army invaded the European state of Georgia on 9 August (9th Av) (http://www.infoplease.com/world/events/2008/aug.html). This invasion demonstrated the renewed assertiveness of Moscow and the loss of will by NATO and the US to act decisively in the face of Russian aggression. This political and military weakness will grow under the Obama administration and be further exploited. On 22 and 23 July 2009 the UN Committee on the Exercise of the Inalienable Rights of the Palestinian People convened a meeting titled "Responsibility of the international community to uphold international humanitarian law to ensure the protection of civilians in the Occupied Palestinian Territory in the wake of the war in Gaza". The objective was to discuss Israeli violations of international humanitarian law during the hostilities in the Gaza Strip and determine how the international community could uphold norms of international humanitarian law and fulfil its obligations with regard to ensuring protection of civilians. Again anti-Israeli bias presupposing the outcome of the investigation.				

Index No.	1010	Event	Total Solar Eclipse		
Date	11 Jul 2010	Hebrew	1 Av	Scripture	NA
Event Defined		Explicit Date		Direct Correlation	Assessed Quality
Yes		Yes		Yes	A
Discussion	This total solar eclipse on 1 Av could signify the beginning of the Time of Jacob's Trouble, but as we now understand this being a very short period (as little as one month for the total destruction on the English speaking people), it is more likely to be a sign of impending war in the Middle East started by Hizballah to draw attention, and the threat of effective sanctions, away from Iran as it culminates its nuclear weapons programme. (http://www.debka.com/article/8745/). What gives even more credence to this scenario is that the Chairman of the Palestinian Authority, Mahmoud Abbas, asked the Chinese President Hu Jintao to support sanctions against Iran as Palestinians would be defenceless and in the line of fire from rockets launched from Syria and Lebanon. China is a staunch supporter of Iran and, so far, has adamantly refused to support sanctions against Iran in an effort to stop the development of an Iranian nuclear weapon. (http://www.debka.com/article/8754/)				

Index No.	1020	Event	Israel attacks Iran's nuclear weapons facilities		
Date	Before 30 November 2010	Hebrew	NA	Scripture	NA
Event Defined		Explicit Date		Direct Correlation	Assessed Quality
Yes		No		No	C

| Discussion | Israel cannot allow Iran to create operational nuclear weapons as a single nuclear strike on Israel would effectively destroy the Jewish state. Iran has now produced enough low enriched uranium for 2 bombs and the discovery of covert, hardened nuclear facilities indicate that the enrichment could be completed in only a few months. The UN sanctions have so far been ineffective and Russia is commissioning a nuclear reactor in Iran which would be capable of producing weapons grade plutonium.

The Obama administration has demonstrated a contempt for Israel as has never before been seen from Washington. This has emboldened the Iranian regime against Israel. At the same time the US attempts to enforce meaningful sanctions against Iran to prevent the production of the Iranian bomb have been totally unproductive with China adamant that it will resist any effort to impose sanctions against Tehran. Also the message coming out of the Obama administration is that the policy towards Iran is one of prevention and that US military force will not be used to pre-empt any Iranian aggression against Israel. In fact, the US seems intent on inhibiting Israel ability to defend itself from the Iranian nuclear threat by diverting a consignment of JDAM Kits (that turn ordinary bombs into smart-bombs aka "bunker busters") that Israel had bought from the US in August 2009.

The Israelis must take action especially as the level of support from the US may weaken even further under the Obama administration. The former Israeli deputy defence minister Brig. Gen. Ephraim Sneh stated that Israel "will be compelled to attack Iran's nuclear weapons facilities by this November unless the U.S. and its allies enact crippling sanctions that will undermine the regime in Tehran" (http://www.newsmax.com/KenTimmerman/Timmerman-Israel-Iran-nuclear/2010/04/02/id/354614). |
|---|---|

Index No.	1030	Event	**Israel attacked with WMD**		
Date	In response to event 1020	Hebrew	Unknown	Scripture	NA
Event Defined		Explicit Date		Direct Correlation	Assessed Quality
Yes		No		No	**C**

Discussion	US defence secretary Robert Gates stated: "Hizballah has far more rockets and missile than most governments in the world." (http://www.debka.com/article/8745/) This extensive array of rockets capable of reaching deep into Israel from their bases in Lebanon and Syria has increased in volume and sophistication from those used during the 2006 Lebanon war. Then none of the rockets had any guidance capability so there was no way to accurately target specific sites. Although 100kg of high explosives available in 2006 would certainly destroy a residential building it would not cause the large scale destruction Iran would want in retaliation for losing its nuclear weapon capability. However, there is now evidence that two brigades of Hizballah fighters have been trained to use Scud missiles, with a warhead of one ton, which are available in Syria and can reach any part of Israel without needing to cross over into Lebanon. Scud missiles could also be used to deploy chemical and biological weapons.

I met Ambassador Richard Butler at a conference in 2003 and in our conversation he told me that during his time as the Chief UN weapons inspector in Iraq he had personally presented chemical weapons to his Iraqi counterparts who were actively denying they had the capability. I was confused when the intelligence services said they could not find any WMD materials after the Gulf War. That question is answered in this article which states that Iraqi WMD's were moved into Syria before Gulf War 2 by Russian Speznatz troops. http://archive.newsmax.com/archives/articles/2005/3/2/230625.shtml.

Hezbollah who are controlled by Iran now have the delivery systems and could easily get access to former Iraqi biological and chemical weapons which are stored in Syria. It doesn't take much imagination to think that Iran would instruct its proxy army in Lebanon to attack Israel with weapons of mass destruction in retaliation for a pre-emptive (possibly tactical nuclear) strike in their nuclear weapons capability. Syria and Iran have re-armed Hezbollah after the 2006 war with Israel – http://cedarsrevolution.net/blog/?p=173 |

The timing for this event is uncertain as it is conditional on the Israeli attack on the Iranian nuclear weapons capability. However, once that condition has been met, it is reasonable to assume that Iran would want retaliation as soon as possible so the attack would likely be conducted within weeks of the Natanz operation.

Index No.	1040	Event	Israel invokes the "Samson Option"			
Date	In response to event 1030	Hebrew	Unknown	Scripture	Jer 49:26-27	
Event Defined		Explicit Date		Direct Correlation		Assessed Quality
Yes		No		NA		C

| Discussion | Israel has a deterrent policy known as "The Samson Option" named after the Biblical hero Samson who pulled down the Temple of Dagon the god of the Philistines killing himself and 3,000 philistines who were in the temple to see him tortured. This policy of mutually assured destruction basically states that Israel would respond with nuclear weapons against any country that attacked Israel with weapons of mass destruction.

The problem Israel has in this case is who would they attack – Iran for ordering the strike, Syria for supporting Hezbollah and providing the chemical and biological weapons or the Lebanon which is the likely launch site. Based on Biblical prophecy it is likely that the response would cover all areas. But one dramatic prophecy is found in Jeremiah 49 **"Therefore her young men shall fall in her streets, and all the men of war shall be cut off in that day, saith the LORD of hosts. And I will kindle a fire in the wall of Damascus, and it shall consume the palaces of Benhadad."**

All the men of war being cut off in one day and fires consuming Damascus certainly sounds like the result of a nuclear attack. If this does occur it will be the most dramatic indicators that we are indeed in the final countdown to the return of Jesus.
http://carolmoore.net/nuclearwar/israelithreats.html
http://archive.newsmax.com/archives/articles/2001/10/15/112430.shtml |

Index No.	1050	Event	1st Seal of Revelation		
Date	Before Spring 2011	Hebrew	NA	Scripture	Rev 6:1-2
Event Defined		Explicit Date		Direct Correlation	Assessed Quality
Yes		No		NA	C

Discussion	Rev 6:2 "And I saw, and behold a white horse: and he that sat on him had a bow; and a crown was given unto him: and he went forth conquering, and to conquer." In chapter 3 we identified that the rider of the white horse matches the description of the 12 Imam, the Mahdi of Shiite Islam.

President Ahmadinejad of Iran believes it is his duty to herald the return of the Mahdi, who will come to liberate Muslims from oppression out of a period of global chaos and destruction. As we see Iranian backed terror organisations provoking violence against Israel from Gaza, the Lebanon and Syria we can see a clear connection between this and the conflict in Gaza.
http://www.worldnetdaily.com/news/article.asp?ARTICLE_ID=48225

In the first edition of this book I used "worst case" dating and placed this event immediately after the beginning of the 70th week of Daniels prophecy. However as I discussed earlier there were flaws in that approach. I felt that Islamic messianic fervour coupled with the increasing Iranian desire to produce a nuclear weapon could provoke Israel into a pre-emptive attack. I now feel that the opening of the first seal of revelation, the revealing of the Islamic messiah who will come out of destruction and chaos will actually occur after the chaos and destruction of a Mideast WMD exchange between Iran, its proxy states and Israel.

This also ties in better with the statement of Matthew Chapter 24 - **And you will hear of wars and rumours of wars. See that you are not troubled; for all these things must come to pass, but the end is not yet. For nation will rise against nation, and kingdom against kingdom. And there will be famines, pestilences and earthquakes in various places. (Mt 24:6-7).** Wars and rumours of war must come before the end which is signified by opening the first and second seals (nations rising against nation) and the third and fourth seals (famine and pestilence). |

Index No.	1100	Event	**2nd Seal of Revelation opened**		
Date	Early in 2011 in response to event 1050	Hebrew	NA	Scripture	Rev 6: 3-4 Hos 8:14

Event Defined	Explicit Date	Direct Correlation	Assessed Quality
Yes	No	No	C

Discussion	**And there went out another horse that was red: and power was given to him that sat thereon to take peace from the earth, and that they should kill one another: and there was given unto him a great sword. (Rev 6:3-4)** As we discussed in Chapter 3 the red horse with a sword signifies military operations from communist dictatorships. We are seeing a renewed aggression from Russia – Georgia invasion, manipulating gas supplies to Europe and increased military cooperation with Venezuela, Iran and China. China is also growing more assertive with Chinese nuclear submarines surfacing next to a US naval task group. http://www.strategypage.com/htmw/htsub/articles/20061114.aspx?comments=Y As the situation in the Middle East deteriorates with the exchange of WMD's between Israel and Iran and its surrogate partners, Syria and Lebanon, America, Russia and China will inevitably be brought to a war footing. Russia's military doctrine is that it could survive a nuclear war and China has upgraded its nuclear weapons capability from a purely defensive retaliatory organisation to have first strike capability. America and Russia signed the New START nuclear warhead reduction treaty in April 2010, however the agreement to reduce warheads to a limit of 1500 will take 7 years. And early in the Obama administration the US backed down from establishing a truly effective missile defence shield at objections from Russia to place radar stations and interceptor missiles in eastern Europe. A pre-emptive Russian nuclear strike (http://www.tldm.org/news2/first_strike.htm) supported by secondary strikes from China would overwhelm US capabilities and fulfil the prophecy of Hosea - **For Israel hath forgotten his Maker, and buildeth temples; and Judah hath multiplied fenced cities: but I will send a fire upon his cities, and it shall devour the palaces thereof. (Hos 8:14).**

Index No.	1110	Event	**Time of Jacob's Trouble**

Date	Results from event 1100	Hebrew	NA	Scripture	Jer 30:1-7 Dt 28:1-65
Event Defined		Explicit Date		Direct Correlation	Assessed Quality
Yes		No		No	C

Discussion	The time of Jacob's Trouble is a short period, possible as little as one month, during which the Israelite nations – US, UK, Canada, Australia, New Zealand, NW Europe are destroyed. There will also be increasing aggression against the Jews in Israel. During this period the curses of Deuteronomy 28 will fall on these nations and as we discussed in Chapter 3 – this period will culminate in a pre-emptive nuclear attack which will result in massive destruction on America, the UK and NW Europe. I initially believed that this was a one year period but that was based on a misinterpretation of the Hebrew word for "Time". There are numerous examples where the wrath of God is delivered as sudden destruction – the Great flood, Pharaoh's army in the Red sea, Sodom and Gomorrah and the death of Sennacherib's army all attest to this fact. Also we are clearly told in 1 Thessalonians **"For when they say, "Peace and safety!" then sudden destruction comes upon them, as labour pains upon a pregnant woman. And they shall not escape". (1 Thes 5:3)** If the destruction of the Israelite people takes as little as one month when will it occur? I believe this sudden destruction will be a coordinated response from Russia and China (fulfilling the Second Seal requirements). It could happen as early as the Spring of 2011 and I would expect no later than the fall of 2011 as there must be a failure of the global harvest in this year to meet the requirements of the third seal. The willingness of European countries to engage in US lead combat initiatives has been clearly demonstrated in both Iraq and Afghanistan. These examples are simply the visible symptoms of the practical dissolution of NATO. The EU Lisbon treaty and the European desire to have its own military capability (led by Germany and France) has raised serious question about the effectiveness and cohesion of NATO - http://www.telegraph.co.uk/comment/4060481/We-didnt-join-the-EU-for-defence-reasons---we-have-Nato-for-that.html, the apathetic response by the West to the Russian invasion of Georgia, the resistance of Germany to fulfil its NATO commitments in Afghanistan - http://www.spiegel.de/international/germany/0,1518,534524,00.html

and the French desire for a parallel command structure in the EU - http://www.timesonline.co.uk/tol/news/world/europe/article4160462. ece.

When the pre-emptive strike against the US and Britain occurs, NATO will fail to stand up to the challenge. The EU, under German and French leadership, will abandon NATO and sue for peace with Russia. This will leave Britain and America facing the combined forces of Russia and China alone setting the basis for the prophecy of Amos **"For thus saith the Lord GOD; The city that went out by a thousand shall leave an hundred, and that which went forth by an hundred shall leave ten, to the house of Israel" (Am 5:3)** to be fulfilled with the death of 90% of the Israelitish people in a nuclear war and its aftermath.

Index No.	1120	Event	**3rd Seal of Revelation – Global Famine**		
Date	By 30 September 2011	Hebrew	NA	Scripture	Rev 6:5-6
Event Defined		Explicit Date		Direct Correlation	Assessed Quality
Y		N		N	C
Discussion		As a direct result of WW3 and harvest failures after destruction of the major food producing nations of the west along with the collapse of the global commercial and delivery infrastructure there will be massive starvation across the entire world. The disappearance of honey bees through colony collapse disorder (http://www.financialpost.com/story.html?id=1061238&p=1) could also play a major contributing factor to this global famine. Mark Biltz raised the idea in a teaching on Deborah (Bee in Hebrew) http://www.elshaddaiministries.us/storefront/notes/20091222hrc_bees.pdf that the collapse of the bee colonies could have a prophetic meaning (Deborah was a prophetess to Israel) as the four crops cited in the passage of Revelation – wheat, barley, oil (olives) and wine (grapes) do not rely on bees for pollination.			

Index No.	1130	Event	**4th Seal of Revelation – Widespread Death**		
Date	After Event 1120	Hebrew	NA	Scripture	Rev 6:7-8

Event Defined	Explicit Date	Direct Correlation	Assessed Quality
Y	N	N	C

Discussion	The remaining global population weakened by famine and the failure of national infrastructure will be devastated by deadly disease epidemics resulting a breakdown in social order causing widespread death.

Index No.	1140	Event	**Calls for One World Government to bring peace**		
Date	Resulting from event 1130	Hebrew	NA	Scripture	Rev 13:1-10

Event Defined	Explicit Date	Direct Correlation	Assessed Quality
Y	N	N	C

Discussion	The Armistice which ended the fighting of WW1 was signed on 11 November 1918. The Paris Peace Conference started on 18 January 1919 and resulted in the Treaty of Versailles which was signed on 28 June 1919. Part 1 of this treaty was the covenant of the League of Nations which held its first council meeting on 16 January 1920, only 14 months after the end of hostilities. After the Second World War the United Nations was established on 24 October 1945, to replace the League of Nations. This was only 5 months after VE day (7 May 1945) and less than two months after official surrender of Japan on 2 September 1945 (VJ day was on 15 August 1945). After the devastation of WW3 and the global social collapse there will be urgent calls for a One World Government to bring lasting peace to the world. Out of this chaos and destruction the Beast Power/Antichrist will emerge as a global saviour. This will occur quickly, probably before the end of 2011, as he will need time to establish himself before the Abomination of Desolation on 1 March 2012.

Index No.	1210	Event	Prophetic 1335 Days of Revelation		
Date	27 January 2012	Hebrew	3 Shevat 5772	Scripture	Dan 12:5-13
Event Defined		Explicit Date	Direct Correlation		Assessed Quality
Yes		Yes	Yes		A
Discussion	Daniel 12:6 tells us that the timings given are "to the end of these wonders". Then it goes on to specifically in verse 11 from the time the daily sacrifice is taken away and abomination of desolation is set up there will be 1290 days. In verse 12 it stated blessed is he that waits and comes to the 1335 days. Taking our prophetic anchor point of 23 September 2015 and the end of these wonders and counting back 1335 days brings us to 27 January 2012.				

Index No.	1220	Event	Temple sacrifice starts		
Date	27 January 2012	Hebrew	3 Shevat 5772	Scripture	Dan 12:5-13
Event Defined		Explicit Date	Direct Correlation		Assessed Quality
Yes		No	No		C
Discussion	According to Daniel 12:6 the daily sacrifice will be taken away 1290 days before the end. For the Jews to start sacrificing again on the Temple Mount will require a massive change in policy and administration, at the moment it is forbidden for Christians and Jews to even pray on the Mount. As the Al Aqsa mosque is situated right on the place where the Holy of Holies once stood it is unlikely the Muslims will welcome this event, so it must come about out of massive social and political changes, such as nuclear war in the Middle East and subsequent World War 3. Ezra chapter 3 tells us that the first thing the Jews did when they returned to Jerusalem from Babylon was to build an altar and offer burnt offerings to God. It was over 6 months later before they even laid the foundation for the temple. There is no need for the Third temple to be built before the morning and evening sacrifices can commence. All that is needed is the political will and a safe environment to complete the appropriate rituals before sacrifice can commence.				

The Rabbis have at least one red heifer, which is required for the purification ritual, meeting the sanctification requirements, so theoretically, this event could happen very quickly but it is extremely unlikely. Dedicating and purifying the altar is more complex than it may sound because the red heifer can be very easily defiled. The Muslims know this so it would be virtually impossible for this ceremony to happen in the current hostile climate around Jerusalem. I do not expect this event to occur until the Jews have a high degree of control in Jerusalem, which will not happen without massive Muslim opposition.

If the next prophetic event is the cessation of the morning and evening sacrifice, it would be logical to think that the preceding event is the start of the sacrifice which is why I have connected this date with the prophetic 1335 days. Although there is a high degree of speculation in making this connection, in the absence of any information to the contrary I believe it is a reasonable assumption. As with all these prophetic indicators, rather than watching calendar dates it is more important to be watching for the signs, so pay particular attentions for any mention of red heifers being prepared in Israel.

Index No.	1230	Event	1290 Days of Revelation - Abomination of Desolation		
Date	12 March 2012	Hebrew	18 Adar 1, 5772	Scripture	Dan 12:5-13 Mt 24:15-20
Event Defined		Explicit Date		Direct Correlation	Assessed Quality
Yes		Yes		Yes	A

Discussion	Daniel 12:11 gives us one of the most accurate timing points of the prophetic calendar **"And from the time that the daily sacrifice shall be taken away, and the abomination that maketh desolate set up, there shall be a thousand two hundred and ninety days."** Counting back from our prophetic end point we arrive at a date of 12 March 2012. This is when the Beast power will betray the Jews and commence to establish himself in the temple as God. Jesus tells us that when we see this abomination "let those in Judea flee to the mountains" because the next event is great tribulation. Witnessing this abomination gives a 30 day warning that the Great Tribulation is about to start.

Index No.	1240	Event	**4th (Middle) Year of Daniel's 70th week starts**				
Date	24 March 2012		Hebrew	1 Nisan 5772	Scripture	Dan 9:27	
Event Defined		Explicit Date		Direct Correlation		Assessed Quality	
Yes		Yes		Yes		**A**	
Discussion	If we take the Biblical New Year (1 Nisan) as our timing point the 4th of Daniels final 7 years starts on 24 March 2012. This is the middle of the final seven years. If we use the Jewish Civil New Year of 1 Tishrei this date would be exactly 3½ years through the final seven year countdown and as the abomination of desolation stopped the sacrificing only 12 days earlier, I think it is fair to say that the requirements of Daniel 9:27 **"And he shall confirm the covenant with many for one week: and in the midst of the week he shall cause the sacrifice and the oblation to cease, and for the overspreading of abominations he shall make it desolate, even until the consummation, and that determined shall be poured upon the desolate."** have been fulfilled.						

Index No.	1250	Event	**Prophetic 1260 Days of Revelations starts**		
Date	11 April 2012	Hebrew	19 Nisan 5772	Scripture	Various
Event Defined		Explicit Date		Direct Correlation	Assessed Quality
Yes		Yes		Yes	A

<table>
<tr><td>scussion</td><td>

The 1260 day period is the most well known of the timing points in the end time chronology. It is variously recorded as 1260 days, 42 months (42 x 30 – the length of the prophetic month = 1260 days) or "time, times and half a time" which means 3½ years (3½ years = 42 months = 1260 days).

In Daniel 12:7 we are told: **"it shall be for a time, times, and an half; and when he shall have accomplished to scatter the power of the holy people, all these things shall be finished."**

Rev 11:2-3 says this: **"But the court which is without the temple leave out, and measure it not; for it is given unto the Gentiles: and the holy city shall they tread under foot forty and two months. And I will give power unto my two witnesses, and they shall prophesy a thousand two hundred and threescore days, clothed in sackcloth."**

Rev 12:14 states: **"And to the woman were given two wings of a great eagle, that she might fly into the wilderness, into her place, where she is nourished for a time, and times, and half a time, from the face of the serpent."**

And Rev 13:5: **"And there was given unto him a mouth speaking great things and blasphemies; and power was given unto him to continue forty and two months."**

A lot happens in this 1260 day period. The Beast power takes control and the holy people are scattered for 42 months; the holy city is trampled under the feet of the gentiles and the two witnesses fulfil their prophetic ministry. Also the woman (Church) is supernaturally protected in the wilderness from the devil and the Beast power continues in power.

Based on Dan 12:7 "all these things are finished" these 1260 days are counted back from the prophetic anchor point which gives us a start date of 11 April 2012.

</td></tr>
</table>

Index No.	1260	Event	5th Seal of Revelation – The Great Tribulation begins			
Date	11 April 2012	Hebrew	19 Nisan 5772	Scripture	Mt 24:7-21 Rev 6:9-11	
Event Defined		Explicit Date		Direct Correlation		Assessed Quality
Yes		Yes		Yes		A

| Discussion | In Matthew 24:7-9 Jesus tells us that **"For nation will rise against nation, and kingdom against kingdom. And there will be famines, pestilences, and earthquakes in various places. All these are the beginning of sorrows. Then they will deliver you up to tribulation and kill you, and you will be hated by all nations for My name's sake."** Nations against nations (2nd Seal); famines (3rd Seal) and pestilence (4th Seal) are the beginning of sorrow.

In the Book of Revelation we read that "When He opened the 5th seal ... until their [the faithful dead] fellow servants and brethren, who would be killed as they were, was complete".

Matthew 24:15 & 21 "When you see the abomination of desolation ... For then there will be great tribulation" tells us that after the abomination of desolation there will be great tribulation. We can see that the Great Tribulation is the period of 1260 days when the saints will be killed.

And as we saw in event 1250 the period of 1260 days which follows 30 days after the abomination of desolation includes the scattering of the holy people and trampling the holy city underfoot. We also saw that the Woman [faithful church] was protected in the wilderness 1260 days.

Rev 12:17 states **"And the dragon was wroth with the woman, and went to make war with the remnant of her seed, which keep the commandments of God, and have the testimony of Jesus Christ."** While the woman is protected in the wilderness [satan] the dragon makes war with the children of God.

This period of persecution against the Children of God who have not been placed under the miraculous protection of God in the wilderness continues for the remaining three and a half years right through until the return of Messiah. |
|---|---|

Index No.	1410	Event	**Total Lunar Eclipse Blood Moon**		
Date	15 April 2014	Hebrew	15 Nisan 5774	Scripture	NA
Event Defined		Explicit Date	Direct Correlation	Assessed Quality	
Yes		Yes	Yes	A	
Discussion	This is the first of the 4 total lunar eclipses which form the tetrad pointing to the return of Messiah. It occurs on 15 Nisan which is the Passover.				

Index No.	1420	Event	**Total Lunar Eclipse Blood Moon**		
Date	8 October 2014	Hebrew	14 Tishrei 5775	Scripture	NA
Event Defined		Explicit Date	Direct Correlation	Assessed Quality	
Yes		Yes	Yes	A	
Discussion	This is the second of the tetrad moons falling on a Biblical Holy day, this time the eve of First Day of Feast of Tabernacles.				

Index No.	1505	Event	**Total Solar Eclipse Sackcloth Sun**		
Date	20 March 2015	Hebrew	29 Adar 1, 5775	Scripture	NA
Event Defined		Explicit Date	Direct Correlation	Assessed Quality	
Yes		Yes	Yes	A	
Discussion	This total solar eclipse falls on the eve of first day of the Biblical New Year which is also the day that the Sabbath year begins. Also this is the date of the vernal (spring) equinox. The total solar eclipse will last for 2 minutes and 47 seconds during which time the sun will appear as black as sackcloth. It is quite remarkable how God has scheduled these events so that the various interpretations of the Biblical calendar (calculated Hebrew calendar, observed Abib barley and spring equinox) will all be running concurrently in this critical final year of man's rule on the earth.				

Index No.	1510	Event	**Total Lunar Eclipse Blood Moon**		
Date	4 April 2015	Hebrew	15 Nisan 5775	Scripture	Rev 6:12 Joel 2:31
Event Defined		Explicit Date	Direct Correlation	Assessed Quality	
Yes		Yes	Yes	A	
Discussion	This is the third of the Tetrad moons - total lunar eclipses falling on a Biblical Holy Day, in this case Passover.				

Index No.	1512	Event	6th Seal of Revelation Opened – Great terrible day of the Lord	
Date	4 April 2015	Hebrew	15 Nisan 5776	Scripture	Joel 2:31 Rev 6:12

Event Defined	Explicit Date	Direct Correlation	Assessed Quality
Yes	Yes	Yes	A

Discussion	Joel 2 states "The sun shall be turned into darkness, and the moon into blood, before the great and the terrible day of the LORD come."

Joel 2 states **"The sun shall be turned into darkness, and the moon into blood, before the great and the terrible day of the LORD come."**

And Rev 6 says **"And I beheld when he had opened the sixth seal, and, lo, there was a great earthquake; and the sun became black as sackcloth of hair, and the moon became as blood"**

Both the spring holy days (Biblical New Year and Passover) and the Autumn Holy Days (Feast of Trumpets and Feast of Tabernacles) in 2015 have dark suns and blood moons and there are two events in the Bible which have these characteristics – the opening of the 6th seal of Revelation and the period known as the "Day of the Lord".

The 6th seal cannot occur on the Autumn holy days as 5 ½ months are required for the subsequent plagues so there would be insufficient time to complete them before the return of Messiah, therefore it must be associated with the Spring Holy Days.

There are numerous references to the Day of the Lord, many describe similar events to the 6th seal but others indicate that it is a one year period (Is 34:8); that the day of the Lord comes after the solar and lunar eclipses (Joel 2:31) and that it occurs in the valley of decision (the Battle of Armageddon) (Joel 3:14).

If we identify the Autumn Holy Days with the day of the Lord we have a problem in that the day of the Lord would start in the Jubilee year and continue for the whole year long period, which doesn't seen to fit in with the concept of the freedom and release of the Jubilee. I am convinced that the 6th seal of Revelation is announcing the Day of the Lord. This is further supported by Rev 6:17 **"For the great day of His wrath has come, and who is able to stand?"**

The eclipses on the Autumn Holy Days are drawing emphasis to the completion which culminates in the pouring out of the bowls of wrath and the war between Jesus and the armies of the world. The fact that the day of the Lord is a year long period could also imply that God's wrath continues on the earth for 6 months after Jesus established his world ruling government in Jerusalem.

For the purpose of developing the timeline I have ascribed both the opening of the 6th seal and the Day of the Lord to the solar and lunar eclipses occurring in the Spring of 2015.

Index No.	1516	Event	144,000 Sealed		
Date	After event 1512	Hebrew	15 Nisan 5776	Scripture	Rev 7:1-17 Rev 14:1-5
Event Defined		Explicit Date		Direct Correlation	Assessed Quality
Yes		Yes		No	B

| Discussion | Revelation 7 tells us that "after these things" [the opening of the 6th seal] the "servants of God are sealed on their foreheads" and they numbered 144,000; 12,000 from each of the 12 tribes of Israel. We also find in Revelation 14 that the 144,000 stand with the Lamb on Mt Zion, they were redeemed from the earth, redeemed from men being firstfruits to God. In Revelation 7:9 we are told of a great multitude which no one could number, of all nations, tribes, people who came out of the great tribulation, were given white robes and were standing before the throne of God and serve Him day and night in His Temple.

What do we make of this? Is this sealing of 144,000 physical human beings who are alive on the earth at this specific time or is it a spiritual sealing of those who have served God throughout history? And who are the great multitude?

None of the dead live until the first resurrection and those who come up in that resurrection are priests of God and reign with Him for 1,000 years. The two witnesses are resurrected after the 6th trumpet blast but before the 7th (Rev Ch 11). We also know that the resurrection of the saints and those who are alive at His return occurs when we are taken up in the clouds to meet Jesus. Revelation chapters 12 and 13 are inset chapters (not part of the main narrative) The next event is Rev 14 – the 144,000 standing on Mt Zion with Jesus.

Based on all these scriptures I believe that the 144,000 are the saints physically alive at the end of the age who are redeemed (saved) from the end time destruction of the world. They will serve with Jesus to establish His physical world ruling 1,000 year government on earth. They have been selected to fulfil the ministry original given to Israel – to be a chosen nation which would attract all the people of the earth into a relationship with God. A ministry which Israel constantly failed to fulfil throughout its history. These are spirit beings who can enter into the temple of God, but whose primary duty is to work on the earth with Jesus. |
|---|---|

	The great multitude consist of all those (Israelite and gentile) who remained faithful to God and kept the Commandments. They include those who were martyred during the great tribulation and all the saints who have died in faith since the beginning of creation. These remain in heaven with God serving Him in His temple until the thousand years are ended and the New Jerusalem comes to reside on the new earth.

Index No.	1520	Event	**7th Seal of Revelation Opened – 7 Trumpet Plagues**		
Date	5 April 2015	Hebrew	16 Nisan 5776	Scripture	Rev 8:1-6

Event Defined	Explicit Date	Direct Correlation	Assessed Quality
Yes	Yes	No	**B**

Discussion	When the 7th seal is broken the next sequence of prophetic events are set in motion – the 7 trumpet plagues. Up to this point all the death and destruction on the earth has been as the result of man's [demonically inspired] behaviour. We are now in the Day of the wrath of the Lord, a year long period where God takes vengeance on those who continue to defy him. All the plagues which follow on from this grow more and more supernatural in nature. Initially they could be ascribed to natural catastrophes but as the sequence of events continue their supernatural nature becomes more and more obvious. The statement "there was silence in heaven for half an hour" could indicate that there is a two week delay (using the day for a year principle and the Biblical definition of a day having 12 hours ½ an hour would equate to just over two weeks). However this would not allow sufficient time for the trumpet plagues to complete so I have taken this to be a literal silence of 30 minutes, not a prophetic one.

Index No.	1522	Event	**1st Trumpet Plague**		
Date	5 Apr 2015	Hebrew	16 Nisan 5775	Scripture	Rev 8:7

Event Defined	Explicit Date	Direct Correlation	Assessed Quality
Yes	Yes	No	**B**

Discussion	Hail and fire fall to the earth and kill 1/3 of the trees and all green grass. This is possibly a meteor shower causing massive firestorms.

Index No.	1524	Event	2nd Trumpet Plague		
Date	5 April 2015	Hebrew	16 Nisan 5775	Scripture	Rev 8:8-9
Event Defined		Explicit Date		Direct Correlation	Assessed Quality
Yes		Yes		No	**B**
Discussion	A burning mountain falls into the sea which turns one third of the sea to blood, killing one third of the creatures and destroying one third of the ships. This is possibly a large comet falling into the Pacific ocean (which covers 28% of the total surface of the earth and 40% of the water coverage, in either case about 1/3). Each of the first 4 trumpet plagues could complete within minutes of each other so I have assumed that they all occur on the same day as there is no indication to the contrary.				

Index No.	1526	Event	3rd Trumpet Plague		
Date	5 April 2015	Hebrew	16 Nisan 5775	Scripture	Rev 8:10-11
Event Defined		Explicit Date		Direct Correlation	Assessed Quality
Yes		Yes		No	**B**
Discussion	A great star called wormwood falls burning from heaven and one third of the rivers and springs became poisoned. This is more difficult to explain but notice that the scripture does not say that the star hit the earth. One theory is that this is caused by the earth passing through the gaseous debris in the wake of a large comet (which would also account for the meteorite storms and the burning mountain). Tim McHyde who wrote the prophetic analysis "Escape all things" ascribes all these events to Planet X, a rogue planet in our solar system which may be returning for a near miss with earth in the near future (http://uk.youtube.com/watch?v=sjjrStDxTrc&feature=related). I do not endorse the alien and new age bias of this site but the basic information on Planet X is worth reviewing although I am sceptical that the whole of the end of the age events can are caused by the passing of Planet X which is Tim's main thesis because we should have some record of a similar global cataclysm from around 1600BC which when it would have previously passed the earth based on its 3600 year orbit.				

Index No.	1528	Event		4th Trumpet Plague			
Date	5 April 2015		Hebrew	16 Nisan 5775	Scripture		Rev 8:12
Event Defined		Explicit Date		Direct Correlation		Assessed Quality	
Yes		Yes		No		B	

Discussion	The results of this plague require careful analysis to understand what is going on. Rev 8:12 states: **"Then the fourth angel sounded: And a third of the sun was struck, a third of the moon, and a third of the stars, so that a third of them were darkened. A third of the day did not shine, and likewise the night."** What is being struck here is not the sun, moon and stars but rather our ability to observe them – the day and night did not shine. We are experiencing massive cloud cover which would be due to the debris and water vapour thrown up by the "burning mountain" falling into the sea. If you saw the recent dramatic pictures of the Icelandic volcano Eyjafjallajokull spewing tons of ash high into the atmosphere it is entirely conceivable to think that hundreds of volcanoes erupting at the same time due to the comet strike described at the second trumpet plague. Sandia National laboratories, a US Government research centre estimates that a 1.4 km wide comet striking the Atlantic ocean would instantaneously vapourise 300 – 500 cubic kilometres of ocean into superheated steam (http://www.sandia.gov/media/comethit.htm). The impact energy is equivalent to that of 300 Gigatons of TNT (this is 10 times the total nuclear weapons capability of the whole planet at the height of the cold war). The vapour, debris and gasses released would collect in the upper atmosphere to create dense cloud resulting in a nuclear winter. It would also cause massive earthquakes, volcanic and tsunami activity. It could also cause a change in the weather patterns. Instead of flowing west to east in the northern hemisphere and east to west in the southern hemisphere; it could cause a band of dense cloud circulating north-south. As the earth rotated west to east into the band of cloud the day and night, sun moon and stars would be darkened until the piece of land you were on rotated from under the cloud.

Index No.	1530	Event	5th Trumpet Plague, the 1st Woe		
Date	5 April 2015	Hebrew	16 Nisan 5775	Scripture	Rev 9:1-12
Event Defined		Explicit Date		Direct Correlation	Assessed Quality
Yes		Yes		No	B
Discussion	Some commentators' make the case that these "locusts shaped like horses prepared for battle, with crowns of gold, men's faces, women's hair, lion's teeth, breastplates of iron, scorpions tails making a sound like horses running to battle" are the Apostle John's attempt to describe Apache attack helicopters using the imagery from his period. However, this does not account for how these weapons could (or why they would) differentiate between those who had the seal of God and those with the mark of the beast. Also it does not make sense that a military force would merely want to torment people and not destroy them, nor how these weapons would affect men but cause no damage to grass, tree or green thing. I've taken a literal interpretation of this plague. Isaiah 14:12 states **"How art thou fallen from heaven, O Lucifer, son of the morning! how art thou cut down to the ground, which didst weaken the nations!"** Also Rev 9:11 tells us the king over these locusts is the angel of the bottomless pit called Abaddon (Heb) and Apollyon (Gk). This is not a natural manmade phenomenon, rather a demonic event. The star fallen from heaven is Satan who releases all the demons that have been constrained in the bottomless pit (where Satan will be held for 1000 years – Rev 19:1-2). This demonic torment falls upon all of mankind who are alive and do not have the seal of God on their foreheads. This is also the first "Woe".				

Index No.	1535	Event	5th Trumpet plague ends		
Date	2 September 2015	Hebrew	18 Elul 5775	Scripture	Rev 9:5
Event Defined		Explicit Date		Direct Correlation	Assessed Quality
Yes		Yes		No	B
Discussion	Rev 9:5 tells us that this torment lasts for 5 months which is 150 days using the prophetic calendar.				

Index No.	1540	Event	6th Trumpet Plague, the Second Woe		
Date	3 September 2015	Hebrew	19 Elul 5775	Scripture	Rev 9:13-21
Event Defined		Explicit Date	Direct Correlation		Assessed Quality
Yes		Yes	No		B
Discussion	The 4 angels are prepared to kill 1/3 of mankind, the questions is whether this is by their own action or by the action of others. The statement about the 200 million man army being released indicates that this is man made destruction, facilitated by the 4 angels (possibly by holding back the Euphrates) so that the 200 million man army from China can cross. This human army would not be able to function while being tormented by the demons. This event occurs after the 5th trumpet plague completes.				

Index No.	1550	Event	Partial Solar Eclipse - Sun Darkened		
Date	13 September 2015	Hebrew	29 Elul 5775	Scripture	NA
Event Defined		Explicit Date	Direct Correlation		Assessed Quality
Yes		Yes	Yes		A
Discussion	The second solar eclipse of this end time period falls on 13 September 2015; this is the eve of the Feast of Trumpets. This indicates that we have entered the final climactic time of the return of Jesus. In the paper on Jubilee cycles I referred to in chapter 5 the author had also done extensive research on the relationship of the "Golden Proportion" and the various Jubilee cycles. It is interesting to note that according to the Golden Proportion between the first and second jubilees of cycle three (see Appendix B for the full analysis) falls on 2015.7. If you calculate 0.7 of the calendar year 2015 you arrive at the exact date of 13 September. Potentially we have a fourth witness to the timing end of the age provided by an independent "clock" embedded in the very growth code of creation. This would be the end of Daniels 70th week if we took 29 September 2008 as the start date. But as the Autumnal New Year is a Jewish civil custom and not Biblical and there are still events which must unfold, I have rejected this date as the start of Daniel's 70th week.				

Index No.	1555	Event	7 Thunders from God				
Date	14 September 2015	Hebrew	1 Tishrei 5776		Scripture		Rev 10:1-7
Event Defined		Explicit Date		Direct Correlation		Assessed Quality	
Yes		No		No		C	

| Discussion | The voice of God is identified as a sound of thunder in several scriptures (Job 40:9, Ps 18:13, Jn 12:29). Rev 10:4 also tells us that the voice in the thunder was understandable by John because he was about to write what he had heard until he was told to seal up what had uttered. Just as God gave the 10 Commandments in His own voice, it would be logical to assume that He will give His final judgement on the world in His own voice.

When God spoke on Mt Sinai to deliver the 10 Commandments there was a sound of a great trumpet. Also Jewish understanding is that the Commandments were given on the day of Pentecost. It would be fitting that the next time man hears God's voice is on the next Holy day – the Feast of Trumpets. It is possible that a Thunder judgement happens each day from 14 – 20 September, similar to the sounding of the trumpets every day for 7 days leading up to the fall of Jericho. |
|---|---|

Index No.	1560	Event	2 Witnesses killed				
Date	20 September 2015	Hebrew	7 Tishrei 5776		Scripture		Rev 11:1-13
Event Defined		Explicit Date		Direct Correlation		Assessed Quality	
Yes		Yes		Yes		A	

| Discussion | The two witnesses prophesy for 1260 days clothed in sackcloth and are killed. Their bodies lie in the streets of Jerusalem for 3½ days while the world rejoices over their death. Then a voice from heaven calls them up and they are resurrected (at the final trump on the Day of Atonement). (Rev 11:3-13)

Their ministry could begin on 8 Apr 2012, not the 11th as the other 1260 day periods do because they were dead for 3 ½ days, alternatively even lying dead in the street they are a witness against rebellious mankind. |
|---|---|

Index No.	1565	Event	Prophetic Anchor Point		
Date	23 September 2015	Hebrew	10 Tishrei	Scripture	Mt 24:29-31
Event Defined		Explicit Date		Direct Correlation	Assessed Quality
Yes		Yes		Yes	A

Discussion	As we clearly demonstrated in Chapter 6, the dual fulfilment of the 7 week portion of Daniels 70 week prophecy gives us 17,640 days from the day Jerusalem was restored to Israel in 7 June 1967 (7/6/67) to the 23 September 2015 (10 Tishrei 5776) – the Day of Atonement.

Jesus tells us in Matthew Chapter 24, **"Immediately after the tribulation of those days the sun will be darkened, and the moon will not give its light; the stars will fall from heaven, and the powers of the heavens will be shaken. Then the sign of the Son of Man will appear in heaven, and then all the tribes of the earth will mourn, and they will see the Son of Man coming on the clouds of heaven with power and great glory. And He will send His angels with a great sound of a trumpet, and they will gather together His elect from the four winds, from one end of heaven to the other. (Mt 24:29-31).** After the tribulation, which started in the spring of 2012, the sun is darkened and the moon will not give light, this is talking of a solar and lunar eclipse, it cannot be the eclipses we identified as the 6th seal of Revelation as the tribulation is still occurring at this time. This scripture points us to the final solar and lunar eclipse in the Autumn holy days.

At this time, sometime between the Feast of Trumpets and the Day of Atonement, the sign of the Son of Man appears in the clouds and at the sound of a great trumpet the elect are gathered together. At the end of the tribulation all the nations of the earth will see Jesus return in the clouds; His people will be resurrected to meet Him in the clouds and be taken to safety and remain with Him forevermore. This is also the catalyst for several other cataclysmic prophetic events to occur and relates to numerous prophetic statements which are discussed below. |

Index No.	1566	Event	Day of Atonement/ Jubilee Year Starts		
Date	23 Sep 2015	Hebrew	10 Tishrei	Scripture	Lev 16:29, 25:9
Event Defined		Explicit Date	Direct Correlation		Assessed Quality
Yes		Yes	Yes		A
Discussion	The Day of Atonement is the 10th day of Tishrei. The atonement ceremony has two main elements – firstly the people are to afflict their souls and secondly it is the one day in the year when the High priest enters in to the Holiest of Holies to atone (make At-One) the people with God. Also the Jubilee year starts with sound of shofar on the Day of Atonement. As we demonstrated in Chapter 6, 2015/2016 is the next Jubilee year. This is the Final Trumpet Sound which heralds the Elect being resurrected and taken up into clouds. I'm not sure if there is any significance to this but 23 September 2015 is also the Autumn Equinox, this may symbolise the end of the harvest season.				

Index No.	1570	Event	The Resurrection of the Dead		
Date	23 September 2015	Hebrew	10 Tishrei	Scripture	Rev 11:7-19
Event Defined		Explicit Date	Direct Correlation		Assessed Quality
Yes		No	No		C
Discussion	The two witnesses are called up by a voice from heaven and they are bodily resurrected and taken up into heaven. This is the beginning of the first resurrection (Rev 20:6) which consists of those who have died in faith and is followed by those still alive at Christ's coming (1 Cor 15:23). 1 Thes 4:16-17 tells us – "For the Lord himself shall descend from heaven with a shout, with the voice of the archangel, and with the trump of God: and the dead in Christ shall rise first: Then we which are alive and remain shall be caught up together with them in the clouds, to meet the Lord in the air: and so shall we ever be with the Lord." This meeting in the clouds is also alluded to in Revelation 14:13-16 which talks of Jesus sitting on a cloud and reaping the harvest of the earth. We also find in verse 1 that the Lamb and the 144,000 stand on				

Mt Zion. Although this was written before the reaping it must occur after because the 144,000 cannot have been taken up before the harvest.

This is the first part of the Atonement ceremony – becoming "At One" with God.

Revelation 11:18 tells us - **And the nations were angry, and thy wrath is come, and the time of the dead, that they should be judged, and that thou shouldest give reward unto thy servants the prophets, and to the saints, and them that fear thy name, small and great; and shouldest destroy them which destroy the earth.** We can see a convergence of three main themes – the anger of the nations (demonstrated by the gathering of the 200 million man army at the 6th trumpet); the resurrection, judgement and reward of the saints and the pouring out of the wrath of God.

Revelation 11:14 tells us that after the two witnesses are resurrected the 3rd woe comes quickly – this is the second requirement of the Atonement ceremony – the afflicting of our souls (in this case it is the affliction of all of mankind) – God's judgement is poured out on the world from the 7 bowls of wrath.

Index No.	1572	Event	7 Bowls of Wrath – The 3rd Woe God's punishment poured out		
Date	23 September 2015	Hebrew	10 Tishrei	Scripture	Rev 15 & 16
Event Defined		Explicit Date		Direct Correlation	Assessed Quality
Yes		No		No	C

Discussion	All the previous plagues **God allowed to happen**, these final 7 plagues **God causes to happen**. It is His judgement on the world which He can now execute because His people have been taken up from the world, out of harms way. It would have been unjust to pour His punishment on those who have obeyed His voice and done His will which is why the bowls of wrath are only poured out after His people have been moved to safety.

This is the third Woe, which we have been told comes quickly after the resurrection of the two witnesses. Revelation 14:4 tells us about the redemption of the firstfruits and starting just two verses later we are told that the hour of His judgement is come, Babylon is fallen and they shall drink of the wine of the wrath of God. All of these events can occur on the later part of the Day of Atonement. The 7 bowls of wrath are:

1) Grievous sores on those who have the mark of the beast
2) The sea is turned to blood
3) Rivers and fountains turn to blood
4) The sun scorches men with fire
5) The kingdom of the beast is full of darkness and pain
6) The Euphrates is dried up to allow the kings of the east to gather at Armageddon.
7) Judgement is executed on Babylon – plagues come on Babylon in one day, the city is destroyed with fire and great violence in one hour.

Index No.	1574	Event	**Judah accepts the Messiah**			
Date	23 September 2015	Hebrew	10 Tishrei	Scripture	Zec 12:9-14	
Event Defined		Explicit Date		Direct Correlation		Assessed Quality
Yes		No		No		C
Discussion	The prophet Zechariah tells us **"It shall be in that day that I will seek to destroy all the nations that come against Jerusalem. And I will pour on the house of David and on the inhabitants of Jerusalem the Spirit of grace and supplication; then they will look on Me whom they pierced. Yes, they will mourn for Him as one mourns for his only son, and grieve for Him as one grieves for a firstborn. In that day there shall be a great mourning in Jerusalem, like the mourning at Hadad Rimmon in the plain of Megiddo. (Zec 12:9-14)** The Children of Judah have been in denial of Messiah since the physical manifestation of Jesus at His first coming. When He appears in the clouds for the entire world to see there will be no way they can deny Him a second time and so there will finally be reconciliation between Judah and YHWH their God.					

Index No.	1576	Event	**Wedding Supper of the Lamb**			
Date	24 September 2015	Hebrew	11 Tishrei	Scripture	Rev 19:5-10	
Event Defined		Explicit Date		Direct Correlation		Assessed Quality
Yes		No		No		C
Discussion	Revelation Chapter 19 comes immediately after the destruction of Babylon at the 7th bowl of wrath (which is detailed in Revelation chapters 17 and 18). At the end of the Day of Atonement people are naturally hungry and often celebrate the end of the day by sharing a meal. It is natural to think that Wedding Supper of the Lamb would occur after His Bride has been made ready (the saints have been resurrected) and the time of affliction has passed. There is no indication how long this heavenly feast lasts, and as heaven is outside of time and space there is no way of knowing. But on the earthly calendar it must complete before 28 September as Jesus has to return and subdue the nations before his world ruling reign of peace starts on the Feast of Tabernacles.					

Index No.	1578	Event	Jesus makes war against the Kings of the Earth		
Date	26 September 2015	Hebrew	13 Tishrei	Scripture	Rev 19:11-21
Event Defined		Explicit Date		Direct Correlation	Assessed Quality
Yes		No		No	C

Discussion	Immediately after the Wedding Supper of the Lamb we are told that Jesus rides out on a white horse with the armies of heaven with Him to strike all those of the nations who stand against him.

Zechariah chapter 14 tells us: "**Then YHWH will go forth and fight against those nations, as He fights in the day of battle. And in that day His feet will stand on the Mount of Olives, which faces Jerusalem on the east. And the Mount of Olives shall be split in two, from east to west, making a very large valley; Half of the mountain shall move toward the north and half of it toward the south. (Zec 15:3-4)**

Later in that chapter we learn: "**And this shall be the plague with which the LORD will strike all the people who fought against Jerusalem: Their flesh shall dissolve while they stand on their feet, their eyes shall dissolve in their sockets, and their tongues shall dissolve in their mouths. (Zec 14:12).**

This is also confirmed in Revelation 14 "**And another angel came out from the altar, who had power over fire, and he cried with a loud cry to him who had the sharp sickle, saying, "Thrust in your sharp sickle and gather the clusters of the vine of the earth, for her grapes are fully ripe." So the angel thrust his sickle into the earth and gathered the vine of the earth, and threw it into the great winepress of the wrath of God. And the winepress was trampled outside the city, and blood came out of the winepress, up to the horses' bridles, for one thousand six hundred furlongs. (Rev 14:18-20)**

Converting bridles and furlongs, this river of blood is 4 feet deep and flows for 200 miles. It comes from the dissolved bodies of all the armies of the world gathered together after the Euphrates was dried up on the Day of Atonement. It must occur after 23 September and before 28 September 2015. |

Index No.	1580	Event	**Satan bound for 1000 years**			
Date	27 September 2015	Hebrew	14 Tishrei	Scripture	Rev 20:1-3	
Event Defined		Explicit Date		Direct Correlation		Assessed Quality
Yes		No		No		C
Discussion	Immediately after the destruction of the armies of the earth, we are told that Satan is bound with a great chain and sealed into the bottomless pit for 1,000 years. (Rev 20:3) This is done so that he should deceive the nations no more. It is the final event which is required to free all of mankind from the curse which was placed upon us through Satan's deception of Eve in the garden of Eden. Only when Satan is bound so that the earth is free from his deception can the true message of Jesus be heard and understood by all those who remain on the earth.					

Index No.	1585	Event	**Total Lunar Eclipse Blood Moon**			
Date	28 September 2015	Hebrew	15 Tishrei	Scripture	NA	
Event Defined		Explicit Date		Direct Correlation		Assessed Quality
Yes		Yes		Yes		A
Discussion	This is the final heavenly sign indicating that this phase of God's plan for the salvation of the earth is complete. This sign appears on the first Day of the Feast of Tabernacles which as we have discussed earlier is the feast that symbolises Jesus living among us (tabernacling with us) and when we can come into His presence and celebrate with Him.					

Index No.	1590	Event	Millennial Sabbath begins				
Date	28 September 2015	Hebrew	15 Tishrei		Scripture		Rev 20:4-6
Event Defined		Explicit Date		Direct Correlation		Assessed Quality	
Yes		No		No		C	
Discussion	After Satan has been bound there will be a one thousand year period when the earth is brought under the authority of Jesus and the resurrected saints. During this period the earth will be repaired and brought back to the state God intended for us to live, in a Garden of Eden type paradise. It is also the time when God's law will be given to all nations of the earth, not just Israel, and they will be required to follow His law or face divine punishment if they choose to break His laws. **And it shall come to pass, that every one that is left of all the nations which came against Jerusalem shall even go up from year to year to worship the King, the LORD of hosts, and to keep the feast of tabernacles. And it shall be, that whoso will not come up of all the families of the earth unto Jerusalem to worship the King, the LORD of hosts, even upon them shall be no rain. And if the family of Egypt go not up, and come not, that have no rain ; there shall be the plague, wherewith the LORD will smite the heathen that come not up to keep the feast of tabernacles. This shall be the punishment of Egypt, and the punishment of all nations that come not up to keep the feast of tabernacles. (Zec 14:16-19)**						

Index No.	3010	Event	Gog Magog War		
Date	Year 3015		Hebrew	NA	Scripture	Rev 20:7-9

Event Defined	Explicit Date	Direct Correlation	Assessed Quality
Y	N	N	C

Discussion	The purpose of this physical life is for us to fulfil the choice made by Adam and Eve, to have knowledge (experience) of good and evil. And under Satan's influence the first 6,000 of human existence have been filled with evil. During the early part of the millennial Sabbath the memory of the horror of the time of the end will be indelibly written on the minds of the people who survive. But as time goes on this memory will fade and those born in the later part of this period will have had neither experience of Satan's corrupting influence nor the vivid memories of those who have. God allows Satan to be released at the end of the 1,000 years as a test and demonstration to those who are alive on the earth. Regrettably, as we have done over the last 6,000 years, the future generations of human kind will turn against God and attempt to destroy the holy city, Jerusalem. At this point God will destroy all those who rebel against Him with fire. (Rev 20:9)

Index No.	3020	Event		Satan destroyed		
Date	Year 3015		Hebrew	NA	Scripture	Rev 20:10
Event Defined		Explicit Date		Direct Correlation		Assessed Quality
Yes		No		No		C

Discussion

The scripture tells us **"And the devil that deceived them was cast into the lake of fire and brimstone, where the beast and the false prophet *are*, and shall be tormented day and night for ever and ever."** (Note the word "are" is italicized indicating that it has been added by the translators so I could equally read "were").

But Ezekiel chapter 28:11-19 tells us that the "King of Tyre" who was created perfect until iniquity was found in him, was in the garden of Eden, was the covering cherub who walked upon the holy mountain and was cast out. This is obviously an allusion to Satan the Dragon, the Serpent of Old. And verses 18 and 19 state: **Thou hast defiled thy sanctuaries by the multitude of thine iniquities, by the iniquity of thy traffick; therefore will I bring forth a fire from the midst of thee, it shall devour thee, and I will bring thee to ashes upon the earth in the sight of all them that behold thee. All they that know thee among the people shall be astonished at thee: thou shalt be a terror, and never shalt thou be any more.** This scripture clearly states that the evil will be burned up and reduced to ashes. This is what we would logically expect to see if a being was cast into a fire that burned forever.

The mistranslation/interpretation of being "tormented forever" is a complex word study outside the scope of this book.

Index No.	3030	Event	**New Heaven and New Earth**		
Date	Year 3015		Hebrew	NA	Scripture	Rev 21:1-8
Event Defined		Explicit Date		Direct Correlation	Assessed Quality
Yes		No		No	C

Discussion	After the 1,000 years of preparing and purifying the earth under leadership of Jesus, God Himself descends to take up residence with all His children on a newly created earth. Death and pain will no longer exist and anyone who chooses to drink of the "water of life" will become a full member of God's family.

And I saw a new heaven and a new earth: for the first heaven and the first earth were passed away; and there was no more sea. And I John saw the holy city, new Jerusalem, coming down from God out of heaven, prepared as a bride adorned for her husband. And I heard a great voice out of heaven saying, Behold, the tabernacle of God is with men, and he will dwell with them, and they shall be his people, and God himself shall be with them, and be their God. And God shall wipe away all tears from their eyes; and there shall be no more death, neither sorrow, nor crying, neither shall there be any more pain: for the former things are passed away. And he that sat upon the throne said, Behold, I make all things new. And he said unto me, Write: for these words are true and faithful. And he said unto me, It is done. I am Alpha and Omega, the beginning and the end. I will give unto him that is athirst of the fountain of the water of life freely. He that overcometh shall inherit all things; and I will be his God, and he shall be my son. But the fearful, and unbelieving, and the abominable, and murderers, and whoremongers, and sorcerers, and idolaters, and all liars, shall have their part in the lake which burneth with fire and brimstone: which is the second death.

Ephesians 5:26 tells us that Jesus cleansed the Church by washing it in the water of the word [the Bible]. The very first event which occurs on the New Earth is the opportunity for all of humanity to be washed in the word of the Bible in preparation for the Great White Throne judgement. |

Index No.	3040	Event	**Great White Throne Judgement**		
Date	Year 3115		Hebrew		Scripture	Rev 20:11-15
Event Defined		Explicit Date		Direct Correlation	Assessed Quality
Yes		No		No	C

<table>
<tr><td rowspan="1">Discussion</td><td>

After Satan is destroyed and the New heaven and new earth are formed there is the resurrection of all mankind who then come before the Great White Throne of God for judgement. Some believe that this large majority of humanity are judged by the works they did in their earthly life. But this makes no sense as if they had never heard of the Bible or Jesus in their earthly life they would have lived a life of sin and have had no opportunity for repentance, so there is no redemption for them at the resurrection and they would automatically be condemned to the lake of fire.

And I saw a great white throne, and him that sat on it, from whose face the earth and the heaven fled away; and there was found no place for them. And I saw the dead, small and great, stand before God; and the books were opened: and another book was opened, which is the book of life: and the dead were judged out of those things which were written in the books, according to their works. And the sea gave up the dead which were in it; and death and hell delivered up the dead which were in them: and they were judged every man according to their works. And death and hell were cast into the lake of fire. This is the second death. And whosoever was not found written in the book of life was cast into the lake of fire. (Rev 20:11-15)

The scripture actually tells us that the books (the Bible) will be opened [to their understanding]. And it is how they receive this information which decides whether they are given eternal life or ultimate destruction.

The prophet Isaiah gives us this information about this period: "**For, behold, I create new heavens and a new earth: and the former shall not be remembered, nor come into mind. But be ye glad and rejoice for ever in that which I create: for, behold, I create Jerusalem a rejoicing, and her people a joy. And I will rejoice in Jerusalem, and joy in my people: and the voice of weeping shall be no more heard in her, nor the voice of crying. There shall be no more thence an infant of days, nor an old man that hath not filled his days: for the child shall die an hundred years old; but the sinner being an hundred years old shall be accursed**". (Is 65:17-20)

</td></tr>
</table>

This tells us that everyone will die at 100 years old, but a sinner reaching 100 years will be cursed. When we combine this understanding with the information about the books being opened we can see that after the resurrection all members of the human race are given a 100 year period to come to accept the teachings of the Bible. Whoever accepts this "drinks of the water of life" becomes a spirit being and full member of God's family. At the end of 100 years anyone who continues to reject the One True God is finally destroyed in the lake of fire. This is in fact an act of mercy to take away the misery they would experience for all eternity for rejecting God.

Chapter 10

Spiritual Survival Guide

The Biblically foretold events which we have discussed in the previous chapters paint a very bleak outlook for the next few years of human existence. In fact, we are literally going to experience death and destruction of Biblical proportions. Pre-emptive nuclear war against America and Britain will result in the death of 90% of our people. Plagues, famine and pestilence will kill many of the survivors. This will be followed by a cosmic catastrophe in the form of an asteroid striking the ocean with an explosive force greater than all the nuclear weapons currently in existence being detonated at exactly the same location at exactly the same moment. This period will continue with demonic attacks on those who remain finally culminating with the very wrath of God Himself being poured out on the earth and its inhabitants. By the end of this period approximately 90% of all of humankind will have been killed.

To put this another way, there is only a one in ten chance that you will be alive in 5 years time. That's only slightly better odds than playing Russian roulette and I'm sure you would not take a revolver loaded with a single round and place it next to the head of each member of your family in turn and pull the trigger. If you're like me married with two children the random chance of me and my family making it through the end time period alive is only 1 in 10,000. Those are not the sort of odds I want to contemplate for the survival of my family and I'm sure you would not be comfortable sitting back in the knowledge that your family have a miniscule chance of surviving the next five years. What can be done?

The first option, and the course of action which will probably chosen by the majority of people, is to ignore the information presented in this book. This will be done in one of two ways. Firstly, the "ostrich defence". People who take this option will just ignore the information presented in this book and go on with their lives assuming that nothing at all can or will go wrong. Jesus spoke of the people who take this option: **"But as the days of Noe [Noah], so shall also the coming of the Son of man be. For as in the days that were before the flood they were eating and drinking, marrying and giving in marriage, until the day that Noe entered into the ark, and knew not until the flood came, and took them all away; so shall also the coming of the Son of man be. (Mt 24:37-39)**

The second defensive option is that of "shoot the messenger". This has been a common response by the children of Israel to those who would bring them the word of God. The Bible tells us that the prophets of the Old Testament were frequently killed for their witness. It was the same during the time of Jesus, John the Baptist, whose

Ministry was to prepare the way of the Lord, was beheaded for preaching the truth and holding fast to his convictions. And the history of the New Testament church follows the same path with all the Apostles, except John (who died in exile on the island of Patmos) being killed for their witness of the truth.

At this time it is unlikely that anyone will try and kill me for writing this book. But in the mind of the reader, it is easy to kill the message. As I have stressed many times this end time understanding based on a literal interpretation of the Word of God revealed to us in the Bible. If you want to undermine the foundational premise of this argument all you have to do is convince yourself that the Bible is in fact allegorical. If you choose to believe that it's a collection of useful stories and examples of what we as humans should be doing to live a nice life, but it really has no more or less authority than the writing of the world's other religions or a whole host of secular personal development guru's then you have no need to worry about what is written here.

However, if you have read your Bible with any degree of honesty and commitment you will undoubtedly have come across these verses:

But he answered and said, It is written, Man shall not live by bread alone, but by every word that proceedeth out of the mouth of God. (Mt 4:4)

All scripture is given by inspiration of God, and is profitable for doctrine, for reproof, for correction, for instruction in righteousness: (2 Tim 3:16)

In hope of eternal life, which God, that cannot lie, promised before the world began: (Tit 1:2)

God, who cannot lie, promised eternal life before the world began. Man is to live by every word of God and all scripture is given by the inspiration of God. If we want to claim the promise of eternal life, we must accept that everything God says is true and we are required to live by His every word and every word of scripture is inspired by God. This means that if you choose the "shoot the messenger" option and take the position of the majority of people today, that the Bible doesn't matter or actually mean what it says, you're calling God a liar and forfeiting this chance of eternal life. Again the Bible tells of those who take this approach: **Enter ye in at the strait gate: for wide is the gate, and broad is the way, that leadeth to destruction, and many there be which go in thereat: (Mt 7:13)**

10.1 The way that seems right to man

If you do believe the Bible for what it says and that the analysis I have presented here is scripturally sound, you're going to have to make a decision about what you are going to do with this information. There are many possible courses of action which people will choose. These fall into four main categories – survivalists, institutionalists, monetarists and religionists.

a. The Survivalists

The survivalists are the ones I spoke of at the very beginning of this book. Those who will place their trust in their own might. Choosing to stock up on weapons, ammunition, food and water and either bunkering down in their own homes or heading to the hills. If this is your preferred option have you really thought the problem through? Even if you were able to survive the nuclear war and subsequent plagues and famine and by force of arms protect yourself from marauding gangs of starving refugees – how will you survive the cosmic catastrophes, demonic plague and divine intervention poured out from the bowls of God's wrath?

An horse is a vain thing for safety: neither shall he deliver any by his great strength. (Ps 33:17)

The horse is prepared against the day of battle: but safety is of the LORD. (Pr 21:31)

The Bible clearly tells us that placing our trust in the weapons of man [represented by the horse which was symbolic of military might in the ancient world] will not deliver us. In fact it makes an even more direct statement in the book of Revelation – **"He that leadeth into captivity shall go into captivity: he that killeth with the sword must be killed with the sword. Here is the patience and the faith of the saints". (Rev 13:10)**

b. The Institutionalists

The position of the institutionalists is that the government should protect them. If this is your preferred approach, you should realize that it is the governments of the world who will have created the chaos in the first place and they will be far too busy worrying about their own survival and clinging on to their personal power to pay any real regard for you or your family.

Remember the adage "power corrupts, absolute power corrupts absolutely". It doesn't matter what form of power people chose – political or economic (in the form of trans-national corporations that wield more power than many national governments) their only desire is personal power. What makes you think they will spend one second considering the well being of you and your family? Again the Bible provides this clear warning:

Put not your trust in princes, nor in the son of man, in whom there is no help. (Ps 146:3)

It is better to trust in the LORD than to put confidence in man. It is better to trust in the LORD than to put confidence in princes. (Ps 118:8-9)

c. The Monetarists

The monetarist position comes from the distorted world view that we have in the West – "it doesn't matter what's going on around me, with enough money I can buy my way out of any problem". We can see this fallacious thought being applied by our governments in response to the financial crisis. The reason we are in the financial mess we're experiencing is due to too much credit, lack of control and oversight of the money supply and a basic lack of fiscal discipline at the individual, corporate and governmental levels. How can throwing trillions of (illusory) dollars, pounds, euro and yen at the problem (without making any attempt at correcting the underlying structural failures of the system) going to fix the problem?

There is a definition of insanity which states "doing the same as you've always done and expecting a different outcome is insanity". What we are witnessing is fiscal insanity on a global scale that will impoverish our nations and destroy the future potential for our children for generations to come.

When there is no food, or clean water and the social infrastructure has failed – how will your money help you? How will bank accounts overflowing with electronic dollars help you in a nuclear attack? And if you draw your money out how will piles of pound notes protect you from plagues and disease? Or what about hording your wealth in gold? Certainly it would be more acceptable as a form of trade than discredited pieces of government paper – but if there's nothing to buy what good will gold do you? You can't eat it, you can't build a shelter with it and it won't keep you warm (at least with piles of worthless dollars and pounds you could burn them for heat!)

God gives this direct warning to the end time church, the Church of Laodicea **"Because thou sayest, I am rich, and increased with goods, and have need of nothing; and knowest not that thou art wretched, and miserable, and poor, and blind, and naked: I counsel thee to buy of me gold tried in the fire, that thou mayest be rich; and white raiment, that thou mayest be clothed, and that the shame of thy nakedness do not appear; and anoint thine eyes with eyesalve, that thou mayest see". (Rev 3:17-18)**

d. The Religionists

Of the four groups, the religionists are without doubt the most pitiful. They say they believe the Bible, they understand that placing their trust in guns, governments and money is a fool's errand. They practice a form of worshiping God but when faced with the difficult truth that the Bible presents them, they turn to man for guidance.

Irrespective of whether that man is called Father, Priest, Vicar, Rabbi, Pastor or Elder, the religionist seeks solace and comfort in the well worn customs, traditions and doctrines of their particular denomination. Organized religion is simply another man made power base right alongside the political and economic ones we have already identified. It is not in the interests of the leaders of corporate churches to introduce *their flock* to the truth God reveals to us in the Bible. Any understanding which induces individuals to turn wholly and solely to Jesus for their guidance and protection will be actively suppressed by the corporate organization.

A subset of the religionists are "rapturists". These people believe in the end time events, the cataclysmic destruction of the world and the horror of the tribulation, but in their fear they have accepted a false doctrine which is going to cause them to abandon their faith just when they need to be getting closest to God. The rapture doctrine is a man made heresy which is leading millions of genuine believers away from God. You can search the Bible from one cover to the other and you will not find one mention of the word "rapture". There are however, three versions of the rapture doctrine – pre-tribulation, mid-tribulation and post-tribulation. The pre-trib and mid-trib doctrines are terribly dangerous as they tempt believers into a laissez faire attitude – "I'm alright, I'll be raptured to safety before all these horrible things happen, I don't need to worry". And this attitude is exactly what Jesus warned the Laodicean church about. When all these people who have placed their faith in a false doctrine suddenly find themselves in the middle of the horror and destruction of the tribulation, do you think they will blame themselves for not studying the scriptures daily and proving all things? No! They'll blame God for letting them down and in doing so they will be swept up by hope of safety and security offered by the false religion of the beast power.

To be fair, I should point out that the post-tribulation rapture doctrine is very close to what the Bible actually describes about the saints being resurrected and taken up at the sound of the last trump. The last trump as we have already described above is the sounding of the heavenly shofar on the Day of Atonement which comes at the very end of the 1,260 day period of tribulation. Although I feel it is still very dangerous to use non Biblical terms (such as the rapture) to describe clear Biblically foretold events as it just serves as a potential cause of confusion.

The information provided in this book is challenging to say the least and if you have taken the time to check it against the Bible references I have provided, it could well be a terrifying realization that you have come to. If you find that this analysis stands in the light of scripture you need to decide to what, or who, you will give precedence – the word of God or the doctrine of men? By all means discuss this with your family members or others in your congregation who may be able to give you better understanding. The Bible clearly states that there is wisdom in a multitude of counsel, but do not let others sway you from your convictions. If the information you are being given contradicts what you have read in the Bible (or what you have read in this book once you have checked it against the Bible) then you must have the discernment and courage to holdfast to your beliefs and politely but firmly rebuff those who try and change your mind. Be forewarned that many ministries declare that the Book of Revelation is wholly allegorical and not to get concerned about what it actually says!

The acid test I use is to ask myself "who is going to be the one who resurrects me?" Will it be my priest, vicar or the Pope? Or is it God? Whoever has the power to resurrect me back to life is the one I choose to obey. And if you choose to diligently follow the instructions God reveals to you through His inspired word, you will find yourself in a minuscule minority, but do not let this dissuade you, listen to the words that Jesus gave us to encourage us in these end times:

Let not your heart be troubled: ye believe in God, believe also in me. In my Father's house are many mansions: if it were not so, I would have told you. I go to prepare a place for you. And if I go and prepare a place for you, I will come again, and receive you unto myself; that where I am, there ye may be also. (Jn 14:1-3)

And I will shew wonders in heaven above, and signs in the earth beneath; blood, and fire, and vapour of smoke: The sun shall be turned into darkness, and the moon into blood, before that great and notable day of the Lord come: And it shall come to pass, that whosoever shall call on the name of the Lord shall be saved. (Ac 2:19-21)

Jesus is clearly telling us that he has prepared a place for us and He will come again to receive us and that to be saved we have to call on the name of the Lord. Is that all there is to do, to call on the name of the Lord and we'll be saved? Actually there is a little more to it than that (but not much if you're truly seeking God). How can we find out what we need to do to be saved?

Let's turn to the instructions Jesus gave us to make sure we get it right!

10.2 Jesus' Instructions for us to be saved

As we've already read above, one thing we need to do to be saved is to call on the name of the Lord. Now many people fall at this first hurdle, mistakenly believing that that name of the Lord, is "The Lord". This is a very wrong understanding. In the Old Testament, when you see the words "THE LORD" in small capitals this is misrepresentation of what was actually written in the original manuscripts.

The Rabbinic tradition has been to build a hedge around the Commandments in the form of layers of additional restrictions and traditions in an attempt to stop people breaking them. Unfortunately all the rabbis have done is to make God's perfect law a burden of rules and regulations and hide the real meaning of the law from the very people it was designed to protect. These burdensome regulations have failed to stop people breaking the Commandments, especially since Jesus' ministry was to fulfil the Law (Mt 5:17) and in doing so He changed the law from physical instructions "Do not murder", "Do not commit adultery" into spiritual requirements "Do not even call your brother a fool", "Do not look at a woman with lust in your heart".

One of the prohibitions of the oral law, the Rabbinic tradition, is that the name of God is so sacred that it must never be spoken out loud in case it is used in an unworthy manner and the name of God be blasphemed. To prevent this they substituted the word "Adonai" (meaning the Lord) and even say "Ha Shem", *the Name*, when they read the scriptures. Unfortunately this burdensome custom has actually caused the people to break the Commandment which reads, **"You shall not take the name of the LORD your God in vain, for the LORD will not hold him guiltless who takes His name in vain." (Ex 20:7).**

By hiding the name of The Lord, they have actually made His name vain, not through misuse, but through none use! What is the name of the God revealed to us through the Bible? The Hebrew letters – יהוה transliterate into YHWH. Hebrew is read from right to left and also the vowels are omitted. Even in the early Hebrew texts the scribes were already omitting the vowel points from the sacred name so it is not the easiest job in the world to work out the correct pronunciation of God's name. The most common translation of YHWH is Yahweh and you will find this used in many Messianic and Sabbattarian assemblies. Unfortunately, this is not the correct translation; it is based on a poor understanding of the Hebrew grammar rules. A little bit of research brings us to the first complete Masoretic text of the Old Testament, known as the Leningrad Codex or Manuscript 19b which was written around 1008AD. Although the scribes had started to remove the vowel points in this manuscript they were inconsistent omitting different vowels at different points in the text. With a little detective work we discover that the real name of the God revealed to us through the Bible is "**YeHoWaH**" and this is the name we must call on if we are to be saved.

Many people argue against the use of the correct name of God because they have been deceived for their entire life and find it difficult to let go of cherished misconceptions. And so counter arguments such as *"if the correct pronunciations is so important does this mean a mute person is denied access to salvation?"* This is a fair argument, but one which denies the instructions provided in scripture. We are told that God knows the heart (Acts 15:8) so those who do not speak the correct name of God, either because they cannot physically make the sound, or intellectually do not know what sound to make, but whose hearts yearn for the law of God, they will be judged as being righteous. Those who are convicted of the correct name of God, but choose not to use it for whatever reason, will be judged as unrighteous transgressors of the 3rd Commandment.

Not every one of the requirements to be saved takes as much research as this one. And in fact, this is probably the most difficult to understand as Satan has been trying to deceive the world for millennia and hiding the name of the one true God who can save us was an important part of this deception. While we're on the subject of names, it's worth pointing out that Jesus was not the name by which the Son of God was known when He walked upon the earth. The most accurate rendering of Jesus' name is Yehoshua, usually pronounced Y'shua. This name actually defines who He is and His purpose on the earth. Yehoshua actually means "Salvation from Yehowah" and you can see God's name "Yeho" in the name of His Son.

Another deception that is widely accepted by the Christian world is that the Law has been nailed to the cross, so the Commandments don't apply to the New Testament church as we're saved by grace not works. Unfortunately this understanding is in direct contradiction to the instructions Jesus gave us in His own words.

Think not that I am come to destroy the law, or the prophets: I am not come to destroy, but to fulfil. For verily I say unto you, Till heaven and earth pass, one jot or one tittle shall in no wise pass from the law, till all be fulfilled. (Mt 5:17-18)

If we take Jesus at His word, he clearly tells us that "till heaven and earth pass away" and as far as I can tell heaven and earth are still here, so it must be fair to accept that the law of God is still valid and applies today, just as it did in Jesus' time here on earth. But what is this law that he is talking about?

There is great misunderstanding on this subject but as quickly as possible I will explain my understanding of the Law. There are four main components which go to make up the doctrine of any Christian church or religious organisation. These are:

- The Ten Commandments
- The books of the Law – these are the statutes and judgements given to the people of Israel in the Old Testament
- Church doctrine – these are beliefs and traditional interpretations developed by a particular church organisation based on their specific understanding and application of the scriptures.
- Church regulations – these are man made rules developed against the civil law of the land so that the "corporate organisation" can legally function.

Obviously civil regulations have no bearing on our spiritual journey, so we can dismiss these immediately. Church doctrine/tradition is fine, providing that it does not conflict with the scriptural requirements or countermand the law of God. Unfortunately in many cases church doctrine has been developed specifically for that purpose. As we saw earlier, the Catholic doctrine requiring worship on a Sunday is openly overturning the clear Biblical Commandment to observe the 7th day Sabbath. Jesus had exactly this problem with the religious elite of His period, prompting Him to rebuke them with this admonition:

Thus have ye made the commandment of God of none effect by your tradition. Ye hypocrites, well did Esaias prophesy of you, saying, This people draweth nigh unto me with their mouth, and honoureth me with their lips; but their heart is far from me. But in vain they do worship me, teaching for doctrines the commandments of men. (Mt 15:6-9)

By all means follow your local traditions and customs as long as they DO NOT CONTRADICT the Holy Scriptures.

What about the Law and The Commandments – are they both equally applicable today as they were 2,000 or even 4,000 years ago?

Let's look at the Law to clearly understand what we are talking about. The Law comprises all the instructions given to the children of Israel in the first 5 books of the Bible, The Torah. According to Rabbinic tradition there are 613 commandments contained in these 5 books. These cover the Ten Commandments, laws of cleanliness, the Levitical law of priestly duties and sacrificial worship, law of sexual propriety and many other areas. Having reviewed these laws I believe that approximately 400 are applicable to Bible observant Christians today. Now this may sound like a tall order but when you explore the Word of God and truly desire to do His will, you will easily come to understanding and a willingness to live His way rather than the way of man.

However, having said this if there are some 200 "laws" we do not, or cannot, follow today, so what was Jesus referring to when He said the Law will not pass away until all is fulfilled? This law was the Ten Commandments which are as binding today as they were when they were first set in our hearts at the beginning of creation. The following chart gives a good comparison between the law and the Commandments.

	Commandments	Law
Author	God – wrote them with His own finger. (Dt 9:10)	Moses prepared them and delivered them after 40 days negotiation with God.
Material	Tablets of stone – indicating permanence and unalterable. (Dt 9:10)	Parchment scrolls written by Moses indicating that they can be modified and are impermanent. (Dt 31:24)
Location	Placed inside the Ark of the Covenant directly under the mercy seat of God. (The two tablets of stone are in fact the foundation stones upon which God's mercy is based. (1 Ki 8:9)	Laid at the side of the ark. (Dt 31:26)

End Time Reference	Jesus said if you want to enter into life, keep the Commandments. Rev 14 – the saints keep the Commandments of God; Rev 12 – the dragon went to make war with those who keep the Commandments of God; Rev 22 – blessed are they that do His Commandments they have the right to the tree of life and may enter into the holy city.	None.

We can see that the Ten Commandments of God were written personally by Him on tablets of stone and placed in the Ark of the Covenant to form the foundation stones of His mercy seat and is referred to several times as an end time requirement. The Law was written by Moses on parchment scrolls, is outside the Ark and is not mentioned as an end time requirement. These Commandments which we are so frequently told are "nailed to the Cross" actually form the very foundation of God's mercy towards us.

Blotting out the handwriting of ordinances that was against us, which was contrary to us, and took it out of the way, nailing it to his cross; (Col 2:14)

What was actually nailed to the cross was the "handwriting of ordinances" which correctly understood means the judicial sentence against a person found guilty, not the law itself. I don't know about you, but I know that I am a sinner and I want to be on the strongest possible basis for receiving His mercy so anything that could undermine the foundation of His mercy towards me is something I want to avoid!

If the Ten Commandments are so important (which they are – your eternal life depends on them!) are you sure you understand them and are following them correctly. Let's just review them here (from Exodus 20:1-17):

> **ONE - And God spake all these words, saying, I am YHWH thy God, which have brought thee out of the land of Egypt, out of the house of bondage. Thou shalt have no other gods before me.**

Have you allowed anything or anyone to come between you and your relationship with God? Does your desire for money, status, beauty or material possessions form a barrier between you and God?

TWO - Thou shalt not make unto thee any graven image, or any likeness of any thing that is in heaven above, or that is in the earth beneath, or that is in the water under the earth: Thou shalt not bow down thyself to them, nor serve them: for I YHWH thy God am a jealous God, visiting the iniquity of the fathers upon the children unto the third and fourth generation of them that hate me; and shewing mercy unto thousands of them that love me, and keep my commandments.

Do you bow down to worship before any icons or false images that can distract you from a personal relationship with YHWH the living God? I know it may be difficult to accept but even the cross is not Biblical (Jesus was executed on a single upright stake) so bowing down before any cross or crucifix is contrary to God's Commandment.

THREE - Thou shalt not take the name of YHWH thy God in vain; for YHWH will not hold him guiltless that taketh his name in vain.

The name of God is NOT the LORD. As we discussed earlier the name of God written as YHWH is **YeHoWaH** (v and w is interchangeable in Hebrew so it is more commonly pronounced YeHoVaH). If you don't know your God, now is the time to start calling on His name and building an intimate relationship with Him.

FOUR - Remember the Sabbath day, to keep it holy. Six days shalt thou labour, and do all thy work: But the seventh day is the Sabbath of the LORD thy God: in it thou shalt not do any work, thou, nor thy son, nor thy daughter, thy manservant, nor thy maidservant, nor thy cattle, nor thy stranger that is within thy gates: For in six days the LORD made heaven and earth, the sea, and all that in them is , and rested the seventh day: wherefore the LORD blessed the Sabbath day, and hallowed it.

This is considered by many to be the test Commandment. In Exodus 31:13 we read **"Verily my Sabbaths ye shall keep: for it is a sign between me and you throughout your generations; that ye may know that I am YHWH that doth sanctify you."** Observing the Sabbaths (weekly and annual celebrations) are a sign between YHWH and the people He sanctifies (makes holy and sets apart). **If you are not observing the weekly and annual Sabbaths, God does not consider you to be part of His people.**

FIVE - Honour thy father and thy mother: that thy days may be long upon the land which YHWH thy God giveth thee.

Just think how much better our society would be if as children we honoured our parents by listening to their wisdom (and learning from their mistakes and not having to make quite so many of our own). And how much better would the quality of life of our older parents be if they were kept with the family and not carted off to an old people's facility where they very conveniently become "out of sight and out of mind".

SIX - Thou shalt not murder.

This Commandment prohibits all forms of taking human life, including abortion and euthanasia, but as Jesus fulfilled it we are not even to hold a grudge or harbour and angry thought against our brother. Can you honestly say that you haven't got angry feelings about anyone on the planet?

SEVEN - Thou shalt not commit adultery.

The epidemic of promiscuous sex, extramarital relationships, divorce and broken homes is destroying the very fabric of our society. And the rise in the use of internet pornography is having a devastating impact on healthy relationships between men and women in all sectors of society. Remember Jesus told us that whoever looks at a woman (or man) with lust in their hearts has already committed adultery.

EIGHT - Thou shalt not steal.

How much needs to be said on this Commandment? As we have become more tolerant of *minor* transgressions and accepted the concept of situational ethics we find that the moral compass of our society in relation to theft has been lost resulting in scandals such as Enron, Worldcom and the whole global financial meltdown we are now witnessing.

NINE - Thou shalt not bear false witness against thy neighbour.

If you have ever had the misfortune of being caught up in any form of legal proceedings you will know that truth is an extremely rare commodity. We have an enormous, cumbersome legal system but there is very little justice. As we saw with the media circus of the OJ Simpson trial, in our countries we now have the best legal system that money can buy!

TEN - Thou shalt not covet thy neighbour's house, thou shalt not covet thy neighbour's wife, nor his manservant, nor his maidservant, nor his ox, nor his ass, nor any thing that is thy neighbour's.

This is the antidote to modern rampant consumerism. If we had only stopped to apply this commandment we would not see our societies struggling under debt levels which are almost beyond comprehension. Two sayings I really like to use in relation to this concept of covetousness and consumerism are "Real wealth is what you have left after all the money is taken away" and "True happiness is wanting what you have, not having what you want".

We can see that we are required to be obedient to ALL TEN of the Commandments if we are going to be saved. But what else do we need to do?

10.3 The Four Steps to Salvation

The Biblical process for being saved by God is extremely simple and clearly explained in the book of Acts.

Then Peter said unto them, Repent, and be baptized every one of you in the name of Jesus Christ for the remission of sins, and ye shall receive the gift of the Holy Ghost. For the promise is unto you, and to your children, and to all that are afar off, even as many as the Lord our God shall call. (Ac 2:38-39)

a.   Repent

True repentance is poorly understood by many Christians. The core meaning of the word from the Hebrew understanding is to "turn back". And this very idea requires action on our part. It's very easy to say that we're sorry and ask God for forgiveness, but without the accompanying action on our part we make His forgiveness void. Unless we make deliberate efforts to turn back from the way of the world we will be swept along the broad path which leads to destruction. And going against the flow is an extremely difficult course of action to follow. The pressure exerted by our family members, peer group, social network and church traditions can be overwhelming. But go against the flow we must – if we are going to find the path to salvation. Jesus made explicit reference to this at the end of His sermon on the mount:

Enter ye in at the strait gate: for wide is the gate, and broad is the way, that leadeth to destruction, and many there be which go in thereat: Because strait is the gate, and narrow is the way, which leadeth unto life, and few there be that find it. (Mt 7:13-14)

b.   Be Baptised

When asked the vast majority of Christians will say they have been baptised, but nearly all of these people are wrong. The act of sprinkling water over an infants head does not meet the Biblical criteria for baptism for three reasons. Before an individual is baptised they must have come to repentance and after their baptism show repentance through their fruits.

And he [John the Baptist] came into all the country about Jordan, preaching the baptism of repentance for the remission of sins; ... Bring forth therefore fruits worthy of repentance. (Lk 3:3, 8)

Firstly, a new born infant does not have the intellect or will to repent and secondly can do nothing to demonstrate the fruits of repentance after being sprinkled.

Finally the Greek word translated as baptism is Strong's G908 "baptisma" which means immersion or submersion. The reason we are to be fully immersed in water is because of the symbolic act it represents.

Therefore we are buried with him by baptism into death: that like as Christ was raised up from the dead by the glory of the Father, even so we also should walk in newness of life. (Ro 6:4)

The act of immersion symbolises our death (to the sins of the world), burial and resurrection into the new life as a follower of Jesus. Again being sprinkled with water as an infant does not fulfil this requirement.

c.   Receive the Gift of the Holy Spirit

There are three examples of the way the Holy Spirit has been given to man in the Bible. The first was when Jesus breathed on His disciples after His resurrection. The second was on the day of Pentecost when the Holy Spirit appearing as tongues of fire descended on the assembled disciples. The final, and most usual, way of receiving the Holy Spirit is by the laying on of hands.

Now when the apostles which were at Jerusalem heard that Samaria had received the word of God, they sent unto them Peter and John: Who, when they were come down, prayed for them, that they might receive the Holy Ghost: (For as yet he was fallen upon none of them: only they were baptized in the name of the Lord Jesus.) Then laid they their hands on them, and they received the Holy Ghost. (Ac 8:14-17)

And this would normally occur immediately after emerging from being immersed in the waters of baptism. Now God can, and on occasion, does give His Spirit to an individual who has not gone through the normal process, but this is an exception, not the norm. If you have not completed these three steps you should seriously consider going through the Biblically correct process of repentance then being fully immersed and receiving the gift of the Holy Spirit through the laying on of hands.

A question which is often asked by people who are newly baptised is how do they know that they have actually received the gift of the Holy Spirit? There are three criteria we can use to make this assessment. Do you feel a growing revulsion for the lusts of the world? Do you have the fruits of the Spirit manifesting in your life? And do you find yourself wanting to obey the word of God rather than argue against it?

This I say then, Walk in the Spirit, and ye shall not fulfil the lust of the flesh. For the flesh lusteth against the Spirit, and the Spirit against the flesh: and these are contrary the one to the other: so that ye cannot do the things that ye would. But if ye be led of the Spirit, ye are not under the law. Now the works of the flesh are manifest, which are these; Adultery, fornication, uncleanness, lasciviousness, idolatry, witchcraft, hatred, variance, emulations, wrath, strife, seditions, heresies, envyings, murders, drunkenness, revellings, and such like: of the which I tell you before, as I have also told you in time past, that they which do such things shall not inherit the kingdom of God. But the fruit of the Spirit is love, joy, peace, longsuffering, gentleness, goodness, faith, meekness, temperance: against such there is no law. And they that are Christ's have crucified the flesh with the affections and lusts. If we live in the Spirit, let us also walk in the Spirit. (Gal 5:16-25)

If you feel yourself drawn to the lust of the world (we are all tempted from time to time but if you prefer this lust to the gifts of the Spirit), or if you cannot sense the gifts of the Spirit growing in you or if you would rather spend your time justifying why the Bible doesn't mean what it says and that you don't have to do what God tells you to do – you need to seriously question whether you have received the Holy Spirit which comes from YHWH our God.

Many genuine, devout Christians have been deceived into accepting a false spirit and because they have accepted the lie that the Commandments have been nailed to the cross, they have no yardstick against which to measure the spirit which is operating in their lives. Remember the urgent warning Jesus gave His disciples before he was crucified.

For there shall arise false Christs, and false prophets, and shall shew great signs and wonders; insomuch that, if it were possible, they shall deceive the very elect. (Mt 24:24)

Beloved, believe not every spirit, but try the spirits whether they are of God: because many false prophets are gone out into the world. Hereby know ye the Spirit of God: Every spirit that confesseth that Jesus Christ is come in the flesh is of God: And every spirit that confesseth not that Jesus Christ is come in the flesh is not of God: and this is that spirit of antichrist, whereof ye have heard that it should come; and even now already is it in the world. (1 Jn 4:1-3)

d. Obey The Commandments

I know that really keeping the Commandments of God is contrary to the teaching of most Christian denominations, but it's exactly what Jesus told us that we must do.
And, behold, one came and said unto him, Good Master, what good thing shall I do, that I may have eternal life? And he said unto him, Why callest thou me good? there is none good but one, that is , God: but if thou wilt enter into life, keep the commandments. (Mt 19:16-17)

Now you have read this book, you must decide what you are going to do with the information.

Do you want to dismiss the information as hysterical nonsense? If you do that's fine. All I would ask is that when you see the events detailed in this book start to unfold, please remember what you have read and then come before God with an open mind and a contrite heart.

Or would you rather dismiss the Bible as a nice book, but not having divine authority. Again, it's your choice; all I have done here is expand on the words of the Bible and lined them up with what I believe to be the prophetically unfolding end time events. If you do choose to dismiss the word of God please do not think that you will be able to stand before God at the day of Judgement and claim ignorance of the Law. That is no defence.

If you have come to the end of this book and are offended by the words you have read please consider why you feel offended. If I have misquoted the Holy Scriptures or falsely interpreted what the Bible says, please do contact me and I would be happy to discuss this with you. My email address is david@spiritandtruthrevival.org. Similarly if you have questions about the end time countdown or feel that there are prophetic events which need to be added, again, please contact me.

If you have checked the scriptures I have provided and proven them to be accurate but still feel offended by what you have read, then that is an issue between you and God. Please take it up with Him in your prayers and ask Him to open your heart to His Word that you may still come to understanding and choose the narrow path of righteousness while there is still time. Remember what we are warned in the final chapter of the Book of Revelation:

He that is unjust, let him be unjust still: and he which is filthy, let him be filthy still: and he that is righteous, let him be righteous still: and he that is holy, let him be holy still. And, behold, I come quickly; and my reward is with me, to give every man according as his work shall be. I am Alpha and Omega, the beginning and the end, the first and the last. Blessed are they that do his commandments, that they may have right to the tree of life, and may enter in through the gates into the city. (Rev 22:11-14)

I call heaven and earth to record this day against you, that I have set before you life and death, blessing and cursing: therefore choose life, that both thou and thy seed may live: That thou mayest love the LORD thy God, and that thou mayest obey his voice, and that thou mayest cleave unto him: for he is thy life, and the length of thy days: that thou mayest dwell in the land which the LORD sware unto thy fathers, to Abraham, to Isaac, and to Jacob, to give them. (Dt 30:19-20)

I have set before you life and death.

Please choose life.

About the Author

David Walters is an independent Apostolic Christian living in Lincolnshire, England. He was raised in the Church of England until at the age of 16, he drifted from the church. After the birth of his first child David and his wife returned to the Church of England. He served as a Weapons Engineer in the Royal Navy submarine service before immigrating to Canada where he served in the Canadian Forces and subsequently the nuclear power industry.

During his time in Canada, David became increasingly disillusioned with the doctrine and worship of the Anglican Church of Canada. After several months of soul searching and being lead firmly by the Lord to study the scriptures for what they really say, he was introduced to the Global Church of God. This started a period of dramatic growth and understanding which resulted in David and his wife, Yvonne, being baptised together in a lake by their home. This growth was further spurred on by the break up of the Global Church of God and the formation of the Living Church of God. It was this event which turned him away from all corporately organised churches to become an independent Sabbath keeping Christian.

Fellowshipping in a number of small independent assemblies around the Toronto area, David was exposed to many of the challenges facing God's people as they strive to serve the Lord and find fellowship with likeminded individuals. David led the Canadian branch of Ron Dart's Christian Educational Ministries, Christian Educational Services Canada, for several years before returning to live in the UK late in 2004. This was a pivotal year in David's education in the scriptures. At the Feast of Tabernacles in 2004 he was introduced to the Hebrew roots of the Christian faith which brought many doctrines and teachings to new life. Shortly before returning to the UK, David was ordained as an elder.

David has served as the co-founder of the Grimsby Bible Assembly and now dedicates his time serving the Lord through internet evangelism with Spirit and Truth Revival Ministry (www.spiritandtruthrevival.org). David lives in Lincolnshire with his wife Yvonne.

If you have any questions about the evidence provided in this book, or have any other questions about following the Way taught to us by Y'shua the Messiah or are simply looking for fellowship with likeminded believers, please feel free to contact David via email david@spiritandtruthrevival.org.

Appendix A

Solar and Lunar Eclipse Analysis

In the period from 2000 BC to 2100 AD the data provided on the NASA website - http://eclipse.gsfc.nasa.gov/LEcat5/LE2101-2200.html indicates that there have been/will be 9878 lunar eclipses.

Searching through all this data for "signs in the heavens" which are of prophetic significance has required some careful thought. Based on the work conducted by Pastor Mark Biltz, the analysis has been completed against the following protocol:

- Identify all lunar tetrads (4 consecutive total lunar eclipses – blood moons)
- Discount those which cannot be holy days (i.e. all four eclipses must occur in March/April or September/October – the period of the spring and autumn holy days.
- Convert the dates to the Hebrew calendar and check whether all four eclipses fall on or around holy days.
- Identify whether there are solar eclipses occurring at the same time.

Of the 9878 eclipses identified in the analysis period there were 111 tetrads of which only 12 meet the requirement that the lunar eclipse falls on the Holy Day (15 Nisan or 15 Tishri) or the Day of Preparation for the Holy Day (14 Nisan or 14 Tishri).

Each tetrad of 4 lunar eclipses is accompanied by 2 solar eclipses preceding each of the final 2 lunar eclipses.

Julian Date					Hebrew Date			
Year	Month	Day	Eclipse Type		Day	Month	Year	Holy Day
-1596	Apr	13	Total Lunar		15	Nisan	2164	Feast of Unleavened Bread
-1596	Oct	6	Total Lunar		14	Tishri	2165	Preparation Day for Tabernacles
-1595	Mar	18	Total Solar		29	Adar	2165	Eve of Biblical New Year
-1595	Apr	2	Total Lunar		15	Nisan	2165	Feast of Unleavened Bread
-1595	Sep	11	Partial Solar		29	Elul	2165	Preparation Day for Trumpets
-1595	Sep	26	Total Lunar		15	Tishri	2166	Feast of Tabernacles
-945	Apr	16	Total Lunar		15	Nisan	2815	Feast of Unleavened Bread
-945	Oct	10	Total Lunar		15	Tishri	2816	Feast of Tabernacles
-944	Mar	21	Partial Solar		29	Adar	2816	Eve of Biblical New Year
-944	Apr	4	Total Lunar		14	Nisan	2816	Passover
-944	Sep	14	Partial Solar		29	Elul	2816	Preparation Day for Trumpets
-944	Sep	28	Total Lunar		14	Tishri	2817	Preparation Day for Tabernacles
-377	Apr	6	Total Lunar		15	Nisan	3383	Feast of Unleavened Bread
-377	Sep	30	Total Lunar		15	Tishri	3384	Feast of Tabernacles
-376	Mar	11	Partial Solar		29	Adar	3384	Eve of Biblical New Year
-376	Mar	26	Total Lunar		15	Nisan	3384	Feast of Unleavened Bread
-376	Sep	4	Annular Solar		29	Elul	3384	Preparation Day for Trumpets
-376	Sep	18	Total Lunar		14	Tishri	3385	Preparation Day for Tabernacles
-312	Apr	7	Total Lunar		14	Nisan	3448	Passover
-312	Oct	1	Total Lunar		14	Tishri	3449	Preparation Day for Tabernacles
-311	Mar	13	Total Solar		1	Nisan	3449	First day of the Biblical New Year
-311	Mar	27	Total Lunar		15	Nisan	3449	Feast of Unleavened Bread
-311	Sep	5	Partial Solar		29	Elul	3449	Preparation Day for Trumpets
-311	Sep	20	Total Lunar		15	Tishri	3450	Feast of Tabernacles
162	Apr	17	Total Lunar		14	Nisan	3992	Passover
162	Oct	11	Total Lunar		14	Tishri	3923	Preparation Day for Tabernacles
163	Mar	22	Annular Solar		29	Adar	3923	Eve of Biblical New Year
163	Apr	6	Total Lunar		15	Nisan	3923	Feast of Unleavened Bread
163	Sep	16	Hybrid Solar		1	Tishri	3924	Feast of Trumpets

| Julian Date | | | | | Hebrew Date | | | |
Year	Month	Day	Eclipse Type		Day	Month	Year	Holy Day
163	Sep	30	Total Lunar		15	Tishri	3924	Feast of Tabernacles
795	Apr	9	Total Lunar		15	Nisan	4555	Feast of Unleavened Bread
795	Oct	3	Total Lunar		15	Tishri	4556	Feast of Tabernacles
796	Mar	14	Total Solar		29	Adar	4556	Eve of Biblical New Year
796	Mar	28	Total Lunar		14	Nisan	4556	Passover
796	Sep	6	Partial Solar		28	Elul	4556	
796	Sep	21	Total Lunar		14	Tishri	4557	Preparation Day for Tabernacles
842	Mar	30	Total Lunar		15	Nisan	4602	First Day of the Feast Unleavened Bread
842	Sep	23	Total Lunar		15	Tishri	4603	Feast of Tabernacles
843	Mar	5	Partial Solar		29	Adar	4603	Eve of Biblical New Year
843	Mar	19	Total Lunar		14	Nisan	4603	Passover
843	Aug	29	Total Solar		29	Elul	4603	Preparation Day for Trumpets
843	Sep	12	Total Lunar		14	Tishri	4604	Preparation Day for Tabernacles
860	Apr	9	Total Lunar		15	Nisan	4620	Feast of Unleavened Bread
860	Oct	3	Total Lunar		15	Tishri	4621	Feast of Tabernacles
861	Mar	15	Partial Solar		29	Adar	4621	Eve of Biblical New Year
861	Mar	30	Total Lunar		15	Nisan	4621	First Day of the Feast Unleavened Bread
861	Sep	8	Total Solar		29	Elul	4621	Preparation Day for Trumpets
861	Sep	22	Total Lunar		14	Tishri	4622	Preparation Day for Tabernacles
1493	Apr	2	Total Lunar		15	Nisan	5253	Feast of Unleavened Bread
1493	Sep	25	Total Lunar		14	Tishri	5254	Preparation Day for Tabernacles
1494	Mar	7	Total Solar		29	Adar	5254	Eve of Biblical New Year
1494	Mar	22	Total Lunar		15	Nisan	5254	Feast of Unleavened Bread
1494	Aug	30	Partial Solar		28	Elul	5254	
1494	Sep	15	Total Lunar		15	Tishri	5255	Feast of Tabernacles

Gregorian Date					Hebrew Date			Holy Day
Year	Month	Day	Eclipse Type		Day	Month	Year	
1949	Apr	13	Total Lunar		14	Nisan	5709	Passover
1949	Oct	7	Total Lunar		14	Tishri	5710	Preparation Day for Tabernacles
1950	Mar	18	Annular Solar		29	Adar	5710	Eve of Biblical New Year
1950	Apr	2	Total Lunar		15	Nisan	5710	Feast of Unleavened Bread
1950	Sep	12	Total Solar		1	Tishri	5711	Feast of Trumpets
1950	Sep	26	Total Lunar		15	Tishri	5711	Feast of Tabernacles
1967	Apr	24	Total Lunar		14	Nisan	5727	Passover
1967	Oct	18	Total Lunar		14	Tishri	5728	Preparation Day for Tabernacles
1968	Mar	28	Partial Solar		28	Adar	5728	
1968	Apr	13	Total Lunar		15	Nisan	5728	Feast of Unleavened Bread
1968	Sep	22	Total Solar		29	Elul	5728	Preparation Day for Trumpets
1968	Oct	6	Total Lunar		14	Tishri	5729	Preparation Day for Tabernacles
2014	Apr	15	Total Lunar		15	Nisan	5774	Feast of Unleavened Bread
2014	Oct	8	Total Lunar		14	Tishri	5775	Preparation Day for Tabernacles
2015	Mar	20	Total Solar		29	Adar	5775	Eve of Biblical New Year
2015	Apr	4	Total Lunar		15	Nisan	5775	Feast of Unleavened Bread
2015	Sep	13	Partial Solar		29	Elul	5775	Preparation Day for Trumpets
2015	Sep	28	Total Lunar		15	Tishri	5776	Feast of Tabernacles

Appendix B

*The Re-Birth of Israel and its Amazing Time-Line Corresponding
to the Jubilees and the Golden Proportion*

by Bonnie Gaunt

According to the Encyclopaedia Judaica, when the exiles in Babylon returned to Jerusalem, under the edict of Cyrus, they began again to count Sabbath Years, but did not continue the original cycle, but began a new cycle which counted from the time of their resettling in the land. The new cycle has continued to be counted to the present day. Some examples of its mention in history can give us a reference point from which to count back and confirm the date that the exiles resettled in the land.

One of the most interesting was in modern times. After the long years of the Diaspora, in the late 1800s Jews began to resettle their homeland; but when the next Sabbath Year approached, they had a problem. They knew that the year 1889 was to be a Sabbath Year, in which they could not plant crops. The leading Rabbis suggested a solution to the problem. They felt that if they sold the fields and vineyards to the Muslims for a specified period of two years, the crops could then be planted and harvested and not violate the law of the Sabbath, because the land was not theirs. A formal statement was issued by R. Isaac Elhanan Spektor of Kovno, stating that for the Sabbath year (Tishri 1888 to Tishri 1889) it was permissible to sell the land to Muslims so that the crops could be harvested. Thus through a legal technicality, they cheated God out of His Sabbath.

But as the Sabbath Year 1909-1910 approached, the debate was once again raised over the policy of selling the land for two years, but some still continued the practice. In Kibbutz Hafez Hayyim they even attempted to grow vegetables in water as a method of technically observing the Sabbath Year while still harvesting food.

Several Sabbath Years have been recorded in history, and since the length of time between them is always evenly divisible by 7, it gives confidence in their authenticity. A Sabbath Year was mentioned in I Maccabees 16:14, which computes to the year 135 B.C. Josephus tells of another in 37 B.C. In fact, years that have been identified as Sabbath Years in history are 331 B.C.; 163 B.C.; 135 B.C.; 37 B.C.; A.D. 41, 55, 69, 132, 433 and 440. These dates give the year in which the larger part was during the Tishri to Tishri Sabbath Year. Thus the Sabbath Year recorded in 135 B.C. would, in fact, be from Tishri 136 B.C. to Tishri 135 B.C. (three months of which were in 136 B.C. and nine months of which were in 135 B.C.) The point is made clear in the Encyclopaedia Judaica where it lists Sabbath Years during the 20th century – they are in perfect harmony with the years mentioned in history, all of which have intervals evenly divisible by 7.

Thus, on the following pages I give tables showing the Jubilee cycle, with its 49th year being a Sabbath Year, and its 50th year being the Jubilee Year. It should be remembered that the year of Jubilee was not only the 50th, but it was also the first year of the next Sabbath cycle, meaning that the time from Jubilee to Jubilee is 49 years.

The Talmud states that Josiah's Great Passover was in the 16th Jubilee. This would have been 623 - 622 B.C. (Tishri to Tishri). The fact that it was a Jubilee year probably gave him cause to celebrate this Great Passover.

The Talmud also states that Ezekiel received his Temple vision in the year of the 17th Jubilee. This would have been 49 years after Josiah's Great Passover. Thus 623 - 622 B.C. minus 49 years would put us in the year 574-573 B.C. for the 17th Jubilee year. Since this is an established date in history, let's begin counting Sabbath and Jubilee years from that point forward. However, when the exiles returned to the land of Israel from the Babylonian captivity, and began the resettlement of Jerusalem, they began to count a new Sabbath and Jubilee cycle, beginning with the building of the Altar in 535 B.C. (Ezra 3:1-2). Zero year for this new cycle (which I will call Cycle 2) was 535 - 534 B.C. (Tishri to Tishri). During that year the foundation of the Temple was laid. Thus Cycle 2 began between the 17th and 18th Jubilees of Cycle 1.

The Talmud states that Josiah's Great Passover was in the year of the 16th Jubilee. This would have been 623 - 622 B.C. (Tishri to Tishri).

The Talmud also states that Ezekiel received the Temple vision in the year of the 17th Jubilee. This would have been 49 years after Josiah's Great Passover. Thus 623 - 622 minus 49 gives us 574 - 573 B.C. for the 17th Jubilee year.

Because these are reliable historical data, let's start counting Sabbath and Jubilee years from those dates forward. When the exiles in Babylon returned to the land of Israel, and the resettlement of Jerusalem, they began to count a new Sabbath and Jubilee cycle – beginning with the building of the Altar in 535 B.C. (Ezra 3:1-2). Zero year for this new cycle was 535 - 534 B.C. (Tishri to Tishri). During that year the foundation of the Temple was laid.

Thus a new cycle began to count between the 17th and 18th Jubilees of the original cycle. On the list of Sabbath and Jubilee years I have circled years that appear to conform to the pattern of the Golden Proportion. Because these events in the restoration of Israel follow this pattern, it appears logical that we could use the pattern to foresee future events.

Jubilee Cycle 1		Jubilee Cycle 2		Jubilee Cycle 3
Sabbath	575-574			
17th Jubilee	574–573			
Sabbath	526-525			
18th Jubilee	525-524	Zero Year	535-534	
		Sabbath	486-485	
		1 st Jubilee	485-484	
		Sabbath	437-436	All Dates BC
		2nd Jubilee	436-435	
		Sabbath	388-387	
		3rd Jubilee	387-386	
		Sabbath	339-338	
		4th Jubilee	338-337	
		Sabbath	290-289	

Jubilee Cycle 1	Jubilee Cycle 2		Jubilee Cycle 3	
	5th Jubilee	289-288		
	Sabbath	241-240		
	6th Jubilee	240-239		
	Sabbath	192-191		
	7th Jubilee	191-190		
	Sabbath	143-142		
	8th Jubilee	142-141		
	Sabbath	94-93		
	9th Jubilee	93-92		
	Sabbath	45-44		
	10th Jubilee	44-43		
	Sabbath	5-6	Absence of Year Zero compensated for here	
	11th Jubilee	6-7		
	Sabbath	54-55		
	12th Jubilee	55-56		
	Sabbath	103-104		
	13th Jubilee	104-105		
	Sabbath	152-153		
	14th Jubilee	153-154		
	Sabbath	201-202		
	15th Jubilee	202-203		
	Sabbath	250-251		
All dates AD	16th Jubilee	251-252		
	Sabbath	299-300		
	17th Jubilee	300-301		
	Sabbath	348-349		
	18th Jubilee	349-350		
	Sabbath	397-398		
	19th Jubilee	398-399		
	Sabbath	446-447		
	Jubilee	447-448		
	Sabbath	495-496		
	20th Jubilee	496-497		
	Sabbath	544-545		
	21st Jubilee	545-546		
	Sabbath	593-594		
	22nd Jubilee	594-595		
	Sabbath	642-643		
	23rd Jubilee	643-644		
	Sabbath	691-692		
	24th Jubilee	692-693		
All dates AD	Sabbath	740-741		
	25th Jubilee	741-742		
	Sabbath	789-790		
	26th Jubilee	790-791		
	Sabbath	838-839		
	27th Jubilee	839-840		
	Sabbath	887- 888		

Jubilee Cycle 1	Jubilee Cycle 2		Jubilee Cycle 3	
	28th Jubilee	888-889		
	Sabbath	936-937		
	29th Jubilee	937-938		
	Sabbath	985-986		
	30th Jubilee	986-987		
	Sabbath	1034-1035		
	31st Jubilee	1035-1036		
	Sabbath	1083-1084		
	32nd Jubilee	1084-1085		
	Sabbath	1132-1133		
	33rd Jubilee	1133-1134		
	Sabbath	1181-1182		
	34th Jubilee	1182-1183		
	Sabbath	1230-1231		
	35th Jubilee	1231-1232		
	Sabbath	1279-1280		
	36th Jubilee	1280-1281		
	Sabbath	1328-1329		
	37th Jubilee	1329-1330		
	Sabbath	1377-1378		
	38th Jubilee	1378-1379		
	Sabbath	1426-1427		
	39th Jubilee	1427-1428		
	Sabbath	1475-1476		
	40th Jubilee	1476-1477		
	Sabbath	1524-1525		
	41st Jubilee	1525-1526		
	Sabbath	1573-1574		
	42nd Jubilee	1574-1575		
	Sabbath	1622-1623		
	43rd Jubilee	1623-1624		
	Sabbath	1671-1672		
	44th Jubilee	1672-1673		
	Sabbath	1720-1721		
	45th Jubilee	1721-1722		
	Sabbath	1769-1770		
	46th Jubilee	1770-1771		
	Sabbath	1818-1819		
All dates AD	47th Jubilee	1819-1820		
	Sabbath	1867-1868		
	48th Jubilee	1868-1869		
	Sabbath	1916-1917		
	49th Jubilee	1917-1918		
The new Jubilee (Cycle 3) began with the re-birth of Israel in 1948. Because a new Jubilee cycle began to count when they came back into the			Zero Year	1947-1948
	Sabbath	1965-1966		
	50th Jubilee	1966-1967		
			Sabbath	1996-1997

Jubilee Cycle 1	Jubilee Cycle 2		Jubilee Cycle 3	
land after the Babylonian captivity, it appears that a new Jubilee cycle would also begin to count when they came back into the land officially in 1948. And Israel today considers it so, because they celebrated their first Jubilee in 1998.			1st Jubilee	1997-1998
	Sabbath	2014-2015		
	51st Jubilee	2015-2016		
			Sabbath	2045-2046
			2nd Jubilee	2046-2047
	Sabbath	2063-2064		
	52nd Jubilee	2064-2065		

The Golden Proportion is a physical constant appearing as the foundation principle of growth in nature. Physicists call it the "growth constant." The appearance of this proportion in the growth process of the restoration and re-birth of Israel is magnificent.

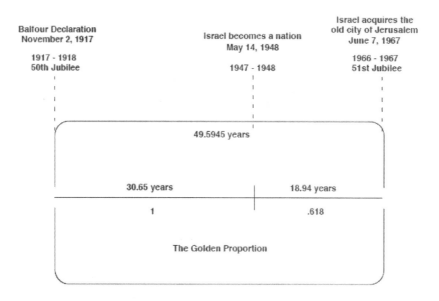

But notice, these three primary dates in the re-birth of Israel are also Sabbath and Jubilee years. It is not likely a blind coincidence, but has the appearance of having been planned. The year 1916 - 1917 was a Sabbath year, and the year 1917 - 1918 was Israel's 50th Jubilee on Cycle 2. Since the Balfour Declaration was dated November 2, 1917, it falls within the 50th Jubilee year.

But it was not until June 7, 1967 in the growth process of Israel that they gained the old city of Jerusalem. That date falls within the 51st Jubilee year in Cycle 2. The exact length of time between these two landmark dates was 49.5945 years. If we multiply these number of years by the Golden Proportion (.618) we find it divides them at May 14, 1948 – another landmark date in the re-birth of Israel, and the Zero year for the beginning of Cycle 3.

The beginning and ending dates in this diagram are Jubilee years. And that beautiful Golden Proportion that says *"Speak to the heart of Jerusalem"* (Isaiah 40:1) points directly to May 14, 1948 – the day they became a nation. How amazing to find that the Gematria value of *"the heart of Jerusalem"* is 618.

The heart of Jerusalem = 618
The Golden Proportion is 0.618

But let's go back in time a bit further, to the very beginning of the re-birth process. In the summer of 1878 the nations of central Europe sent representatives to the Berlin Congress of Nations. Queen Victoria, of England, sent her beloved Prime Minister, Benjamin Disraeli, known also as Lord Beaconsfield, to the Congress, with a proposal regarding Jewish emancipation. It opened the way for the First Aliyah to begin a settlement in Palestine. In 1878 the first settlers came, and their village later became known as Petah Tikvah, which means "Door of Hope."

From this small beginning to the occupation of Jerusalem on June 7, 1967 was a span of 89 years. Its Golden Proportion would be in the year 1933 – the year Hitler came to power and began his plan for the annihilation of Jews in Europe. Graphically it looks like this.

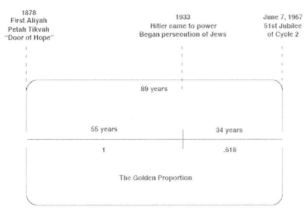

This growth of the restoration of Israel not only follows the principle of the "growth constant" – the Golden Proportion – but additionally it conforms to the Jubilee cycles.

So, let's go back to the two Jubilee dates – 1917 - 1918 to 1966 - 1967 – and look more closely at the remarkable structure of the Golden Proportion.

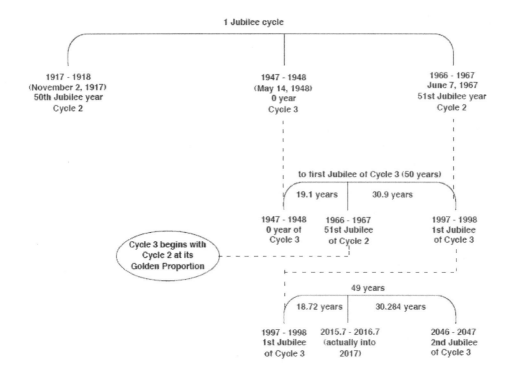

These relationships of the Golden Proportion to the Jubilees suggest that some event regarding the restoration of Israel will happen in the early part of 2017.

The covenant that God gave to Moses on Mt. Sinai was, in fact, a marriage covenant. It was identified by the Golden Proportion, because the Hebrew word for "His covenant" has a Gematria value of 618. Therefore it is logical that we look for evidence of Golden Proportions in the course of that marriage, the divorce, and the re-marriage.

His covenant = 618
The Golden Proportion is 0.618

Isaiah used the Golden Proportion when he prophesied concerning the time when the breach between God and Israel would be healed.

"The light of the sun shall be sevenfold, as the light of seven days, in the day that the Lord bindeth up the breach of his people, and healeth the stroke of their wound." (Isaiah 30:26)

The *"breach of his people"* began when Jesus hung on the cross in A.D. 33. It was the legal divorce. The healing of the breach began with the First Aliyah which became their door of hope, through which their restoration could be acquired. How amazing to find *"the breach of his people"* has a Gematria value of 618, (the Golden Proportion is .618). In that year God began again to "woo" his people back to Him.

"Therefore, behold I will lure (woo) her and bring her to the wilderness and speak to her heart. And I will give her her vineyards from there, and the valley of Achor for a door of hope (Petah Tikvah). And she shall answer there as in the days of her youth, and as in the day when she came up out of the land of Egypt. And at that day, says Jehovah, you shall call me 'My Husband' ... and I will betroth you to me forever ...." (Hosea 2:14 - 23)

Israel will answer as she did at Sinai – for there she had said "I do" to the covenant of marriage. For reasons too lengthy to include in this paper, it appears that the new marriage covenant (the re-marriage) will take place in the year 2032, just prior to the fulfilment of 2,000 years from the death of Jesus in A.D. 33. If this is the correct date, observe the beauty of the Golden Proportion.

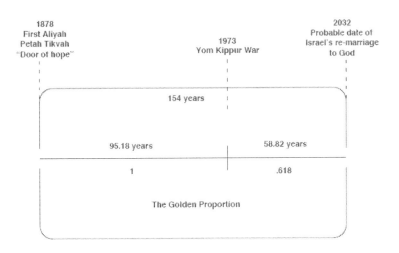

The Yom Kippur war was a pivotal point in the restoration of Israel. If we calculated the span of time from the year that Israel again came into possession of the old city of Jerusalem (1967) to the re-marriage (2032), it would place the Golden Proportion on the year 2007. With the present war in Israel and the Middle East, I suggest the possibility of a landmark victory for Israel in 2007.

177

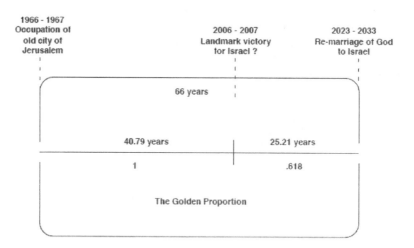

When ancient Israel left Egypt under the leadership of Moses, they could have gone directly into the Promised Land and possessed it, but through fear of the people of the land, they did not go in, but rather, spent 40 years in the desert. The number 40 indicates a time of trial and testing. When modern Israel took the city of Jerusalem and the Temple Mount in 1967, through fear of the Arabs they gave back the Temple Mount. As a result, they have had 40 years of trial and testing (1967 + 40 years = 2007). I don't know (as of July 2006) what great event will happen in the years 2006 - 2007, but it appears to be victorious.

Bonnie Gaunt, July 20, 2006

Reproduced with permission from Bonnie Gaunt.

For more information, updates, discussion and questions please feel welcome to visit www.armageddon2015.com.

LaVergne, TN USA
17 January 2011
212719LV00002B/1-24/P